Marie Antoinette
and the
Downfall of Royalty

marie antoinette

MARIE ANTOINETTE

Marie Antoinette and the Downfall of Royalty

The Queen of France
and the French Revolution

Imbert de Saint-Amand

LEONAUR

Marie Antoinette and the Downfall of Royalty
The Queen of France and the French Revolution
by Imbert de Saint-Amand

First published under the title
Marie Antoinette and the Downfall of Royalty

Leonaur is an imprint
of Oakpast Ltd

ISBN: 978-0-85706-273-4 (hardcover)
ISBN: 978-0-85706-274-1 (softcover)

http://www.leonaur.com

Publisher's Notes

The opinions of the authors represent a view of events in which she
was a participant related from her own perspective,
as such the text is relevant as an historical document.

The views expressed in this book are not necessarily
those of the publisher.

Contents

1.

Paris at the Beginning of 1792

Paris in 1792 is no longer what it was in 1789. In 1789, the old French society was still brilliant. The past endured beside the present. Neither names nor escutcheons, neither liveries nor places at court, had been suppressed. The aristocracy and the Revolution lived face to face. In 1792, the scene has changed. The Paris of the nobility is no longer in Paris, but at Coblentz. The Faubourg Saint-Germain is like a desert. Since June, 1790, armorial bearings have been taken down. The blazons of ancient houses have been broken and thrown into the gutters. No more display, no more liveries, no more carriages with coats-of-arms on their panels. Titles and manorial names are done away with. The Duke de Brissac is called M. Cossé; the Duke de Caraman, M. Riquet; the Duke d'Aiguillon, M. Vignerot. The *Almanach royal* of 1792 mentions not a single court appointment.

In 1789, it was still an exceptional thing for the nobility to emigrate. In 1792, it is the rule. Those among the nobles who have had the courage to remain at Paris in the midst of the furnace, so as to make a rampart for the King of their bodies, seem half ashamed of their generous conduct. The illusions of worldliness have been dispelled. Nearly every salon was open in 1789. In 1792, they are nearly all closed; those of the magistrates and the great capitalists as well as those of the aristocracy. Etiquette is still observed at the Tuileries, but there is no question of *fêtes*; no balls, no concerts, none of that elegance and animation which once made the court a rendezvous of pleasures.

In 1789, illusions, dreams, a naïve expectation of the age of gold, were to be found everywhere. In 1792, eclogues and pastoral poetry are beginning to go out of fashion. The diapason of hatred is pitched higher. Already there is powder and a smell of blood in the air. A general instinct forebodes that France and Europe are on the verge of a terrible duel. On both sides passions have touched their culminating point. Distrust and uneasiness are universal. Every day the despotism of the clubs becomes more threatening. The Jacobins do not reign yet, but they govern. Deputies who, if left to their own impulses, would vote on the conservative side, pronounce for the Revolution solely through fear of the demagogues. In 1789, the religious sentiment still retained power among the masses. In 1792, irreligion and atheism have wrought their havoc. In 1789, the most ardent revolutionists, Marat, Danton, Robespierre, were all royalists. At the beginning of 1792, the republic begins to show its face beneath the monarchical mask.

The Tuileries, menaced by the neighbouring lanes of the Carrousel and the Palais Royal, resembles a besieged fortress. The Revolution daily augments its trenches and parallels around the sanctuary of the monarchy. Its barracks are the *faubourgs*; its soldiers, red-bonneted pikemen. Louis XVI. in his palace is like a general-in-chief in a stronghold, who should have voluntarily dampened his powder, spiked his cannon, and torn his flags. He no longer inspires his troops with confidence. A capitulation seems imminent. The unfortunate monarch still hopes vaguely for assistance from abroad, for the arrival of some liberating army. Vain hope! He is blockaded in his castle, and the moment is at hand when he will be compelled to play the buffoon in a red bonnet.

Glance at the palace and see how closely it is hemmed in by the earthworks of the Revolution. The abode of luxury and display, intended for *fêtes* rather than for war, Philibert Delorme's *chef-d'oeuvre* has in its architecture none of those means of defence by which the military and feudal sovereignties of old times fortified their dwellings. On the side of the courtyards a multitude of little streets contain a hostile population ready to swell every riot. Near the Pavilion of Marsan is the Palais Royal, that headquarters of insurrection, with its cafés, its gambling-dens, its houses of ill-fame, its wooden galleries which are known as the camp of the Tartars. It is the Duke of Orleans who has democratized the Palais Royal. In spite of the sarcasms of the aristocracy and the lawsuits of neighbouring proprietors, he has destroyed the fine gardens bounded by the rue de Richelieu, the rue des Petit-Champs, and the rue des Bons-Enfants.

In the place it occupied he has caused the rue de Valois, the rue de Beaujolais, and the rue de Montpensier to be opened, all of them inhabited by a revolutionary population. The remaining space he has surrounded on three sides with constructions pierced by galleries, where he has built the shops that form the finest bazaar in Europe. The fourth side of these new constructions was originally intended to form part of the Prince's palace, and to be composed of an open colonnade supporting suites of apartments. But this side has not been erected. In place of it the Duke of Orleans has run up some temporary wooden sheds, containing three rows of shops separated by two large passage-ways, the ground of which has not even been made level.

The privileges pertaining to the Orleans family prevent the police from entering the enclosure of the Palais Royal. Hence it becomes the rendezvous of all conspirators. The taking of the Bastille was plotted there, and there the 20th of June and the 10th of August will yet be organized.

A little further off is the National Assembly. Its sessions are held in the riding-school built when the little Louis XV. was to be taught horsemanship. It adjoins the terrace of the Feuillants. One of its courtyards which looks towards the front of the edifice, is at the upper end of the *rue de Dauphin*. The other extremity occupies the site where the rue Castiglione will be opened later on. There, close beside the Tuileries, sits the National Assembly, the rival and victorious power that will overcome the monarchy.

The Assembly terrorizes the Tuileries. The Jacobin Club terrorizes the Assembly. Close beside the Hall of the Manège, on the site to be occupied afterward by the market of Saint-Honoré, the revolutionary club holds its tumultuous sessions in the former convent founded in 1611 by the Jacobin, or Dominican, friars. The club meets three times a week, at seven in the evening. The hall is a long rectangle with a vaulted roof. Four rows of stalls occupy the longer sides, while the two ends serve as public galleries. Nearly in the middle of the hall, the speaker's platform and the president's writing-table stand opposite each other. Hither come all ambitious revolutionists who desire to talk, to agitate, to make themselves conspicuous. Here Robespierre lords it, not being a deputy in consequence of the law forbidding members of the Constituent Assembly to belong to the legislative body.

Those who love disorder come here to seek emotions. Some find lucrative employment, applause being paid for, and the different parties having each its *claque* in the galleries. Since April, 1791, the Jacobin Club has affiliations in two thousand French towns and villages. At its orders and in its pay is an army of agents whose business it is to make stump speeches, to sing in the streets, to make propositions in cafés, to applaud or to hiss in the galleries of the National Assembly. These hirelings usually receive about five *francs* a day, but as the number of the chevaliers of the revolutionary lustrum increases, the pay diminishes, until it is finally reduced to forty *sous*. Deserters and soldiers dismissed from their regiments for misconduct are admitted by preference.

For some days past, the Club of Moderate Revolutionists, friends of Lafayette, who might have closed the old clubs after the sanguinary repression of the riot in the Champ-de-Mars, and who contented themselves with opening a new one, have been meeting in the convent of the Feuillants, rue Saint-Honoré. But this new club has not been a great success; moderation is not the order of the day; the Jacobins have regained their empire, and on December 26, 1791, seals are placed on the door of the Club of the Feuillants.

At the other extremity of Paris there is a club still more inflammatory than that of the Jacobins: that of the Cordeliers. "The Jacobins," said Barbaroux, "have no common aim, although they act in concert. The Cordeliers are bent on blood, gold, and offices." Speaking as a rule, the Cordeliers belong to the Jacobin Club, while hardly a single Jacobin is a Cordelier. The Cordeliers are the advance-guard of the Revolution. They are, as Camille Desmoulins has said, Jacobins of the Jacobins. The chiefs are Danton, Marat, Hébert, Chaumette. They take their names from those religious democrats, the Minorite friars of Saint Francis, who wear a girdle of rope over their coarse gray habit. They meet in the Place of the School of Medicine, in a monastery whose church was built in the reign of Saint Louis, in 1259, with the fine paid as indemnity for a murder. In 1590, it became the resort of the most famous Leaguers.

Chateaubriand says:

There are places which seem to be the laboratory of seditions." How well this expression of the author of the *Mémoires d'Outre-tombe* describes the club-room of the Cordeliers! The pictures, the sculptured or painted images, the veils and curtains of the convent, have been torn down. The basilica displays nothing but its bare bones to the eyes of the spectator. At the apse, where wind and rain enter through the unglazed rose-window, joiners' work-benches serve as a desk for the president and as places on which to deposit the red caps. Do you see the fallen beams, the wooden benches, the dismantled stalls, the relics of saints pushed or rolled against the walls to serve as benches for "dirty, dusty, drunken, sweaty spectators in torn jackets, pikes on their shoulders, or with their bare arms crossed"

Do you hear the orators who "call each other beggars, pickpockets, robbers, assassins, to the discordant noise of hisses and those proper to their different groups of devils? They find the material of their metaphors in murder, they borrow them from the filthiest of sewers and dungheaps, and from places set apart for the prostitution of men and women. Gestures render their figures of speech more comprehensible; with the cynicism of dogs, they call everything by its own name, in an impious and obscene parade of oaths and curses. To destroy and to produce, death and generation, nothing else can be disentangled from the savage jargon which deafens one's ear."

And what is it that interrupts the speakers? "The little black owls of the cloister without monks and the steeple without bells, making themselves merry in the broken windows in expectation of their prey. At first they are called to order by the tinkling of an ineffectual bell; but as their cries do not cease, they are shot at to make them keep silence. They fall, palpitating, bleeding, and ominous, into the midst of the pandemonium."

So, then, clubs take the place of convents. Since the Constituent Assembly had decreed the abolition of monastic vows by its vote of February 13, 1790, many persons, rudely detached from their usual way of life and its duties, had abandoned their vocation. The nun became a working-woman; the shaved Capuchin read his journal in suburban taverns; and grinning crowds visited the profaned and open convents "as, in Grenada, travellers pass through the abandoned halls of the Alhambra, or as they pause, at Tivoli, under the columns of the Sibyl's temple."

The Jacobin Club and the Club of the *Cordeliers* will destroy the monarchy. In the Memoirs of Lafayette it is remarked that "it is hard to understand how the Jacobin minority and a handful of pretended Marseillais made themselves masters of Paris when nearly all the forty thousand citizens composing the National Guard desired the Constitution; but the clubs had succeeded in scattering the true patriots and in creating a dread of vigorous measures. Experience had not yet taught what this feebleness and disorganization must needs cost."

The dark side of the picture is plainly far more evident than it was in 1789. But how vivid it is still! Those who hunger after sensations are in their element. When has there been more noise, more tumult, more movement, more unexpected or more varied scenes? Listen once more to Chateaubriand who, on his return from America,

11

passed through Paris at this epoch:

> When I read the *Histoire des troubles publics ches divers peuples* be-
> fore the Revolution, I could not conceive how it was possible
> to live in those times. I was surprised that Montaigne wrote so
> cheerfully in a castle which he could not walk around without
> risk of being abducted by bands of Leaguers or Protestants. The
> Revolution has enabled me to comprehend this possibility of
> existence. With us men, critical moments produce an increase
> of life. In a society which is dissolving and forming itself anew,
> the strife between the two tendencies, the collision of the past
> and the future, the medley of ancient and modern manners,
> form a transitory combination which does not admit a mo-
> ment of ennui. Passions and characters, freed from restraint,
> display themselves with an energy they do not possess in well-
> regulated cities. The infraction of laws, the emancipation from
> duties, usages, and the rules of decorum, even perils themselves,
> increase the interest of this disorder.

Yes, people complain, grow angry, suffer, but they are not bored.
How many incidents, episodes, emotions, there are in this strange
tragi-comedy! Everywhere there is something to be seen; in the Assembly, the clubs, the public places, the promenades, streets, cafés, and
theatres. Brawls and discussions are heard on every side. If by chance a
salon is still open, disputes go on there as they would at a club. What
quarrels take place in the cafés! Men stand on chairs and tables to
spout. And what dissensions in the theatres! The actors meddle with
politics as well as the spectators. In the greenroom of the *Comédie-
Française* there is a right side, whose chief is the royalist Naudet, and
a left side led by the republican Talma. Neither actor goes out except
well armed. There are pistols underneath their togas.

The kings of tragedy, threatened by their political adversaries, have
real poniards wherewith to defend themselves. *Les Horaces, Brutus,
La Mort de César, Barnevelt, Guillaume Tell, Charles IX.*, are plays containing in each tirade allusions which inflame the boxes and the pit.
The theatre is a tilting-ground. If the royalists are there in force, they
cause the orchestra to play their favourite airs: *Charmante Gabrielle,
Vive Henri Quatre! O! Richard, O! mon roi!* The revolutionists protest,
and sing their own chosen melody, the *Ça ira*. Sometimes they come
to blows, swords are drawn, and, the play over, elegant women are
dragged through the gutters. There is a general outbreak of insults and

violence. The journals play the chief part in this universal madness. Sometimes the press is eloquent, but it is oftener ribald or atrocious. To borrow an expression from Montaigne, "it lowers itself even to the worthless esteem of extreme inferiority." The beautiful French tongue, once so correct and pure, is no longer recognizable. Vulgar words fall thick as hail. To the language of the Academy has succeeded the jargon of the markets.

What a swarm! what a swirl! How noisy, how restless, is this revolutionary Paris! What excited crowds fill the clubs, the Assembly, the Palais Royal, the gambling-houses, and the tumultuous *faubourgs*! Riotous gatherings, popular deputations, detachments of cavalry, companies of foot-soldiers; gentlemen in French coats, powdered hair, swords at their sides, hats under their arms, silk stockings and low shoes; democrats close-cropped and unpowdered, with English frock coats and American cravats; ragged *sans-culottes* in red caps, weave in and out in ceaseless motion.

Do you know what was the chief distraction of this crowd in April, 1792? The debut of that new and fashionable machine, the guillotine. It was used for the first time on the 25th, for a criminal guilty of rape. Sensitive people congratulated each other on the mitigated torment, which they were pleased to consider a humanitarian improvement. The excellent philanthropist, Doctor Guillotin, was lauded to the skies. His machine was named guillotine in his honour, just as the stage-coaches established by Turgot had been called turgotines.

What enthusiasm, what infatuation, for this guillotine, already so famous and destined to be so much more so! The editors of the *Moniteur* declare in a lyric outburst that it is worthy of the approaching century. The truth is that it accelerates and makes less difficult the executioner's task. In the end the crowd would become disgusted with massacres. The delays of the gibbet would weary their patience. The *sans-culottes*, who doubtless have a presentiment of all that is going to happen, welcome the guillotine, then, with acclamations. At the *Ambigu* theatre a ballet-pantomime, called *Les Quatre Fils Aymon*, is given, and all Paris runs to see the heads of all four fall at once, in the midst of loud applause, under the blade of the good doctor's machine. People amuse themselves with their future instrument of torture as if it were a toy.

In a Girondin *salon* they play at guillotine with a moveable screen that is lifted and let fall again. At elegant dinners a little guillotine is brought in with the dessert and takes the place of a sweet dish. A pretty woman places a doll representing some political adversary under the knife; it is decapitated in the neatest possible style, and out of it runs something red that smells good, a liqueur perfumed with ambergris, into which every lady hastens to dip her lace handkerchief. French gaiety would make a *vaudeville* out of the day of judgment. Poor society, which passes so quick from gay to grave, from lively to severe, and which, like the Figaro of Beaumarchais, laughs at everything so that it may not weep!

2

Count de Fersen's Last Journey to Paris

It has been supposed until lately that after the day when he bade farewell to the royal family at the beginning of the Varennes journey, Count de Fersen never again saw Marie Antoinette. A new publication of very great importance proves that this is an error, and that the Swedish nobleman came to Paris for the last time in 1792, and had several interviews with the King and Queen. This publication is entitled: *Extraits des papiers du grand maréchal de Suède, Comte Jean Axel de Fersen*, and is published by his great-nephew, Baron de Kinckowstrom, a Swedish colonel. There is something romantic in this episode of the mysterious journey made by Marie Antoinette's loyal *chevalier*, which merits to leave a trace in history.

Fersen was one of those men whose sentiments are all the more profound because they know how to veil them under an apparently imperturbable calm. A soul of fire under an exterior of ice, as the Baroness de Korff describes him, courageous to temerity, devoted to heroism, he had conceived for Marie Antoinette one of those disinterested and ardent friendships which lie midway between love and religion. Almost as much a Frenchman as he was a Swede, he did not forget that he had fought in America under the standard of the Most Christian King, and had been colonel of a regiment in the service of France. Having been the courtier of the happy and brilliant Queen, he remained the courtier of the Queen overcome by anguish. He had enkindled in the soul of his sovereign, Gustavus III., the same chivalrous sentiment which animated his own, and was impatiently awaiting the time when he could hasten to the aid of Louis XVI. and Marie Antoinette under the Swedish flag.

His dearest ambition was to draw his sword in the Queen's defence. From the Varennes journey up to the day of Marie Antoinette's execution, he had but one thought: to rescue the woman for whom he would willingly have shed the last drop of his blood. This fixed idea has left its trace on every line of his journal. The sad and melancholy countenance of Fersen, the courtier of misfortune, the friend of unhappy days, is assuredly one of the celebrated types in the drama of Versailles and the Tuileries. This man, who would have made no mark in history but for the martyr Queen, is certain, thanks to her, not to be forgotten by posterity. Marie Antoinette was to return him in glory what he gave her in devotion.

On her return to the Tuileries after the disastrous journey to Varennes, the Queen wrote to Fersen, June 27, 1791: "Be at ease about us; we are living," and Fersen replied: "I am well, and live only to serve you."

June 29, she wrote him another letter in which she said:

Do not write to me; it would endanger us; and, above all, do not return here under any pretext; all would be lost if you should make your appearance. They never lose sight of us by night or day; which is a matter of indifference to me. Be tranquil; nothing will happen to me. The Assembly desires to treat us with gentleness. *Adieu.* I shall not be able to write to you again.

Marie Antoinette was in error when she supposed she would not write again. She was in error, likewise, when she imagined that Fersen, in spite of all dangers and difficulties, would not find means to see her again. Their correspondence was not interrupted. After the acceptance of the Constitution, Marie Antoinette wrote to him:

Can you understand my position and the part I am continually obliged to play? Sometimes I do not understand myself, and am obliged to consider whether it is really I who am speaking; but what is to be done? It is all necessary, and be sure our position would be still worse than it is if I had not at once assumed this attitude; we at least gain time by it, and that is all that is required. I keep up better than could be expected, seeing that I go out so little and endure constantly such immense fatigue of mind. What with the persons whom I must see, my writing, and the time I spend with my children, I have not a moment to myself. The last occupation, which is not the least, gives me my sole happiness. When I am very sad, I take my little boy in my arms, embrace him with my whole heart, and for a moment am consoled.

Fersen, touched and pitying, was constantly thinking of that fatal palace of the Tuileries where the Queen was so much to be compassionated. An invincible attraction drew him thither. There, he thought, was the post of devotion and of honour. November 26, he wrote: "Tell me whether there is any possibility of going to see you entirely alone, without a servant, in case I receive the order to do so from the King (Gustavus III.); he has already spoken to me of his desire to bring this about." Of all the sovereigns who interested themselves in the fate of Louis XVI. and Marie Antoinette, Gustavus was the most active, brave, and resolute; he was also the only one in whom Marie Antoinette placed absolute confidence. She expected less from her own brother, the Emperor Leopold, and it was to Stockholm above all that she turned her eyes.

Gustavus ordered Fersen to go secretly to Paris, and on December 22, 1791, he sent him a memoir and certain letters, commissioning him to deliver them to Louis XVI. and Marie Antoinette. He recommended, as forcibly as he could, a new attempt at flight, but with precautions suggested by the lesson of Varennes. He thought the members of the royal family should depart separately and in disguise, and that, once outside of his kingdom, Louis XVI. should call for the intervention of a congress. The following passage occurs in the letter of the Swedish King to Marie Antoinette:

> I beg Your Majesty to consider seriously that violent disorders can only be cured by violent remedies, and that if moderation is a virtue in the course of ordinary life, it often becomes a vice when there is question of public matters. The King of France can re-establish his dominion only by resuming his former rights; every other remedy is illusory; anything except this would merely open the way to endless discussions which would augment the confusion instead of ending it. The King's rights were torn from him by the sword; it is by the sword that they must be reconquered. But I refrain; I should remember that I am addressing a princess who, in the most terrible moments of her life, has shown the most intrepid courage.

Fersen obtained permission from Louis XVI. to accomplish the mission confided to him by Gustavus III. He left Stockholm under an assumed name and with the passport of a Swedish courier, and reached Paris without accident, February 13, 1792. He was so adroit and prudent that no one suspected his presence. On the very evening of his arrival he wrote in his journal: "Went to the Queen by my usual road; very few National Guards; did not see the King."

Fersen, therefore, only reappeared at the Tuileries in the darkness, like a fugitive or an outlaw. He found the Queen pale with grief and with hair whitened by sorrow and emotion. It was a solemn moment. The storm was raging within France and beyond it. Terrible omens, snares, and dangers lay on every side. One might have said that the Tuileries were about to be swallowed up in a gulf of fire and blood.

The next day Fersen saw the King. He wrote in his journal:

Tuesday, 14. Saw the King at six in the evening. He will not go and cannot, on account of the extreme vigilance. In fact, he scruples at it, having so often promised to remain, for he is an honest man. . . . He sees that force is the only resource; but, being weak, he thinks it impossible to resume all his authority. . . . Unless he were constantly encouraged, I am not sure he would not be tempted to negotiate with the rebels. He said to me afterwards: 'That's all very well! We are by ourselves and we can talk; but nobody ever found himself in my position. I know I missed the right moment; it was the 14th of July; we ought to have gone then, and I wanted to, but how could I when *Monsieur* himself begged me to stay, and Marshal de Broglie, who was in command, said to me: "Yes, we can go to Metz. But what shall we do when we get there?" I lost the opportunity and never found it again. I have been abandoned by everybody.'

Louis XVI. desired Fersen to warn the Powers that they must not be surprised at anything he might be forced to do; that he was obliged, that it was the effect of constraint. "They must put me out of the question," he added, "and let me do what I can."

Fersen had a long talk with Marie Antoinette the same day. She entered into full details about the present and especially about the past. She explained why the flight to Varennes, in which Fersen had taken such a prominent part, and which had succeeded so well so long as he directed it, had ended in failure. The Queen described the anguish of the arrest and the return. To the project of a new effort to escape, she replied by pointing out the implacable surveillance of which she was the object, and the effervescence of popular passions, which this time would overleap all restraint if the fugitives were taken. It would be better for the royal family to suffer together than to expose themselves to die separately. It would be better to die like princes, who abdicate majesty only with life, than as vagabonds, under a vulgar disguise.

"The Queen," adds Fersen, "told me that she saw Alexander Lameth and Duport; that they always tell her that there is no remedy but foreign troops; failing that, all is lost, that this cannot last, that they have gone farther than they wished to. In spite of all this, she thinks them malicious, does not trust them, but uses them as best she can. All the ministers are traitors who betray the King."

Fersen had a final interview with Louis XVI. and Marie Antoinette on February 21, 1792. By February 24, he had returned to Brussels. He was profoundly moved on quitting the Tuileries, but, dismal and lugubrious as his forebodings may have been, how much more sombre was the reality to prove!

What a terrible fate was reserved for the chief actors in this drama! Yet a few days, and the chivalrous Gustavus was to be assassinated. The hour of execution was approaching for Louis XVI. and Marie Antoinette. Fersen, likewise, was to have a most tragic end. From the moment when he bade his last *adieu* to the unhappy Queen, his life was but one long torment. His disposition, already inclined to melancholy, became incurably sad. His loyal and devoted soul could not accustom itself to the thought of the calamities weighing so cruelly upon that good and beautiful sovereign of whom he said in 1778: "The Queen is the prettiest and most amiable princess that I know." On October 14, 1793, he will still be endeavoring, with the aid of Baron de Breteuil, to bring to completion a thousandth plot to extricate the august captive from her fate. He will learn the fatal tidings on the 20th.

"I can think of nothing but my loss," he will write in his journal. "It is frightful to have no positive details. It is horrible that she should have been alone in her last moments, with no one to speak to, or to receive her last wishes. No; without vengeance, my heart will never be content."

Covered with honours under the reign of Gustavus IV., senator, chancellor of the Academy of Upsal, member of the Seraphim Order, grand marshal of the kingdom of Sweden, there will remain in the depths of his heart a wound which nothing can heal. An inveterate fatality will pursue him as it had done the unfortunate sovereign of whom he had been the *chevalier*. He will perish in a riot at Stockholm, June 20, 1810, at the time of the obsequies of the Prince Royal. Struck down by fists and walking-sticks, his hair pulled out, his clothes torn to rags, he will be dragged about half-naked, rolled underfoot, assassinated by a maddened populace. Before rendering his last sigh, he will succeed in rising to his knees, and, joining his hands, he will utter these words from the stoning of Saint Stephen: "*O my God, who callest me to Thee, I implore Thee for my tormentors, whom I pardon.*" If not the same words, they are at least the same thoughts as those of Marie Antoinette on the platform of the scaffold.

3

The Death of the Emperor Leopold

One after another, Marie Antoinette lost her last chances of safety; blows as unforeseen as terrible beat down the combinations on which she had built her hopes. Within a fortnight she was to see the two sovereigns disappear from whom she had expected succour: her brother, the Emperor Leopold, and Gustavus III., the King of Sweden. Leopold had not been equal to all the illusions which his sister had cherished with regard to him, but, nevertheless, he showed great interest in French affairs, and a lively desire to be useful to Louis XVI. Pacific by disposition, he had temporized at first, and adopted a conciliatory policy. He desired a reconciliation with the new principles, and, moreover, he was not blind to the inexperience and levity of the *émigrés*.

But the obligation, to which he was bound by treaties, to defend the rights of princes holding property in Alsace, his fear of the propaganda of sedition, the aggressive language of the National Assembly and the Parisian press, had ended by determining him to take a more resolute attitude, and it was at the moment when he was seriously intending to come to his sister's aid that he was carried off by sudden death. Though she did not desire a war between Austria and France, the Queen had persisted in wishing for an armed congress, which would have been a compromise between peace and war, but which the National Assembly would have regarded as an intolerable humiliation. It must not be denied, the situation was a false one. Between the true sentiments of Louis XVI. and his new *rôle* as a constitutional sovereign, there was a real incompatibility. As to the Queen, she was on good terms neither with the *émigrés* nor with the Assembly.

In order to get a just idea of the sentiments shown by the *émigrés*, it is necessary to read a letter written from Trèves, October 16, 1791, by

Madame de Raigecourt, the friend of Madame Elisabeth, to another friend of the Princess, the Marquise de Bombelles:

> I see with pain that Paris and Coblentz are not on good terms. The Emperor treats the Princes like children. . . . The Princes cannot avoid suspecting that it is the influence of the Queen and her agents which thwarts their plans and causes the Emperor to behave so strangely. . . . Some trickery on the part of the Tuileries is still suspected in this country. They ought to explain themselves to each other once for all. Is the Queen afraid lest the Count d'Artois should arrogate an authority in the realm which would diminish her own? Let her be at ease on that score; she will always be the King's wife and always dominant. What is she afraid of, then? She complains that she is not sufficiently respected. But you know the good heart and the uprightness of our Prince; he is incapable of the remarks attributed to him, and which have certainly been reported to the Queen with the intention of estranging them entirely.

Madame de Raigecourt ends her letter with this complaint against Louis XVI.:

> Our wretched King lowers himself more and more every day; for he is doing too much, even if he still intends to escape. . . . The emigration, meanwhile, increases daily, and presently there will be more Frenchmen than Germans in this region.

At this very time, the Queen was having recourse to her brother Leopold as to a saviour. She wrote to him, October 4, 1791:

> My only consolation is in writing to you, my dear brother; I am surrounded by so many atrocities that I need all your friendship to tranquillize my mind. . . . A point of primary importance is to regulate the conduct of the *émigrés*. If they re-enter France in arms, all is lost, and it will be impossible to make it believed that we are not in connivance with them. Even the existence of an army of *émigrés* on the frontier would be enough to keep up the irritation and afford ground for accusations against us; it appears to me that a congress would make the task of restraining them less difficult. . . . This idea of a congress pleases me greatly; it would second the efforts we are making to maintain confidence. In the first place, I repeat, it would put a check on the *émigrés*, and, moreover, it would make an impression here from which I hope much. I submit that to your better judgment. .

. . *Adieu*, my dear brother; we love you, and my daughter has particularly charged me to embrace her good uncle.

While Marie Antoinette was thus turning towards Austria for assistance, the National Assembly at Paris repelled with energy all thought of any intervention whatsoever on the part of foreign powers. January 1, 1792, it issued a decree of impeachment against the King's brothers, the Prince de Conde, and Calonne. The confiscation of the property of the *émigrés* and the taxation of their revenues for the benefit of the State had been prescribed by another decree to which Louis XVI. had offered no opposition. January 14, Guadet said in the tribune, while speaking of the congress:

If it is true that by delays and discouragement they wish to bring us to accept this shameful mediation, ought the National Assembly to close its eyes to such a danger? Let us all swear to die here rather than—

He was not allowed to finish. The whole assembly rose to their feet, crying: "Yes, yes; we swear it!" And in a burst of enthusiasm, every Frenchman who would take part in a congress having for its object the modification of the Constitution, was declared an infamous traitor. January 17, it was decreed that the King should require the Emperor Leopold to explain himself definitely before March 1.

By a curious coincidence, this date of March 1 was precisely that on which the Emperor Leopold was to die of a dreadful malady. He was in perfect health on February 27, when he gave audience to the Turkish envoy; he was in his agony, February 28, and on March 1, he died. His usual physician asserted that he had been poisoned. The idea that a crime had been committed spread among the people. Vague rumours got about concerning a woman who had caused remark at the last masked ball at court. This unknown person, under shelter of her disguise, might have presented the sovereign with poisoned *bonbons*.

The Jacobins, who might have desired to get rid of the armed chief of the empire, and the *émigrés*, who might have reproached him as too luke-warm in his opposition to the principles of the French Revolution, were alternately suspected. The last hypothesis was hardly probable, nor does anything prove that the Jacobins had any hand in the possibly natural death of the Emperor Leopold. But minds were so overexcited at the time that the parties mutually accused each other, on all occasions, of the most execrable crimes. For that matter, there were Jacobins who, out of mere bravado, would willingly have gloried in crimes of which they were not guilty, provided that these crimes had been committed against kings.

What is certain is, that Marie Antoinette believed in poison.

"The death of the Emperor Leopold," says Madame Campan, "occurred on March 1, 1792. The Queen was out when the news arrived at the Tuileries. On her return, I gave her the letter announcing it. She cried out that the Emperor had been poisoned; that she had remarked and preserved a gazette in which, in an article on the session of the Jacobin Club at the time when Leopold had declared for the Coalition, it was said, in speaking of him, that a bit of piecrust could settle that affair. From that moment the Queen had regarded this phrase as an inadvertence of the propagandists."

On the very day when Marie Antoinette's brother died, Louis XVI.'s Minister of Foreign Affairs, De Lessart, had enraged the National Assembly by reading them extracts from his diplomatic correspondence, which they found not sufficiently firm. They were indignant at a despatch in which Prince de Kaunitz said:

> The latest events give us hopes; it appears that the majority of the French nation, impressed with the evils they have prepared, are returning to more moderate principles, and incline to render to the throne the dignity and authority which are the essence of monarchical government.

When De Lessart came down from the tribune, the whispering changed into cries of rage and threats against the minister and the court, which, it was said, was planning a counter-revolution at the Tuileries, and dictating to the cabinet of Vienna the language by which it hoped to intimidate France. At the evening session of the same day, Rouyer, a deputy, proposed to impeach the Minister of Foreign Affairs. "Is it possible," cried he, "that a perfidious minister should come here to make a parade of his work and lay the responsibility of it on a foreign power? Will the time never arrive when ministers shall cease to betray us? Were my head to be the price of the denunciation I am making, I would none the less go on with it."

At the session of March 6, Guadet said: "It is time to know whether the ministers wish to make Louis XVI. King of the French, or the King of Coblentz."

On the 10th the storm broke. The day before, Narbonne had received his dismission. Brissot accused De Lessart of having compromised the safety of France, withheld from the Assembly the documents

24

establishing the alliance between the Emperor and the King of Prussia, discredited the *assignats*, depreciated the credit, lowered the rate of exchange, and encouraged interior disorder. Vergniaud followed him, exclaiming:

> From the tribune where I am speaking may be seen the palace where perverse counsellors lead astray and deceive the King given to you by the Constitution; where they forge chains for the nation, and arrange the manoeuvres which are to deliver us up to Austria, after having caused us to pass through the horrors of civil war. Terror and dismay have often issued from that famous palace. Let them re-enter it today in the name of the law, let them penetrate all hearts, and teach all who dwell there, that our Constitution accords inviolability to the King alone. Let them know that the law will overtake all the guilty without exception, and that there will not be a single head convicted of crime which can escape its sword.

The decree of impeachment against the ministers was voted by a very large majority. De Lessart was advised to take flight, but he refused. "I owe it to my country," said he, "I owe it to my King and to myself to make my innocence and the regularity of my conduct plain before the tribunal of the high court, and I have decided to give myself up at Orleans." He was conducted by *gendarmes* to that city, where he was imprisoned. Louis XVI. dared not do anything to save his favourite minister. On March 11, Pétion, the mayor of Paris, came to the bar of the Assembly, and read, in the name of the Commune, an address in which it was said:

> When the atmosphere surrounding us is heavy with noisome vapours, Nature can relieve herself only by a thunder-storm. So, too, society can purge itself from the abuses which disturb it only by a formidable explosion. . . . It is true, then, that responsibility is not an idle word; that all men, whatever may be their stations, are equal before the law; that the sword of justice is poised over all heads without distinction.

Was not this language like a prognostic of the 21st of January and the 16th of October? Encompassed by a thousand snares, hated by each of the extreme parties, by the *émigrés* as well as by the Jacobins, Marie Antoinette no longer beheld anything but aspects of sorrow. Abroad, as in France, her gaze fell on dismal spectacles only. Her imagination was affected. She hardly dared taste the dishes served at her table. All had conspired to betray her. She had experienced so many deceptions and so much anguish; fate had pursued her with so much bitterness, that her heart, exhausted with emotions, and overwhelmed with sadness, was weary of all things, even of hope.

4

The Death of Gustavus III

The drama of the Revolution is not French alone; it is European. It has its afterclap in every empire, in every kingdom, even to the most distant lands. It excites minds in Stockholm almost as much as in Paris. Among the Swedes there are people whose greatest desire would be to parody the October Days, and to carry about on pikes the bleeding heads of their adversaries. The new ideas take fire and spread like a train of gunpowder. It is the fashion to go to extremes; a nameless frenzy and fatality seem let loose upon this epoch of agitations and catastrophes. All those who, at one time or another, have been guests at the palace of Versailles, are condemned, as by a mysterious sentence, either to exile or to death.

How will terminate the career of that brilliant King of Sweden, who had received from Versailles and from Paris, from the court and from the city, such an enthusiastic reception? Gustavus, the idol of the great lords, the philosophers, and the fashionable beauties, who, after being the hero of the encyclopædists, came to hold his court at Aix-la-Chapelle amid the French *émigrés*, and who, on his return to Stockholm, prepared there the great crusade for authority, announcing himself as the avenger of divine right, the saviour of all thrones?

The last days of his life, his presentiments, which recall those of Cæsar, his superstitions, his belief in prophecies, his magic incantations, that warning which he scorns, as the Duke de Guise did at the castle of Blois, that masked ball where the costumes, the music, the flowers, the lights, offer a painfully strange contrast to the horror of the attack; all is sinister, lugubrious, in these fantastic and fatal scenes which have already tempted more than one dramatist, more than one musician, and whose phases a Shakespeare only could retrace. The crime of Stockholm is linked closely to the death-struggle of French

27

royalty. The funeral knell which tolled at this extremity of the North had echoes in Paris. The Swedish regicides set the example to the regicides of France.

M. Geffroy has remarked very justly in his work, *Gustave III. et la cour de France*, that the bloody deed which put an end to the reign and the life of Gustavus is not an isolated fact:

> The faults committed by this Prince would not have sufficed to arm his assassins. The true source whence Ankarstroem and his accomplices drew their first inspiration was that vertigo caused during the last years of the century by the annihilation of all religious and even all philosophical faith. . . . No moment of modern history has presented an intellectual and moral anarchy comparable to that which accompanied the revolutionary period in Europe.

The eighteenth century was punished for incredulity by superstition. Having refused to believe the most holy truths, it lent credence to the most fantastic chimeras. For priests it substituted sorcerers; for Christian ceremonies, the rites of freemasonry. The time was coming when, because it had rejected the Sacred Heart of Jesus, it was going to bow before the sacred heart of Marat. The adepts of Mesmer and of De Puysegur, the seekers after the philosopher's stone, the Nicolaites of Berlin, the illuminati of Bavaria, enlarged the boundaries of human credulity, and the men who succumbed in the most naïve and foolish manner to these wretched weaknesses of mind, were precisely the haughtiest philosophers, those who had prided themselves the most on their distinction as free-thinkers. Such a one was Gustavus III.

This Voltairean Prince, who had held the Christian verities so cheap, was superstitious even to puerility. He did not believe in the Gospels, but he believed in books of magic. In a corner of his palace he had arranged a cupboard with a censer and a pair of candlesticks, before which he performed cabalistic operations in nothing but his shirt. Throughout his entire reign he consulted a fortune-teller named Madame Arfwedsson, who read the future for him in coffee-grounds. Around his neck he wore a gold box containing a sachet in which there was a powder that, according to his belief, would drive away evil spirits. All this apparatus of incantation and sorcery was one of the causes of Gustavus's fall. It multiplied the snares around the unfortunate monarch, and served to mask his enemies. Prophecies announced his approaching end, and conspirators took care to fulfil the prophecies.

The Duke of Sudermania, the King's brother, without being an accomplice in the project of crime, encouraged underhand practices. Sectarians approached Gustavus to reproach him for his luxury, his prodigalities, his entertainments, or addressed him anonymous warnings which, in Biblical language, declared him accursed and rejected by the Lord. Their insolence knew no bounds. Madame Arfwedsson had counselled the King to beware if he should meet a man dressed in red. Count de Ribbing, one of the future conspirators, having heard of this, ordered a red costume out of bravado, and presented himself in it before his sovereign, whom such an apparition caused to reflect if not to tremble.

Gustavus, like Cæsar, was to see his Ides of March. It had been predicted to him that the month of March would be fatal to him. This month approached, and the monarch diverted himself by *fêtes* and boisterous entertainments in order to banish the presentiments which never ceased to assail him. He said to himself that all this phantasmagoria would probably soon vanish; that the funereal images would of themselves depart; and that the spectres would disappear at the sound of arms. The monarchical crusade of which he proposed to be the leader grew upon him as the best means by which to escape the incessant obsessions haunting his spirit. In vain was he reminded that Sweden was in need of money, and that a war of intervention in the affairs of France was not popular. His resolution remained unshaken. He counted the days and hours which still separated him from the moment of action: his sole idea was to chastise the Jacobins and avenge the majesty of thrones.

Returned to Stockholm from Aix-la-Chapelle, at the beginning of August, 1791, the impetuous monarch began to be very active in his warlike preparations. The Marquis de Bouillé, who had been obliged to quit France at the time of the unsuccessful journey to Varennes, had entered his service and was to counsel him and fight at his side under the Swedish flag. At the same time Gustavus officially renewed his promises of aid to the King of France. Louis XVI. replied:—

Monsieur My Brother and Cousin: I have just received the lines with which you have honoured me on the occasion of your return. It is always a great consolation to have such proofs of a friendly sentiment as are given me by this letter. The concern, Sire, which you take in all that relates to my interest touches me more and more, and I recognize in each word the august soul of a king whom the world admires as much for his magnanimous heart as for his wisdom.

Meanwhile the conspirators, animated either by personal rancour or the passions common to nobles hostile to their king, were secretly preparing for an attack. The five leaders were Captain Ankarstroem, Count de Ribbing, Count de Horn, Count de Lilienhorn, major of the Blue Guards, and Baron Pechlin, an old man of seventy-two, who had been distinguished in the civil wars, and was the soul of the plot. The conspirators had doubts before committing the crime. During the Diet, which met at Gefle, January 25, 1792, they refrained at the very moment when they were about to strike.

Gustavus was in his castle of Haga, about a league from Stockholm, without guards or attendants. Three of the conspirators approached the castle at five in the evening. They were armed with carbines, and, having placed themselves in ambush near the King's apartment on the ground-floor, were awaiting an opportunity to kill their sovereign. Gustavus coming in from a long walk, went in his dressing-gown to sit in the library, the windows of which opened like doors into the garden. He fell asleep in his armchair. Whether they were alarmed by the sound of footsteps, or whether the contrast between the slumber of the unsuspicious King and the death poising above his head awakened some remorse, the assassins once more abandoned their meditated crime.

Weary of the attempts they had been planning for six months, and which never came to anything, the conspirators might possibly have given them up altogether if a circumstance which they considered providential had not come to rekindle their regicidal zeal. The last masked ball of the season was to be given in the Opera-house on the night of March 16-17, and it was known that Gustavus would be present. To strike the monarch in the midst of the festival, in order to chastise him for his love of pleasure, was an idea which charmed the assassins. Moreover, the mask alone could embolden them; they thought that if the august victim were enveloped in a *domino* they need no longer dread that royal prestige which had more than once caused them to recoil.

Gustavus was counselled to be on his guard. The young Count Louis de Bouillé, who was then at Stockholm, and who had been informed by a letter from Germany that the King was about to be assassinated, begged him to profit by the warnings reaching him from every quarter. Gustavus replied that he would rather go blindly to meet his fate than torment himself with the numberless precautions which such suspicions would demand. "If I listened," added he, "to all the advice I receive, I could not even drink a glass of water; besides, I am far from believing in the execution of such a plot. My subjects, although very brave in war, are extremely timid in politics. The successes I expect to gain in France, the trophies of which I shall bring back to Stockholm, will speedily augment my power by the confidence and general respect which will be their result."

Meantime the fatal hour was approaching. The masked ball of March 16 was about to open. Before going there, Gustavus took supper with a few of the persons belonging to his household. While he was at table he received a note, written in French and unsigned, in which he was entreated not to enter the playhouse, where he was about to be stricken to death. The author of the note urgently recommended the King not to make his appearance at the ball, and, if he persisted in going, to suspect the crowd which would press around him, because this gathering was to be the prelude and signal of the blow aimed at him. The really bizarre thing about this was that the man who wrote these lines was himself one of the conspirators, Count de Lilienhorn.

"It is impossible to tell," says the Marquis de Bouillé in his Memoirs, "whether his conscience wished to acquit itself in this manner towards the King, to whom he owed everything, without forfeiting his word to his party, or whether, knowing the fearless character of this prince, he did not offer his anonymous advice as a bait to his courage. It certainly produced the latter effect." Gustavus made no reflections on reading this note, and went fearlessly to the ball.

The orchestra is playing wildly. The dances are animated. The hall, adorned with flowers, sparkles under the glow of the chandeliers. Gustavus appears for a moment in his box. It is only then that he shows to Baron d'Essen, his first equerry, the anonymous note he had received while at supper. That faithful servant begs him not to go down into the hall. Gustavus disregards the prudent counsel. He says that hereafter he will wear a coat of mail, but that, for this time, he is perfectly determined to be reckless about danger. The King and his equerry go into the *saloon* in front of the royal box, where each puts on a *domino*. Then they enter the hall by way of the stage. There are men essentially courageous, who love danger for its own sake. Gustavus is one of them. Hence he takes pleasure in braving all his assassins.

As he is crossing the greenroom with Baron d'Essen on his arm,

"Let us see," says he, "whether they will really dare to kill me." Yes, they will dare it. The moment that the King enters he is recognized in spite of his mask and his *domino*. He walks slowly around the hall, and then goes into the pit, where he strolls about during several minutes. He is about to retrace his steps, when he finds himself surrounded, as had been predicted, by a group of maskers who get between him and the officers of his suite. Several black *dominos* approach. They are the assassins. One of them, Count de Horn, lays a hand on his shoulder: "Good day, fine masker!" he says. This Judas salute, this ironical welcome given by the murderers to their victim, is the signal for the attack. On the instant, Ankarstroem fires on the King with a pistol loaded with old iron.

Gustavus, struck in the left hip, cries, "I am wounded!" The pistol, which had been wrapped in wool, made only a muffled report, and the smoke spreading throughout the room, the crowd does not think of a murder, but a fire. Cries of "Fire! fire!" augment the confusion. Baron d'Essen, all covered with his master's blood, helps him to gain a little box called the Œil-de-Boeuf, and from there a salon, where he is laid upon a sofa. Baron d'Armfelt orders the doors of the theatre to be closed, and every one to unmask. A man, brazening it out, lifts his mask before the officer of police, and says to him with assurance, "As for me, sir, I hope that you will not suspect me." It is Ankarstroem, the assassin. He goes out quietly. But, after the crime was committed, his weapons, a pistol and a knife like that of Ravaillac, had fallen on the floor. A gunsmith of Stockholm will recognize the pistol and declare that he had sold it a few days before to a former officer of the guards, Captain Ankarstroem. It is the token which will cause the arrest of the assassin, and his punishment by the penalty of parricides,—decapitation and the cutting off of his right hand.

The King showed admirable calm and resignation during the thirteen days he had still to live. He asked with anxiety if the murderer had been arrested, and being answered that his name was not yet known: "Ah! God grant," said he, "that he may not be discovered!" As soon as the first bandages were put on, the wounded man was taken to his apartments at the castle. There he received his courtiers and the foreign ministers. When he saw the Duke d'Escars, who represented the brothers of Louis XVI. at Stockholm: "This is a blow," said he, "which is going to rejoice your Parisian Jacobins; but write to the Princes that if I recover from it, it will change neither my sentiments nor my zeal for their just cause."

In the midst of his sufferings he preserved a dignity above all praise. Neither recriminations nor murmurs issued from his lips. He summoned to his death-bed both his friends and those who had been among the number of his enemies, but would have been horrified to have been accomplices in a crime. When the old Count de Brahé, leader of the nobles of the opposition, presented himself, Gustavus said, as he pressed him in his arms: "I bless my wound, since it has brought back an old friend who had withdrawn from me. Embrace me, my dear count, and let all be forgotten between us."

The fate of his son, who was about to ascend the throne at the age of thirteen, was the chief preoccupation of the King. "Let them put me on a litter," cried he; "I will go to the public square and speak to the people."

And he said to Baron d'Armfelt: "Go, and like another Antony, show the bloody vestments of Cæsar."

It was also to D'Armfelt that he said as he was signing with his dying hand his commission as Governor of Stockholm: "Give me your knightly word that you will serve my son as faithfully as you have served me."

He made his confession to his grand-almoner: "I fear," he said to him, "that I have no great merit before God, but at least I am sure that I have never done harm to any one intentionally." He meant to receive the sacraments according to the Lutheran form, and to have the Queen brought to him, as he had not seen her since his illness. But while seeking sleep in order to tranquillize his mind before this emotion, he found the slumber of death, March 29, 1792, at eleven in the morning. He was forty-six years old.

Thus terminated the brilliant and stormy career of the prince on whom the Marquis de Bouillé has pronounced the following judgment:

"His manners and his politeness rendered him the most amiable and attractive man in his country, although the Swedes are naturally intelligent. He had a vivid imagination, a mind enlightened and adorned by a taste for letters, a masculine and persuasive eloquence, and an easy elocution even when speaking French; useful and agreeable acquirements, a prodigious memory, polite and affable manners, accompanied by a certain oddity which did not displease. His strong and ardent soul was enkindled with an inordinate love of glory; but a chivalrous spirit and loyalty dominated there. His sensitive heart rendered him clement, when he ought, perhaps, to have been severe; he was even susceptible of friendship, and this prince has had and has preserved friends whom I have known, and who were worthy to be such. He had a firm and decided character, and, above all, that resolution so necessary to statesmen, without which wit, prudence, talents, experience, are not only useless, but often injurious."

According to the Marquis de Bouillé, Gustavus should have been the King of France, and Louis XVI. King of Sweden.

As the sovereign of France, Gustavus would have been, beyond all doubt, one of its greatest kings. He would have preserved that beautiful realm from a revolution; he would have governed with glory and with splendour. . . . Louis XVI., on the other hand, placed on the throne of Sweden, would have obtained the respect and esteem of that simple people by his moral and religious virtues, his economy, his spirit of justice, and his good and benevolent sentiments. He would have contributed to the happiness of the Swedes, who would have wept above his tomb; whereas both these monarchs perished at the hands of their subjects. But the designs of Providence are impenetrable, and we ought, in respect and silence, to obey its unalterable decrees.

The Jacobins of Paris, who affected to despise the projects of Gustavus III., showed how much they had feared him by the mad joy they displayed on learning of his death. They lavished praises on "Brutus Ankarstroem." Although it had been committed by the nobles, there was a certain reminiscence of the French Revolution about the assault. In their secret meetings the conspirators had agreed to carry around on pikes the heads of Gustavus's principal friends, "in the French style," as was said in those days. Count de Lilienhorn, brought up, nourished, and drawn from poverty and obscurity by Gustavus, and overwhelmed to the last moment by the benefits of the generous monarch, explained his monstrous ingratitude and the part he had taken in the attack, by saying he had been led astray by the idea of commanding the National Guards of Stockholm after the Revolution, and playing the same part as Lafayette.

The Girondin ministry attained to power in France a few days after Gustavus had been struck down in Sweden. There was no connecting link between the two facts; but at Paris, as at Stockholm, the cause of kings sustained a terrible repulse. The tragic death of their faithful friend must have caused Louis XVI. and Marie Antoinette some painful forebodings concerning their own fate. The murder of Gustavus was the first of a series of great catastrophes. The pistol of the Swedish regicide heralded the blade of the Parisian guillotine. The 16th of March was the prelude of the 21st of January.

5.

The Beginnings of Madame Roland

The moment is at hand when a woman of the middle class, born in humble circumstances, is about to make her appearance on the scene of politics; a woman who, after living in obscurity during thirty-eight years, was to become famous in a few days, and attract the attention of all France first and afterwards that of Europe entire. No figure is more curious to study than hers, and it is not surprising that of late years it has tempted men of great merit, such as MM. Daubant and Faugère, whose publications have shed great light on the Egeria of the Girondins.

At every epoch of history there are certain women who become as it were living symbols, and sum up in their own persons the passions, prejudices, and illusions of their time. They reflect at once its vices and its virtues, its qualities and its defects. Such was Madame Roland. All the distinctive characteristics of the close of the eighteenth century are resumed in her: ardent enthusiasm, generous ideals, aspiration towards progress, passion for liberty, heroic courage in view of persecution, captivity, and death; an absence of religious faith, an implacable vanity, a thirst for emotions, plagiarism of antiquity, declamatory language and sentiments, and childish imitation of Greece and Rome.

Nothing is more interesting than to analyze the conceptions of this mind, count the pulsations of this heart, and surprise the inmost secrets of a woman whose psychological importance is as considerable as her place in history. Intellectually as well as morally, Madame Roland is the daughter of Jean-Jacques Rousseau; socially she is the personification of that third estate which, having been nothing, wished at first to be something and afterwards to be all; politically, she is by turns the heroine and the victim of the Revolution, which, under pretext of liberty, engendered tyranny, which used the guillotine and perished by the guillotine, and which after dreaming of light expired in mire and blood.

How was it that this little *bourgeoise*, the daughter of Philipon the engraver, a man midway between an artisan and an artist, whose very origin seemed to remove her so far from any political *rôle*, attained to high renown? What influences formed this woman whose qualities were masculine? Whence was drawn the inspiration of this siren, destined to be taken in her own snares and die the victim of her own incantations? A rapid glance at the earliest years of Marie-Jeanne Philipon, the future Madame Roland, is enough to explain her passions and her hopes, her errors and her talents, her rages and her enthusiasms.

She was born in Paris, March 18, 1754, of an intelligent but frivolous father, and a simple, devoted, honestly commonplace mother. From infancy she felt herself superior to those by whom she was surrounded. Thence sprang an unmeasured pride and a continual hunger to produce an impression. The infant prodigy preluded the female politician. Speaking of herself in her *Memoirs*, she becomes ecstatic over the child who "read serious works, explained very well the circles of the celestial globe, used crayons and the *burin*, found at eight years that she was the best dancer in an assembly of young persons older than herself," and who, nevertheless, "was often summoned to the kitchen to make an omelette, clean the vegetables, or skim the pot."

She admires her own willingness to descend to domestic cares: "I was never out of my element," she says; "I could make soup as skilfully as Philopoemen could chop wood; but no one, observing me, could imagine that this was suitable employment."

Still speaking of herself, she celebrates "the little person who on Sundays went to church or out walking in a spick-and-span costume whose appearance was fully sustained by her demeanour and her language." She calls attention to the contrast by which, on week-days, the same child went out alone, in a little cloth frock, to buy parsley and salad at a short distance from home.

"It must be owned," she adds, "that I did not like this very well; but I did not show it, and I had the art of doing my errands in such a way as to find some pleasure in it. I united such great politeness to a certain dignity, that the fruit-seller or other person of the sort, took pleasure in serving me first, and even those who came before me thought this proper."

So the little Philipon wanted to take the chief place in the fruiterer's shop, just as, later on, she desired it on the political stage or the Ministry of the Interior. This enemy of privileges will admit them only for herself. In everything she made pretentions: pretentions to elegance, beauty, distinction, talent, knowledge, eloquence, genius, and, when she wanted to be simple, to simplicity. In her style as in her conversation, in her public as in her private life, what she sought before all things was effect. It was absolutely essential that people should talk about her, that she should be playing a part, or standing on a pedestal.

Assuredly, if she had a fault, it was not excess of modesty. She regarded herself as the flower of her sex, a superior woman, made to be loved, flattered, and adored. She speaks of her charms with the precision of a doctor and the enthusiasm of a poet. Not one of her perfections escapes her. It is through a magnifying-glass and before a mirror that she studies and admires herself. She discovers that a society in which a woman so remarkable and so attractive is not thoroughly well known, must be badly organized. Middle-class by birth, and aristocratic by instinct, she represents what one might then have called the new social strata. A secret voice told her that the day was to come when she would make herself feared by the powerful of the earth, those giants with feet of clay who, at the beginning of her career, were still looked at kneeling.

Banished by fate from the theatre where the human tragi-comedy is played, she said to herself: "I too will have a part one of these days." In the earliest stage of her existence there was in her a confused medley of uneasiness and ambition, of spite and anger. She had a horror of the slightly disdainful protection of people of quality. She conceived an aversion for persons like that Demoiselle d'Hannaches, "big, awkward, dry, and yellow," infatuated with her nobility, annoying everybody with her titles, and yet, in spite of her ignorance, her stiff manners, her old-fashioned dress and her follies, well received everywhere on account of her birth.

Slowly, but steadily, the future Amazon of the Revolution prepared herself for the combat. The books which she read and re-read incessantly were the arsenal whence she drew her weapons. One of those presentiments which do not deceive, promised her a stormy but illustrious destiny. More Roman than French, more pagan than Christian, she longed for glory like that of the heroines of Plutarch, her favourite author. In the humble dwelling of her father, situated at the corner of the Pont-Neuf and the Quai des Orfévres, she caught a glimpse of horizons as wide as her thoughts.

"From the upper part of our house," she says, "a great expanse offered itself to my dreamy and romantic imagination. How often from my north window have I contemplated with emotion the deserts of the sky, its superb azure vault splendidly outlined from the bluish dawn far behind the Pont du Change, to the sunset gilded with a faint purplish lustre behind the trees of the Champs Elysées and the houses of Chaillot."

Irritated with the obscurity to which she was condemned by fate, there was but one resource which could have consoled her for the social inequalities which bruised her vanity and her pride. That resource would have been religion. Nothing but an ideal of humility could have appeased the interior revolts of this soul of fire. To such a woman, what is lacking is heaven. Earth, no matter what happens, can give her nothing but deceptions. The only moment of her life when she felt herself really happy was that when she enjoyed the supreme good, peace of heart. Of all parts of her *Memoirs*, the most pure and touching are those she devotes to her recollections of the convent. One might think that the author of *Rolla* had remembered them when he described in such penetrating terms the mystic poetry of the cloister, and the regrets often engendered by the loss of faith in the minds and hearts of people who have become unbelievers.

The little Philipon, being in her twelfth year, asked to be sent to a convent, in order to prepare better for her first communion. She was placed with the Ladies of the Congregation, rue Neuve-Saint-Étienne, in the Faubourg Saint-Marcel, near Sainte-Pélagie, her future prison:

> How I pressed my dear mamma in my arms at the moment of parting from her for the first time! I was stifled, overwhelmed; but I obeyed the voice of God, and crossed the threshold of the cloister, offering Him with tears the greatest sacrifice that I could make. The first night I spent at the convent was agitated: I was no longer under the paternal roof. I felt that I was far from that good mother who was surely thinking of me with tenderness. There was a feeble light in the room where I had been put to bed, with four other children of my own age; I rose quietly and went to the window. The moonlight permitted me to see the garden upon which it looked. The most profound silence reigned; I listened to it, so to say, with a sort of respect; great trees cast their gigantic shadows here and there, and promised a

safe refuge for tranquil meditation. I lifted my eyes to the pure and serene sky, and thought I felt the presence of the Divinity, who smiled at my sacrifice and already offered me its recompense in the peace of a celestial abode. Delicious tears flowed slowly down my cheeks; I reiterated my vows with a holy transport, and I enjoyed the slumber of the elect.

As if in these silent cloisters, which she crossed slowly so as to enjoy their solitude more fully, she had a presentiment of the storms in her destiny and her heart, she sometimes stopped beside a tomb on which was engraven the eulogy of a holy maiden. "She is happy!" she said to herself with a sigh. While she was in prison she remembered with emotion a novice's taking the veil:

> I experience yet the thrill caused by her faintly tremulous voice when she chanted melodiously the customary versicle: '*Elegi*: Here I have chosen my abode, and I will not depart from it forever.' I have not forgotten the notes of this little air; I can repeat them as exactly as if I had heard them yesterday.

Unhappily, religious ideas were soon to undergo a change in the mind of the future Madame Roland. Returning to the paternal dwelling, she was badly brought up there; her mother let her read everything, even *Candide*. Voltaire, Helvétius, Diderot, had no secrets for this young girl. Extreme disorder and confusion in mind and heart were the result. When she had the misfortune to lose her mother at the age of twenty-one, the book in which she sought consolation was the *Nouvelle Héloïse*. Jean-Jacques became her god.

"It seems," she says, "as if he were my natural aliment and the interpreter of the sentiment I had already, and which he alone knew how to explain to me. . . . To have the whole of Jean-Jacques," she says again, "to be able to consult him incessantly, to enlighten and elevate one's self with him at all times of life, is a felicity which can only be tasted by adoring him as I did." Such reading robbed her of faith. It made her a free-thinker and a bluestocking. It inspired her with an unhealthy ambition, sullied her imagination, and troubled the peace of her heart. It deprived her of that moral delicacy, lacking which, even virtue itself loses its charms. She was no longer anything but a young girl, well-conducted but not pure, honest but shameless.

Was not a day coming when, a prisoner and on the point of getting into the fatal cart, she would throw off the terrible anxieties of her situation in order to imitate the impurities of the *Confessions* of Jean-

Jacques, and retrace indecent details with complacency? Do not seek in her that flower of innocence which is the young girl's grace. The charming puritan does not commit great faults, but she has astonishing licenses of thought and speech. For her, Louvet's *Faublas* is "one of those charming romances known to persons of taste, in which the graces of imagination ally themselves to the tone of philosophy." Is not this woman, who begins her life like a saint and ends it as a pupil of Voltaire and Jean-Jacques Rousseau, the symbol of that troubled eighteenth century which opened in fidelity to religious faith and closed in the depths of the abyss of incredulity? The ravages caused by bad reading in the soul of this young girl explain the catastrophes of the entire century.

From the time when she replaced the Gospels by the *Contrat Social* and the *Imitation of Jesus Christ* by the *Nouvelle Héloise*, there was no longer anything simple or natural remaining in the young philosopher. All her thoughts and actions became declamatory. There was something theatrical in her attitudes and gestures, and even in the sound of her voice. Her speech was rhythmical, cadenced, marked by a special accent. Even her private letters often resemble the amplifications of rhetoric rather than the effusions of friendship. One might say that their author had a presentiment that they would be printed. She wrote to Mademoiselle Sophie Cannet, January 3, 1776:

> In any case, burn nothing. Though my letters were one day to
> be read by all the world, I would not hide the only monuments
> of my weakness, and my sentiments.

Monuments of weakness—is not the expression worthy of the bombast of the time?

Not finding love, Mademoiselle Philipon married philosophically. Her union bears a striking imitation to that of Héloise with M. de Volmar. "Looking her destiny peacefully and tenderly in the face, greatly moved but not infatuated," she united herself to a man whom she esteemed but did not love. This was Roland de la Platière, who was descended from an ancient and very honourable middle class family. Though not rich, he was at least comfortably well off. "Well educated, honest, simple in his tastes and manners, he fulfilled his duties as inspector of manufactures in a notable way. The marriage was celebrated on February 4, 1780.

Roland was forty-six years old, while his wife was not yet twenty-six. Thin, bald, careless in his dress, the husband was not at all an ideal person. It had taken him five years to declare his passion, and this hesitation, as his wife was to write thirteen years later, "left not a vestige of illusion in his sentiments."

"I have often felt," says she, "that there was no similarity between us. If we lived in retirement, I spent many painful hours; if we mingled in society, I was loved by persons among whom I perceived there were some who might affect me too much; I plunged into labour with my husband. . . . It was a long time before I gained courage to contradict him."

M. Roland was sent to Amiens, where his wife presented him with a daughter, whom she nursed, and afterwards brought up with the utmost tenderness and devotion. In 1784, he was summoned to Lyons, where he found himself once more in his native region. Thenceforward he spent two of the winter months in Lyons, and the remainder of the year on his paternal domain, the Close of Platière, two leagues from Villefranche, surrounded by woods and vineyards, and opposite the mountains of Beaujolais. While her husband went to take possession of his new post, Madame Roland, not yet a republican, remained a few weeks in Paris in order to obtain, if possible, the patent of nobility so ardently desired by the family. Her solicitations proved unsuccessful, and the married pair, despairing of becoming nobles, consoled themselves by a frank avowal of democracy.

Up to the time of the Revolution, Madame Roland's life glided peacefully away without any remarkable incidents. In the Close of Platière, which she calls her dovecot, she appears as a good housekeeper who looks after everything, from the cellar to the garret; who plays the doctor among the poor villagers; who is delighted to find in nature a savour of frank and free rusticity. The life she leads is not merely honest, but edifying. She is very careful at this period to hide her philosophy. She writes to Bosc, one of her friends, February 9, 1785:

> My brother-in-law, whose disposition is extremely gentle and sensitive, is also very religious; I leave him the satisfaction of thinking that the dogmas are as evident to me as they appear to him, and my exterior actions are such as become the mother of a family out in the country, who is bound to edify everybody. As I was very devout in my early youth, I know my prayers as well as my philosophy, and I prefer to make use of my first erudition.

She wrote again to Bosc, October 12, 1785:

I have hardly touched a pen for a month, and I think I am acquiring some of the inclinations of the beast whose milk refreshes me; I am extremely *asinine*, and I busy myself with all the petty cares of the *hoggish* country life. I make preserved pears that are delicious; we dry grapes and plums; we wash and make up linen; we have white wine for breakfast, and we lie down on the grass to rest; we follow the vintagers; we repose in the woods and fields.

Before looking at the female politician, let us glance once more at the woman in private life, the charitable, devoted, honourable mother of a family, such as she paints herself in a letter of November 10, 1786:

From the corner of my fire, at eleven o'clock, after a quiet night and the various morning cares, my husband at his desk, my little girl knitting, and I chatting with one and superintending the other's work, enjoying the happiness of being snugly in the bosom of my dear little family, writing to a friend, while the snow is falling on so many wretches weighed down by poverty and sorrow, I am touched with compassion for their fate; I turn back sweetly to my own, and at this moment I count as nothing the annoyances of relations or circumstances which seem occasionally to mar its felicity.

Alas, why did not Madame Roland stay in her modest country-house to dry her grapes and plums, to superintend her washing, mend her linen, and spread out in her garret the fruits for winter use? Were not obscurity, repose, peace of heart, better for her than that fictitious glory which was to pass so quickly and end upon the scaffold? One might say that before quitting nature, that great consoler which calms and does not betray, in order to plunge herself into the odious world of politics, which spoils and embitters the most beautiful souls, she experiences a certain vague regret for the sweet and tranquil joys which her folly was about to cause her to renounce forever.

"The weather is delightful," wrote Madame Roland, May 17, 1790; "the country has changed almost beyond recognition in only six days; the vines and walnuts were as black as they are in winter, but a stroke of the magic wand does not alter the aspect of things more quickly than the heat of a few fine days has done; everything turns green and leafs out; a soft verdure is visible where there was nothing but the dull and faded tint of torpor and inaction. I could easily forget public affairs and men's controversies here; content to arrange the manor, to see my fowls brood, and take care of my rabbits, I would care nothing more about the revolutions of empires. But, as soon as I am in the city, the poverty of the people and the insolence of the rich rouse my hatred of injustice and oppression: I have no longer any soul or desire except for the triumph of great truths and the success of our regeneration."

The die is cast. The daughter of Philipon the engraver is about to become a political woman. The hour is come when this great actress, who has long known her part, is at last going on the stage. She has a presentiment of the risk she is running in assuming a task which is beyond her sex. But, like soldiers who love danger for danger's sake, and prefer the emotions of the battlefield to garrison life, she will joyfully quit her province and throw herself into the seething furnace of Paris. Even though she is to meet persecution and death at the end of her new career, she will not recoil. A short but agitated life will seem better to her than a long and fortunate existence without violent emotions. A clear sky pleases her no longer. She is homesick for storms and lightning flashes.

6

Madame Roland's Entrance on the Scene

The hour of the Revolution had struck, and, ambitious, unbeliev-
ing, full of disdain for the leading classes, full of confidence in her own
superiority, active, eloquent, impassioned, uniting the language of an
orator to the seductions of a charming woman, Madame Roland was
ripe for the Revolution. Her epoch suited her, and she suited her epoch. This pagan who, according to her own expression, roamed men-
tally in Greece, attended the Olympic games, and despised herself for
being French; this fanatical admirer of antiquity who, at eight years of
age, carried Plutarch to church with her instead of a missal, who styled
Roland *the virtuous* as the Athenians called Aristides the *just*, who will
die like her heroes, Socrates and Phocion; this student who, at another
period, would have been rated as an under-bred woman of the middle
class, a more or less ridiculous bluestocking, suddenly found herself, in
consequence of a general panic and circumstances as strange as they
were unforeseen, the very ideal of the society in which she lived. For
several months she was to be its fashionable type, its favourite heroine.
But the Revolution was a Saturn who devoured his children, male
and female, and the Egeria of the Girondins expiated bitterly the intoxication caused by her brief popularity.

In 1777, at the age of twenty-three, she had written:

Gay and jesting speeches fall from this mouth which sobs at
night upon its pillow; a laugh dwells on my lips, while my tears,
shut up within my heart, at length make on it, in spite of its
hardness, the effect produced by water on a stone: falling drop
by drop, they insensibly wear it away.

In 1791, when she was thirty-eight, she wrote:

> The phenomena of nature, which make the vulgar grow pale, and which are imposing even to the philosophical eye, offer nothing to a sensitive person preoccupied with great concerns, but scenes inferior to those of which her own heart is the theatre.

The flame consuming the eloquent and ardent disciple of Rousseau was in need of fuel, and, finding this in politics, she threw herself upon it with a sort of ravenous fury, just as she had once abandoned herself to study. At twenty-two she had written to one of her young friends:

> You scold me for studying too hard. Bear in mind, then, that unless I did so, love might perhaps excite my imagination to frenzy. It is a necessary distraction. I am not trying to become a learned woman; I study because I need to study, as I do to eat.

It was thus that Madame Roland plunged into politics. All her unappeased instincts and repressed forces found their outlet in that direction.

Woman being formed by nature to be dominated, nothing is more agreeable to her than to invert the parts, and in her turn to domineer. To exert influence in public affairs, to designate or support the candidates for great offices of State, to organize or direct a ministry, to make themselves listened to by serious men, to inspire opinions or systems, is to ambitious women a kind of revenge for their sex. Those who have acquired a habit of exercising this sort of power cannot relinquish it without extreme reluctance. If they have once persuaded themselves of their superiority to men, nothing can ever root the conviction from their minds. To be protected humiliates them; what they long for most of all is to be acknowledged as protectresses. Self-deluded, they attribute to their passion for the public welfare what is, especially in their case, the need of petty glory, the thirst for emotions, or the amusement of pride and vanity.

The Revolutionary bluestocking, Madame Roland, was from the very start delighted to see that her works were printed, and that they produced as much effect as if they had been written by some great statesman. These first successes seemed to her to justify the excellent opinion she had always entertained of herself. She got into a habit of playing the oracle. No sooner had her lips touched the cup containing this poisonous but intoxicating beverage than she would have no other. That alone could refresh, even while it killed her.

Politics has the immense defect of exasperating, troubling, and disfiguring souls. Madame Roland was born good, sensible, and generous. Politics made her at times wicked, vindictive, and cruel. July 26, 1789, she wrote this odious letter:

"You are nothing but children; your enthusiasm is a fire of straw, and if the National Assembly does not order the trial of two illustrious heads, or some generous Decius does not strike them down, you are all . . . lost" (Madame Roland employed a more trivial expression). "If this letter does not reach you, may the cowards who read it redden to learn that it is from a woman, and tremble in reflecting that she can create a hundred enthusiasts from whom will proceed a million others."

Roland had been employed by the Agricultural Society of Lyons to draw up its reports for the States-General. Madame Roland wrote much more of them than her husband did. She sent article on article to a journal founded by Champagneux to forward the revolutionary propaganda. Sixty thousand copies were printed of one of them in which she described the festival of the Federation at Lyons. Imagine the joy felt by the *femme-auteur*, the pupil of Jean-Jacques, the model of George Sand! Soon afterwards, the municipality deputed Roland to the Constituent Assembly to advocate the interests of the city, which was involved to the extent of forty millions, and which asked to have this debt assumed by the State. Roland and his wife arrived in Paris, February 20, 1791.

The married pair installed themselves on the third floor of the hotel Britannique, in rue Guénégaud. There a sort of political reunion was formed, of which Brissot was the first link. Four times a week a few friends, and certain deputies and journalists, met around this still unknown woman, whose wit, charm, and beauty were not long in making a sensation. It was at this period that she made Buzot's acquaintance. The day of her first interview with the young and brilliant deputy was an epoch in her sentimental life. Thenceforward, two passions, love and ambition, the one as fierce and devouring as the other, were to occupy her ardent soul.

Comparing the young orator, whom she perhaps transformed in her imagination into the president of a more or less Athenian republic, with the austere and prosaic companion of her existence, she perceived that, according to her own expression, there was no equality between her and her husband, and that "the ascendency of a domineering character, joined to twenty years' seniority, rendered one of these superiorities too great"—that of age. She was herself six years older than Buzot. Even though her love for him may have remained Platonic, she gave him all her heart and soul.

For the majority of women, still beautiful, who mingle in public affairs, love is the principal thing; politics but the accessory, the pretext. They imagine they are attaching themselves to ideas, and it is to men. In this respect the heroines of the Revolution resemble those of the Fronde. The stateswoman in Madame Roland plays second to the lover of Buzot. In her mind the Republic and the handsome republican blend into one. Believing herself a patriot when she is above all a woman in love, she carries the emotions, the infatuations, the ardours and exaggerations of her private life into her public one. With her, angers and enthusiasms rise to paroxysm. She is extreme in all things.

She detests Louis XVI. as much as she loves Buzot. After the flight to Varennes, she wrote:

To replace the King on the throne is a folly, an absurdity, if it is not a horror; to declare him demented is to make obligatory the appointment of a regent. To impeach Louis XVI. would be, beyond all contradiction, the greatest and most righteous step, but you are incapable of taking it. Well then, put him not exactly under interdict, but suspend him.

Here begins the influence of Madame Roland. The suspension of the royal authority is one of her ideas.

"So long as peace lasted," she says, "I adhered to the peaceful *rôle* and to that kind of influence which I thought fitting to my sex; when war was declared by the King's departure, it appeared to me that everyone should devote himself unreservedly. I joined the fraternal societies, being persuaded that zeal and good intentions might be very useful in critical moments. I was unable to stay at home any longer, and I went to the houses of worthy people of my acquaintance that we might excite each other to great measures."

One knows what the Revolution meant by that expression: great measures. Madame Roland became furious. She wanted a freedom of the press without check or limit. She was angry because Marat's newspapers were destroyed by the satellites of Lafayette. "It is a cruel thing to think of," she exclaims, "but it becomes every day more evident that peace means retrogression, and that we can only be regenerated by blood."

Her hatred includes both Louis XVI. and Marie Antoinette. June 25, 1791, she writes:

It appears to me that the King ought to be sequestered and his wife impeached.

And on July 1:

The King has sunk to the lowest depths of degradation; his trick has exposed him completely, and he inspires nothing but contempt. His name, his portrait, and his arms have been effaced everywhere. Notaries have been obliged to take down the *escutcheons* marked with a *flower-de-luce* which served to designate their houses. He is called nothing but Louis the False, or the great hog. Caricatures of every sort represent him under emblems which, though not the most odious, are the most suitable to nourish and augment popular disdain. The people tend of their own accord to all that can express this sentiment, and it is impossible that they should ever again be willing to see seated on the throne a being they despise so completely.

Things did not go fast enough to suit Madame Roland's furious hatred. The popular gathering in the Champ-de-Mars, whose aim was to bring about the deposition of the King, was forcibly dispersed on July 17. With six exceptions, all the deputies who had belonged either to the Jacobin Club or that of the Cordeliers, left them on account of their demand that Louis XVI. should be brought to trial. The time for great measures, to use Madame Roland's expression, had not yet arrived. The ardent democrat laments it.

"I cannot describe our situation to you," she writes at this moment of the revolutionary recoil; "I feel environed by a silent horror; my heart grows steadfast in a mournful and solemn silence, ready to sacrifice all rather than cease to defend principles, but not knowing the moment when they can triumph, and forming no resolution but that of giving a great example."

The mission which had kept Roland in Paris for seven months being ended, the discouraged pair returned to their province in September. After stopping a few days in Lyons, in order to found a popular society affiliated to the Jacobins of the capital, they went to spend the remainder of the autumn at their country place, the Close of Platière. But calm and silence no longer suited Madame Roland. Repose exasperated her. She missed the struggle and the emotions of revolutionary Paris, of which she had said:

> One lives ten years here in twenty-four hours; events and affec-
> tions blend with and succeed each other with singular rapidity;
> no such great events ever occupied minds.

The pleasure of seeing her daughter again was not enough to com-
pensate her for the chagrin of having parted from Buzot. Just as she
was despairing at the thought of sinking back into all the nullity of
the province, as she expresses it, the news came that the inspectors of
agriculture had been suppressed. Roland, no longer an official, delib-
erated with his wife as to their next step. His own inclination was to
settle permanently in the country and devote himself to agricultural
labours which would surely and safely augment his fortune. But his
wife was by no means of the same mind. She must see her dear Buzot
again at any cost. She flattered the self-love of her unsuspecting spouse,
and persuaded him that Paris was the sole theatre worthy of the virtuous Roland. Roland allowed himself to be convinced. His wife, no
longer mistress of herself, was drawn into the Parisian abyss as by an
irresistible force. And yet was it not she who had proposed to herself
this ideal, so easily to have been realized?

> I have never imagined anything more desirable than a life di-
> vided between domestic cares and those of agriculture, spent
> on a healthy and fertile farm, with a little family where the
> example of its heads and common labor maintain attachment,
> peace, and freedom.

Was it not she who had uttered this profoundly true thought:

> I see neither pleasure nor happiness except in the reunion of
> that which charms the heart as well as the senses, and costs no
> regrets?

In the most beautiful days of her youth had she not written:

> There was a time when I was never content except when I had
> a book or a pen in my hand; at present I am as well satisfied
> when I have made a shirt for my father or added up an account
> of expenses as if I had read something profound. I do not care at
> all to be learned; I want to be good and happy; that is my chief
> business. What is necessary but good, honest common sense?

Is it not she, too, who will write at the beginning of her *Memoirs*:

> I have observed that in all classes, ambition is generally fatal;
> for the few happy ones whom it exalts, it makes a multitude

of victims.

Why did she not more frequently remind herself of the sentiment so just and well expressed in a letter dated in 1790:

Women are not made to share in all the occupations of men: they are altogether bound to domestic cares and virtues, and they cannot turn away from them without destroying their happiness.

But, alas! passion does not reason. Farewell common sense, wisdom, and experience, when ambition and love have taken possession of a woman's heart. Returning to Paris, December 15, 1791, the Rolands established themselves in the rue de la Harpe, and plunged head-long into politics. The wife redoubled her activity, eloquence, and passion. The husband, instead of attending quietly to the management of his retiring pension, was named a member of the Jacobin corresponding committee at the beginning of 1792, a revolutionary centre of which Brissot was the leader. At this period, we are informed by Madame Roland, the intimidated court imagined that the nomination of a minister chosen from among the patriots of the Assembly would cause it to regain a little popularity. Brissot proposed Roland, who, on March 24, 1792, accepted the portfolio of the Interior.

Madame, behold yourself, then, the wife of a minister, and in fact more of a minister than your husband. Your ambitious projects, which have been treated as chimerical, are now realized. You have a *cortège* like Marie Antoinette. Men seek the favour of a smile, a word, from you. They court, they solicit, they fear you. The monarchy, which you detest, is at last obliged to reckon with you and your friends. Your beauty, your talent, and your eloquence are boasted of. Your name is in every mouth. You are powerful, you are celebrated. Well! you will find out for yourself what bitterness there is at the bottom of this cup of pride which has tempted your lips so long.

You will learn at your own expense that renown does not produce happiness, and that, for a woman, twilight is better than the full glare of day. Yes, you will long for the obscurity which weighed upon you. You will long for the house of your father, the engraver, on the Quai des Orfèvres. You will dream of the sunsets which affected you, and of the monotonous but peaceful succession of your days. You, the deist, the female philosopher, will recall with regret the cloisters where in your adolescence you tasted the peace of the elect. In the time of your supreme trial Buzot's miniature will not console you; it is not his image you should cover with your kisses. No; that miniature is not the viaticum for eternity. What you will need is the crucifix, and you respect the crucifix no longer. And yet your imagination will evoke the mystic cloister, with its altars decked with flowers, its painted windows, its penetrating and ineffable poesy.

And in thought, also, you will see the country once more, the harvest time, the month of the vintage, the poor who come to the door asking for bread and who go away with blessings on their lips and gratitude in their hearts. Why have you quitted these honest people? What have you come to do in the midst of these ferocious Jacobins, who flatter you today and will assassinate you tomorrow? Do you fancy that Marie Antoinette is the only woman who will be insulted, calumniated, and betrayed? Why do you seat at your hospitable table this livid-faced Robespierre, who today, perhaps, will address you a madrigal, and tomorrow send you to the scaffold?

You will pay very dear for these false and artificial joys, these gusts of commonplace vanity, this pride of a *parvenu*, and the pleasure of presiding for a few evenings at the dinners given to the Minister of the Interior in Calonne's dining-room. The Legislative Assembly, the Jacobin Club, the journals and the ministry, the souvenirs of Plutarch and the parodies of Jean-Jacques, the noisy crowd of flatterers who are the courtiers of demagogues as they would have been the courtiers of kings, these adulators who are going to change into executioners,—all are vanity! Poor woman, whose power will be so ephemeral, why do you make yourself a persecutor? You will so soon be persecuted. Why labour so relentlessly to shake the foundations of a throne that will bury you beneath its ruins?

7

Marie Antoinette and
Madame Roland

Two women find themselves confronted across the chessboard and about to move the pieces in a terrible game in which each stakes her head, and each is foredoomed to lose. One is the woman who represents the old *régime*—the daughter of the German Cæsars, the Queen of France and Navarre; the other stands for the new *régime*, the Parisian middle classes—the daughter of the engraver of the Quai des Orfèvres. They are nearly the same age. Madame Roland was born March 18, 1754; and Marie Antoinette, November 2, 1755. Both are beautiful, and both are conscious of their charm. Each exercises a sort of domination over all who approach her.

In 1792, when Roland enters the ministry, Marie Antoinette is no longer thinking of coquetry, luxury, or dress. The heroine of the Gallery of the Mirrors, the crowned shepherdess of the Trianon, the queen of elegance, pleasure, and fashion is not recognizable in her. The time for splendours is over, like the time for pastorals. No more festivals, no more distractions, no more theatres. Incessant anxieties and unremitting labour; writing throughout the day and reading, meditating, and praying throughout the night, are now the unfortunate sovereign's whole existence. She hardly sleeps. Her eyes are reddened by tears.

A single night, that of the arrest on the journey to Varennes, had sufficed to whiten her hair. She wears mourning for her brother, the Emperor Leopold, and for her ally, the King of Sweden, Gustavus III., and one might say that she is also wearing it for the French monarchy. All trace of frivolity has disappeared. The severe and majestic countenance of the woman who suffers so cruelly as queen, spouse, and mother, is sanctified by the double poetry of religion and sorrow.

Madame Roland, on the other hand, is more coquettish than she has ever been. The actress who has at last found her theatre and is very proud to play her part, wishes to allure, desires to reign. She delights in presiding at these political dinners where all the guests are men, and of which her grace and eloquence constitute the charm. She has just completed her thirty-eighth year. Her husband is nearly fifty-eight; Buzot is only thirty-two. Possibly she is still more preoccupied with love than with ambition. To use one of her own expressions, "her heart swells with the desire to please," to please Buzot above all; she takes pains to celebrate her own beauty, which, in spite of showing symptoms of decline, has the brilliance of sunset.

In her *Memoirs* she describes her "large and superbly modelled bust, her light, quick step, her frank and open glance, at once keen and soft, which sometimes amazes, but which caresses still more, and always quickens." She writes: "My mouth is rather large; there are a thousand prettier, but none that has a softer and more seductive smile." In prison, when she is nearly forty, she states that if she has lost some of her attractions, yet she needs no help from art to make her look five or six years younger.

"Even those who see me every day," she adds, "require to be told my age, in order to believe me more than thirty-two or thirty-three." Madame Roland had at first written thirty-three or thirty-four. But after reflection, finding herself too modest, she made an erasure and retrenched another year. She adds that she made very little use of her charms; avowing at the same time, and with the most absolute frankness, that if she could reconcile her duty with her inclination to utilize them more fully, she would not be sorry.

Both Marie Antoinette and Madame Roland were political women. But the one became so in her own despite, in the hope of saving the life of her husband and the heritage of her son; the other, through ambition and the desire to play a part for which her origin had not destined her. In the one, everything is at once noble and simple, natural and majestic; in the other there is always something affected and theatrical; one scents the *parvenue* who will never be a *grande dame*, even in the Ministry of the Interior or at the house of Calonne. All is unstudied in Marie Antoinette; Madame Roland, on the contrary, is an artist in *coquetry*.

Bizarre caprice of fate which makes political rivals and adversaries treating with each other on equal terms of these two women, of whom one was so much above the other by rank and birth. The Tuileries and the house of the Minister of the Interior are like two hostile citadels at a stone's throw from each other. On both sides there is watchfulness and fear. An impassable abyss, hollowed out by the vanity of the commoner still more than by the pride of the Queen, forever separates these two courageous women who, had they united instead of antagonizing each other, might have saved both their country and themselves.

It is necessary to go back a few years in order to comprehend the motive of Madame Roland's hatred for Marie Antoinette. It was inspired in the vain commoner by envy, the worst and vilest of all counsellors. Madame Roland's special characteristic was the passion for making an effect. Now the effect produced by Marie Antoinette under the old *régime* was immense; that produced by the future Egeria of the Girondin group was almost null. A simple mortal, regarding Olympus from below, she said to herself with vexation, that in spite of her talents and her charms there was no place for her among the gods and goddesses. Versailles was like a superior world from which it maddened her to be excluded. She was twenty years old when, in 1774, she visited it with her mother, her uncle, the Abbé Bimont, and an aged gentlewoman, Mademoiselle d'Hannaches. They all lodged at the palace. One of Marie Antoinette's women, who was acquainted with the *abbé*, and who was not then on duty, lent them her apartment. The only object of the excursion was to give the young girl a near view of the court.

In recalling this souvenir in her Memoirs, Madame Roland displays her aversion for the old society. She is annoyed even with the companion of her visit, because she was, according to the expression then in use, a person of quality. "Mademoiselle d'Hannaches," she says, "went boldly wherever she chose, ready to fling her name in the face of anyone who tried to stop her, thinking they ought to be able to read on her grotesque visage her six hundred years of established nobility. The fine figure of a pedantic little cleric like the Abbé Bimont, and the imbecile pride of the ugly d'Hannaches were not out of keeping in those scenes; but the unpainted face of my worthy mamma, and the modesty of my dress, announced that we were commoners; if my eyes or my youth provoked remark, it was almost patronizing, and caused me nearly as much displeasure as Madame de Boismorel's compliments."

It was this Madame de Boismorel who, although she found the little Philipon very pleasing, had said to the grandmother of the future Madame Roland: "Take care that she does not become a learned woman; it would be a great pity."

The splendours of Versailles did not dazzle the daughter of the engraver of the Quai des Orfèvres. The apartment she occupied was at the top of the palace, in the same corridor as that of the Archbishop of Paris, and so near it that it was necessary for the prelate to take precautions lest she should overhear him talk. "Two poorly furnished rooms," she says, "in the upper end of one of which space had been contrived for a valet's bed, was the habitation which a duke and peer of France esteemed himself honoured in possessing, in order to be closer at hand to cringe every morning at the *levée* of Their Majesties: and yet he was the rigorist Beaumont. . . . The ordinary and the ceremonial table-service of the entire family, eating separately or all together, the masses, the promenades, the gaming, the presentations, had us for spectators during a week."

What impression was made on her by this excursion to the royal palace? She herself will tell us nineteen years later, in her prison. "I was not insensible," she says, "to the effect of so much pomp and ceremony, but I was indignant that its object should be to exalt certain individuals already too powerful and of very slight personal importance: I liked much better to look at the statues in the gardens than at the persons in the palace; and when my mother asked if I was satisfied with my visit, 'Yes,' I replied, 'provided it will soon be over; if I stay here many days longer, I shall detest the people so much that I shall be unable to hide my hatred.' 'What harm are they doing you, then?' 'Making me feel injustice, and constantly behold absurdity.'"

How this impression is emphasized in the really prophetic letter written by the future heroine of the Revolution to her friend, Mademoiselle Sophie Cannet, October 4, 1774:

> To return to Versailles. I cannot tell you how greatly all I have examined has made me value my own situation, and thank Heaven that I was born in an obscure condition. You think, perhaps, that this sentiment is based on the slight esteem I attach to the worth of opinion, and my sense of the reality of the penalties attached to greatness. Not at all. It is based on the knowledge I have of my own character, which would be very detrimental both to me and to the State if I were placed at a little distance from the throne; because I would be keenly shocked by the extreme inequality which sets so many thousands of men below a single individual of the same species!

What a prediction! The most unforeseen events were one day to bring this young plebeian near that royalty formerly so far above her. The engraver's daughter will be the wife of a minister of State. And then what will happen? According to her own expression, her *rôle* will be very detrimental to herself and to the State.

In the same letter she had written:

> A beneficent king seems to me an almost adorable being; but if, before coming into the world, the choice of a government had been given me, my character would have made me decide for a republic.

She will end by hating the beneficent King, and probably no one will contribute more than she towards establishing the republican *régime* in France.

Supposing that, instead of being merely an insignificant commoner, Madame Roland had been born in the ranks of aristocracy, had enjoyed the right of sitting down in the presence of Their Majesties at Versailles, and had shone at the familiar entertainments of the Trianon, she would doubtless have shared the sentiments and ideas of the women of the old *régime*, and, like the Princess de Lamballe or the Duchess de Polignac, have shed tears of compassion over the Queen's misfortunes. Fate, in placing her in a subordinate position, made her an enemy and a rebel. She anathematized the society in which her rank bore no relation to her lofty intelligence and her need of domination. When, from the upper window of her father's house on the Quai des Orfèvres, beside the Pont-Neuf, she saw the brilliant retinue of Marie Antoinette pass by on their way to Notre Dame to return thanks to God for some happy event, she grew angry at all this pomp and glitter, so much in contrast with her own obscure condition.

What crimes have been engendered by the sentiment of envy! The furies of the guillotine were above all things envious. They were delighted to see in the fatal cart the woman whom they had formerly beheld in gala carriages resplendent with gold. Madame Roland certainly ought not to have carried her hatred to such a pitch; but had she not demanded in 1789, when speaking of Louis XVI. and the Queen, that "two illustrious heads" should be brought to trial? Who knows? If, in 1784, she had obtained the patent of nobility for her husband which at that period she solicited so ardently, she might have become sincerely royalist!

But having remained, despite herself, in the citizen class, she retained and personified, to her latest hour, its rancour, pettiness, and wrath. What figure could she have made at Versailles, or even at the Tuileries? In the midst of great lords and noble ladies the haughty commoner would have been out of place; she would have stifled. It was chiefly on that account that she attached herself to the new ideas. She told herself that so long as royalty lasted, she would always be of small importance; while, if the republic were established, she might aspire to anything. Though her husband was one of the King's ministers, she became daily more adverse to the monarchy, and Roland, following her counsels, was like a pilot whose whole intent is to make the vessel founder, even though he were to perish with its crew.

It is a sad thing to say, but even their community in suffering did not disarm Madame Roland's hate for Marie Antoinette. It was in prison, on the eve of ascending the scaffold herself, that she wrote concerning Louis XVI. and the Queen:

> He was led away by a giddy creature who united the presumption of youth and grandeur to Austrian insolence, the intoxication of the senses, and the heedlessness of levity, and was herself seduced by all the vices of an Asiatic court, for which she had been too well prepared by the example of her mother.

Ah! why were not these cruel lines effaced by the tears Madame Roland shed in floods over the pages she was writing, and of which the traces still remain on the manuscript of her *Memoirs*? Why did she not sympathize in the grief of Marie Antoinette, separated from her children, when in speaking of her daughter Eudora, she wrote:

> Good God! I am a prisoner, and she is living far from me! I dare not even send for her to receive my embraces; hatred pursues even the children of those whom tyranny persecutes, and mine, with her eleven years, her virginal figure, and her beautiful fair hair, could hardly appear in the streets without creatures suborned or deluded by falsehood pointing her out as the offspring of a conspirator. Cruel wretches! how well they know how to tear a mother's heart!

Why were these two women political adversaries? Both sensitive, both artistic, with inexhaustible sources of poetry and tenderness at heart, they were born for gentle emotions and not for horrible catastrophes. Who, at their dawning, could have predicted for them such an appalling night? Like Marie Antoinette, Madame Roland loved nature and the arts. She felt the profound and penetrating charm of the fields. She drew, she played on the harp, guitar, and violin, and she sang.

"No one knows," she wrote a few moments before her death, "what an alleviation music is in solitude and anguish, nor from how many temptations it can save one in prosperity." She had sung the same romances as the Queen. The same poets had inspired and affected each.

Does not this most feminine passage in Madame Roland's *Memoirs* recall the character of the mistress of the Little Trianon?

I always remember the singular effect produced on me by a bunch of violets at Christmas; when I received them I was in that condition of soul often induced by a season favourable to serious thought. My imagination slumbered, I reflected coldly, and I hardly felt at all; suddenly the colour of these violets and their delicate perfume struck my senses; it was an awakening to life.... A rosy tinge suffused the horizon of the day.

Would not this cry of Madame Roland in her captivity suit Marie Antoinette as well? "Ah! when shall I breathe pure air and those soft exhalations so agreeable to my heart?" And might not the daughter of the great Maria Theresa have cried, like the daughter of Philipon the engraver? "*Adieu*! my child, my husband, my friends. *Adieu*! sun whose brilliant rays brought serenity to my soul, as if they were recalling it to the skies. *Adieu*! ye solitary fields which have so often moved me."

What must not these two keenly sensitive women have had to suffer at the epoch when France became a hell? They have each believed in the amelioration of the human species and the return of the golden age to earth, and what will their awakening be, after such alluring dreams? Men will be as unjust, as wicked, as cruel to the republican as to the queen. She, too, will be drenched with calumnies and outrages. They will insult her also in the most cowardly and ferocious manner. Under the very windows of her dungeon she will hear the hawkers crying: "Great visit of Père Duchesne to Citizeness Roland, in the Abbey prison, for the purpose of pumping her."

The ignoble journalist will call her "old sack of the counter-revolution." He will say to her with his habitual oaths: "Weep for your crimes, old fright, before you expiate them on the scaffold!" The wife of Louis XVI. and the wife of Roland will die within twenty-three days of each other: one on October 16, the other on November 8, 1793. They will start from the same prison of the Conciergerie, to be led to the same Place Louis XV., to have their heads cut off by the blade of the same guillotine. The commoner who had been so jealous of the Queen, can no longer complain. If the lives of the two women have been different, they will at least have the same death; and the doer of the noble deeds of the *régime* of equality, the headsman, will make no distinction between the two victims, between the veritable sovereign, the Queen of France and Navarre, and the sovereign of a day, whom Père Duchesne, as insolent to one as to the other, will no longer speak of except under the *sobriquet* of Queen Coco.

8

Madame Roland at the Ministry of the Interior

Roland took the portfolio of the Interior, March 24, 1792, and installed himself and his wife in the ministerial residence, then occupying the site afterwards built on by the *Théâtre Italien*. This very beautiful and luxurious mansion had formerly been the controller's office, and both Calonne and Necker had lived in it. Madame Roland found no small pleasure in queening it under the gilded canopies of the old *régime*. It was not at all disagreeable to her to give dinners in the sumptuous banqueting hall erected by the elegant Calonne, nor did the austere admirer of the ancients set the black broth of Sparta before her guests. Once arrived at power, was this great enemy of nobility and prescription simple, and easy of approach?

Not in the least. There is often more arrogance displayed by *parvenus* of both sexes than by those who are aristocrats by birth. Madame Roland was extremely proud of her new dignity, and at once resolved, as she tells us in her Memoirs, neither to make nor receive visits. Her attitude and manners while at the ministry were those of an Asiatic sovereign. She secluded herself, permitting only a small number of privileged courtiers to enter her presence. Under the old *régime*, the wives of ministers and ambassadors, dukes and peers, had never felicitated themselves on "cultivating their private tastes" to the detriment of the proprieties and obligations of good breeding. But the Revolution had changed all that. French politeness was now mere old-fashioned rubbish.

At the Ministry of the Interior, the etiquette whose "severity" is vaunted by Madame Roland was more rigorous than that of the court of Versailles, and it was easier to see the wife of the King than the wife

MADAME ROLAND

of the minister. With what *hauteur* the latter expresses herself concerning "the self-seeking crowds who throng about those who hold great places"! Assuredly, the Queen had never spoken of her subjects in this tone of disdainful patronage.

Madame Roland, who "was tired of fools," incommoded herself for nobody. The agreeable side of power was all she wanted. Suppressing the receptions which annoyed her, she gave none but men's dinners, where she perorated and paraded, and where, being the only woman present, she had no rivals to fear. Self-sufficiency and insufficiency are, for the most part, what fall to the share of parvenus. What would have been said in the old days of a noble dame who did the honours of a ministry so strangely, who never invited another woman to dinner, and admitted no one to her presence but a little *clique* of flatterers? Everybody would have accused such a lady as lacking in good breeding. But to Madame Roland all that she did was right in her own eyes. How could a woman so superior be expected to submit to the tyranny of polite usages? Was not the first of all despotisms the very one to be shaken off? and ought not a person so proud of the originality of her genius feel bound before all things, as she said herself, "to preserve her own mode of being"? Madame Roland did at the ministry just what she did from her cradle to her grave: she posed.

"To listen to Madame Roland," said Count Beugnot in his witty and curious *Memoirs*, "you would have thought she had imbibed the passion for liberty from reading the great writers of antiquity. . . . Cato the Elder was her hero, and it was probably out of respect for this hero that she showed a lack of courtesy towards her husband. She was unwilling to see that there was as much difference between Roland's wife and the Roman minister as there was between the Brutus of the Revolutionary Tribunal and him of the Capitol. Self-love was the means by which this woman had been elevated to the point where we have seen her; she was incessantly actuated by it, and does not dissimulate the fact."

It was she, and not her husband, who was Minister of the Interior. If the aristocrats treated Roland as a minister *sans-culottes*, it might have been added that the breeches which he lacked were worn by his spouse. Out of all the rooms composing a vast apartment, she had chosen for her own daily use the smallest that could be converted into a study, and kept her books and writing-table in it. It was from this *boudoir*, half literary, half political, that she conducted the ministry according to her own whims.

"It often happened," says she, "that friends or colleagues desiring to speak confidentially with the minister, instead of going to his own room, where he was surrounded by his clerks and the public, came to mine and begged me to have him called thither. Thus I found myself in the stream of affairs without either intrigue or idle curiosity. Roland took pleasure in talking these subjects over with me afterwards with that confidence which has always reigned between us, and which has brought our knowledge and our opinions into community."

On this head, M. Dauban makes the very just remark: "A community in which there is no equilibrium of forces, becomes a sort of omnipotence for the strongest." The omnipotence in this case was not on the side of the beard, but of Madame Roland. The wife wrote, thought, and acted for her husband. It was she who drew up his circulars and reports to the National Assembly.

"My husband," she tells us, "had nothing to lose in passing through my hands. Roland, without me, would have been none the less a good administrator; with me, he has made more sensation, because I imparted to my writings that mixture of force and sweetness, that authority of reason and charm of sentiment, which perhaps belongs only to a sensitive woman, endowed with sound understanding."

And the "virtuous" Roland took pride in the magnificent phrases which he *naïvely* believed to be the expression of his own genius, when his wife had saved him not merely the trouble of writing, but even of thinking. "He often ended," she says, "by persuading himself that he had really been in a good vein when he had written such or such a passage which proceeded from my pen."

Madame Roland had at her orders a man of letters, salaried by the Ministry of the Interior, who was the official defender of the minister and his policy. "It had been felt," she tells us, "that it was needful to counteract the influence of the court, the aristocracy, the civil list and their journals, by popular instructions to which great publicity should be given. A journal posted up in public places seemed to be the proper thing, and a wise and enlightened man had to be found for its editor." This wise and enlightened man was Louvet, the author of the *Amours de Faublas*. He was the writer whom Madame Roland esteemed most capable of instructing and of moralizing the masses.

"Men of letters and persons of taste," she says, "know his charming romances, in which the graces of imagination are allied to lightness of style, a philosophical tone, and the salt of criticism. He has proved that his skilful hand could alternately shake the bells of folly, hold the burin of history, and launch the thunderbolts of eloquence. Courageous as a lion, simple as a child, a sensible man, a good citizen, a vigorous writer, he could make Catiline tremble from the tribune, dine with the Graces, and sup with Bachaumont."

Madame Roland admired the author of *Faublas*, now become the editor-in-chief of the *Sentinelle*; but among her intimates there was a man whom she admired much more. This was Buzot. With what complacency she draws in her *Memoirs* the portrait of this man "of an elevated character, a haughty spirit, and a vehement courage, sensitive, ardent, melancholy; an impassioned lover of nature, nourishing his imagination with all the charms she has to offer, and his soul with the principles of the most touching philosophy; he seems formed to enjoy and to procure domestic happiness; he could forget the universe in the sweetness of private virtues practised with a heart worthy of his own."

Needless to say that in Madame Roland's thought, this heart worthy of the heart of Buzot was her own. "He is susceptible," says she, "of the tenderest affections" (always for Madame Roland), "capable of sublime flights and the most generous resolutions." Into what ecstasies she falls over the noble face and elegant figure of this handsome man, in whose costume "reigns that care, cleanliness, and decency which manifest the spirit of order, taste, the sentiment of decorum, and the respect of an honest man for the public and himself"! How she contrasts with men who think patriotism consists in "swearing, drinking, and dressing like porters, in order to fraternize with their equals," this attractive, this irresistible Buzot, who "professes the morality of Socrates and the politeness of Scipio"!

Clearly, the veritable idol of the Egeria of the Girondins is not the republic, but Buzot. He is so elegant, so distinguished! His mind and his person have so many charms! Poor Roland! You think that your better half is solely occupied with your ministry. Alas! this learned woman has other thoughts in her head. Your position as a minister has not augmented your prestige in the region of sentiment. Though you lord it in the Hotel Calonne, yet, in spite of the throng of petitioners and flatterers who surround you, you will never be a Lovelace, and your romantic spouse will not allow herself to be affected by your appearance, like that of a Quaker in Sunday clothes. You thought you were doing wonders in presenting yourself at the council of ministers with lanky, unpowdered locks, a round hat, and shoes minus buckles. This peasant costume, which so greatly scandalized the master of ceremonies, doubtless made the best impression at the Jacobin Club, but your wife prefers the careful dress of her too dear Buzot.

Madame Roland, who had just completed her thirty-eighth year, was still very charming. Lémontey thus paints her portrait as she appeared at this epoch:

> Her eyes and hair were remarkably beautiful; her delicate complexion had a freshness and colour which made her look singularly young. At the beginning of her husband's ministry she had lost nothing of her air of youth and simplicity; her husband resembled a Quaker whose daughter she might have been, and her child hovered round her with hair floating to her waist; one might have thought them natives of Pennsylvania transported to the drawing-room of M. de Calonne.

Count Beugnot, who was the companion of her captivity in the Conciergerie, is severe on the female politician, but he admires the pretty woman. "Her figure was graceful," he says, "and her hands perfectly modelled. Her glance was expressive, and even in repose her face had something noble and subtly attractive in it. One surmised her wit without needing to hear her speak, but no woman whom I have ever listened to, spoke with more purity and elegance. She must have owed her faculty of giving to French a rhythm and cadence veritably new, to her familiar knowledge of Italian. The harmony of her voice was still further heightened by graceful and appropriate gestures and the expression of her eyes, which grew animated in conversation. I daily experienced new charm in listening to her, less on account of what she said than because of the magic of her delivery."

If Madame Roland, a prisoner, crushed by misfortune, on the very threshold of the scaffold, after so many sleepless nights and so many tears, had preserved such attractions, what a charm must she not have exercised at the Ministry of the Interior, when hope and pride illumined her beautiful face, and when, after appearing to her electrified adorers as the Muse of the new *régime*, the magician, the *Circe* of the Revolution, she touched so profoundly their minds and hearts! She who knew so well how to love and how to hate, who felt so keenly, who had so much energy, so much vigour, what fascination must she not have exerted with her glance of fire, her long black tresses, her more than ornate eloquence, her inspired, lyric, enthusiastic bearing, and that consummate art which, according to the remark of Fontanes, made one believe that in her everything was the work of nature!

9

Dumouriez, Minister
of Foreign Affairs

Madam Roland had wished to reign alone. She saw an influential rival in Dumouriez, and at once conceived for him an instinctive repugnance and suspicion. She met him first on March 23, 1792, at the time when, as Minister of Foreign Affairs, he came to salute Roland, just named Minister of the Interior, as his colleague. As soon as he departed: "There," said she to her husband, "is a man with a crafty mind and a false glance, against whom it is probably more necessary to be on one's guard than any other person; he expressed great satisfaction at the patriotic choice he was deputed to announce; but I should not be at all surprised if he were to have you dismissed some day." She thought she recognized in Dumouriez at first sight, "a witty *roué*, an insolent *chevalier* who makes sport of everything except his own interests and glory."

Later on she drew the following portrait of him:

Among all his colleagues, he had most of what is called wit, and less than any of morality. Diligent and brave, a good general, a skilful courtier, writing well and expressing himself with ease, capable of great enterprises, all he lacked was character enough to balance his mind, or a cooler brain to carry out the plans he had conceived. Agreeable to his friends, and ready to betray them, gallant to women, but not at all suited to succeed with those among them who are susceptible to affectionate relations, he was made for the ministerial intrigues of a corrupt court.

The nomination of Dumouriez as Minister of Foreign Affairs is one of the most curious and unforeseen events of this strange epoch. Few men have had a career so adventurous and agitated as his. A complex and mobile nature, where the intriguer and the great man were blended into one, he never commanded esteem, but at certain moments he secured admiration. Napoleon I. seems to have been too severe when he said of him that he was "only a miserable intriguer." The man who opened the series of great French victories, and who saved his country from invasion by his admirable defence of the defiles of Argonne, merited more than this disdainful mention.

It is none the less certain, however, that one scents, as it were, an air of Beaumarchais in the *Memoirs* of Dumouriez, and that there is more than one link of character and existence between the author of the *Mariage de Figaro* and the victor of Jemmapes. Both were men without principles, but full of resource, wit, and fascination. Both were lovable in spite of their great defects, because of their humanity and kindness. Both belonged at the same time to the old *régime* and the Revolution. Before arriving at celebrity, each had a stormy youth, tormented by the love of pleasure, the need of money, and a sort of perpetual restlessness: they flattered every power of the time, sought fortune by the most circuitous ways, were diplomatic couriers, and secret agents; before coming out into open daylight, they made trial of their marvellous address in obscurity, and signalized themselves among those men of action and initiative whom governments, which make use of them in occult ways, first launch, then compromise, disavow, and sometimes imprison.

Born at Cambrai, January 25, 1739, Dumouriez belonged to a family of the upper middle class. Entering the army early, he distinguished himself by his high spirits and courage. As a cornet of the Penthièvre cavalry, he served in the German campaigns from 1758 to 1761, and was invalided in 1763. He spent twenty-four years at the wars and brought back nothing but twenty-two wounds, the rank of captain, a decoration, and some debts. Seeking then a new career, he entered, thanks to his connection with Favier, the secret diplomacy of Louis XV., and was sent to Corsica, Italy, and Portugal. He returned to the army in 1768, and made a brilliant record in the Corsican campaign, obtaining successively the grades of adjutant-major general, adjutant-quartermaster, and colonel of cavalry.

It was he who seized the castle of Corte, Paoli's last asylum. In 1771, he again became a secret agent. Louis XV. wished to befriend Poland in its death-struggle, but without betraying his hand. Dumouriez was sent to the Polish confederates. He was reputed to be merely acting on his own impulses. He organized troops and fought successfully against Souvaroff, the future adversary of the French Republic, but could not save Poland—that Asiatic nation of Europe, as he called it. He came back to Paris in 1772, and the government, complying with the demands of Russia, shut him up for a year in the Bastille, where he had leisure to meditate on the ingratitude of courts. This captivity strengthened his taste for study, and, far from allaying his ambition, gave it renewed force.

Louis XVI. put him in command at Cherbourg, and it was he who conceived the plan of making that town a station for the French marine. He was fifty years old when the Revolution of 1789 broke out. At once he saw in it an opportunity for success and glory. Full of confidence in his own superiority, he merely awaited the hour when events should second his ambition. He said to himself that the emigration, by making a void in the upper ranks of the army, was going to leave him free scope, and that he would be commander-in-chief of the French troops under the new *régime*. To attain this end he decided to serve the King, the Assembly, and the factions; to assume all parts and all masks, and to be in turn, and simultaneously if need were, the courtier of Louis XVI. and the favourite of the Jacobins.

As has been very well said by M. Frédéric Masson in an excellent book, as novel as it is interesting, *Le Département des affaires étrangères sous la Révolution*, Dumouriez had been accustomed to make his way everywhere, to eat at all tables, and listen at all doors. One of the agents of Count d'Artois brought him into relations with Mirabeau. He was protected by the minister Montmorin. He drew up plans of campaign for Narbonne. He used the intimate "thou" to Laporte, the King's confidant and intendant of the civil list. He made use of women also. Separated from his lawful wife, he lived in marital relations with a sister of Rivarol, the Baroness de Beauvert, a charming person who had much intercourse with aristocratic society, who speculated in arms, and who was pensioned by the Duke of Orleans, as appears from a letter of Latouche de Tréville, the prince's chancellor, dated April 17, 1789.

Dumouriez, who had expensive tastes, sought at the same time for gold and honours. Either by means of the court or the Revolution, he desired to gain a great fortune and much glory, to become a statesman, a minister, commander-in-chief, and realize his great military plan, the conquest of the natural frontiers of France. He said to himself: He who wills the end wills the means, and managed as adroitly with parties as with soldiers. At Niort, where he was in command at the beginning of the Revolution, he made himself remarkable by his enthusiasm for the new ideas, and became president of the club and honorary citizen of the town. He contracted an intimacy with Gensonné, whom the Assembly had sent into the departments of the west to observe their spirit. In January, 1792, the emigration of general officers had become so considerable that he rose by seniority to the rank of lieutenant-general.

Thereafter, he believed his hour had come, and threw himself boldly into the political arena. The Gironde and the Jacobins were the two powers then in vogue; he flattered both the Jacobins and the Gironde. Brissot was the corypheus of the diplomatic committee and the chief of the war party. He became the familiar of Brissot. Already, in 1791, he had prepared a memoir on the subject of the Ministry of Foreign Affairs which he dedicated and read to the Jacobins. In it he announced (singular prediction for the future minister of a king!) that before fifty years had passed, Europe would be republican. He demanded an immediate and radical change in the diplomatic personnel.

"It is of small importance," said he in the same memoir, "that our representatives would lack experience. In the first place, our interests are greatly simplified; moreover, our former representatives were young men belonging to the court who had had no political education. In a word, it is the majesty of the nation which gives our negotiations weight. The minister," he added, "should be a man of approved patriotism, above all suspicion, like the wife of Cæsar. Absolute integrity, great knowledge of men, great firmness, a broad and upright mind, should complete his character."

Dumouriez perhaps imagined that all these qualities of an ideal minister were reunited in his person. However that may be, he accepted, without any mistrust of his own abilities, the portfolio of Foreign Affairs, confided to him March 15, 1792, on account of his relations with the Gironde and his popularity with the Jacobins. He had a high opinion of himself, and, even after his cruel disappointments, he was to write in his *Memoirs*, in 1794:

> Dumouriez sometimes laughs sardonically in his retreat over the judgments passed upon him. When he arrived at the ministry, the courtiers said and published that he was only a soldier of fortune, incapable of conducting political affairs, in which he would make nothing but blunders. When he commanded

an army, they told the Prussians and the German Emperor's troops that he was a mere writer, who had never made war and understood nothing about it. Since he retired with reputation from public employments, they have published that up to the date of the Revolution he had been an intriguing adventurer, a ministerial spy, an office-sweeper. Would to God, they had employed the adventures of their youth in similar espionages! They would not have begun the Revolution like factionists, they would have conducted it with wisdom, they would have preserved the esteem of the nation, they would not have been the prime authors of the King's death, either by betraying or abandoning him.

The new Minister of Foreign Affairs began to play his *rôle* of leader of French diplomacy in a singular fashion. Repairing to the Jacobin Club, he described himself as their liegeman, assumed the red bonnet in their presence, and, with it on his head, announced that as soon as war should be declared, he would throw away his pen in order to resume his sword. Let us add that he was simultaneously trying to conciliate the good graces of Louis XVI. and to persuade him that if he leaned upon the Jacobins, it was solely in the hope of serving the King and consolidating the throne. At the same time he appointed as director of foreign affairs that Bonne-Carrère whose portrait has been traced in this wise by Brissot:

Falling with all his vices and perverse habits into the midst of a revolution whereby the people had recovered sovereignty, he merely changed his idol without changing his idolatry. He caressed the people instead of caressing the great, made the hall of the Jacobins his Œil-de-Boeuf, played valet to the successful parties one after another, the Lameths and the Mirabeaus, and succeeded in raising himself from the secretaryship of the Jacobins to the embassy of Liège, by the aid of that very Montmorin who detested the Jacobins, and could but advance a man who betrayed them.

Dumouriez then, following the example of Mirabeau, was about to play a double game; to be revolutionary with the Revolution and a courtier with the court. As to Madame Roland, he never placed himself at her feet. The despotism of this female minister, the pretentious of this demagogic bluestocking, her affectation of puritan rigor, her mania for directing everything, shocked the good sense of a man who believed that woman is made to please, not to reign. It was repugnant to this soldier to take his orders from the Egeria of the Girondins. On the other hand, Dumouriez was displeasing to Madame Roland. She found him too dissolute and not sentimental enough. She could not pardon his having Madame de Beauvert for mistress and Bonne-Carrère for confidant. She admitted neither his free-and-easy tone, his Gallic humor, nor his natural gaiety, so unlike the declamatory tone and pretentious jargon of the disciples of Jean-Jacques Rousseau. Moreover, she found him too much of a royalist, too accustomed to the old *régime*. The ministry, apparently so homogeneous, was soon to be divided against itself.

10

The Council of Ministers

Louis XVI. had been persuaded that the only means of regaining public confidence would be to name a ministry chosen by the Gironde and accepted by the Jacobins. The six ministers—Dumouriez of Foreign Affairs, Roland of the Interior, De Grave of War, Claviére of Finances, Duranton of Justice, Lacoste of Marine—formed what was called the Girondin ministry; the reactionists named it the *sans-culottes* ministry. The revolutionists rejoiced in its advent, while the royalists sought to cover it with ridicule.

On the day when the Council met for the first time at the Tuileries (in the great royal cabinet on the first floor, afterwards called the Salon of Louis XIV.), Roland created a scandal by his plebeian dress. The simplicity of his costume, his round hat, his shoes fastened with ribbons instead of buckles, caused, as his wife disdainfully remarks, "astonishment to all the valets, those creatures who, existing only for the sake of etiquette, thought the safety of the empire depended on its preservation."

The master of ceremonies, approaching Dumouriez with an uneasy frown, glanced at Roland, and said in an undertone, "Eh! sir, no buckles on his shoes!"

"Ah! sir, all is lost!" replied Dumouriez so coolly that it raised a laugh.

Louis XVI., who wished, as one might say, to enlarge the borders of gentleness and resignation, displayed more than good-will towards the ministers; he showed them deference. This was the more meritorious because to him this ministry was like a reunion of the seditious, like the Revolution in arms against his crown; his pretended advisers seemed much more like enemies than auxiliaries. He tried, however, to attach them to him by kindness, and made a sincere trial of his

73

rights and duties as a constitutional sovereign.

Madame Roland herself, bitter and violent as she is, renders him a certain justice. "Louis XVI.," says she, "showed the greatest good nature towards his new ministers; this man was not precisely such as he has been painted by those who seek to degrade him."

As to Dumouriez, he says in his *Memoirs*:

Dumouriez had been greatly deceived concerning the character of Louis XVI., who had been represented to him as a violent and wrathful man, who swore a great deal and maltreated his ministers. He must, on the contrary, do him the justice to say that during three' months when he observed him closely and in very delicate circumstances, he always found him polite, gentle, affable, and even very patient. This prince had a great timidity arising from his education and his distrust of himself, some difficulty in speaking, a just and dispassionate mind, upright sentiments, great knowledge of history, geography, and the arts, and an astonishing memory.

Madame Roland also owns that he had an excellent memory and much activity; that he was never idle; that he read often, and had a distinct knowledge of all the different treaties concluded by France with neighbouring powers; that he knew history well, and was the best geographer in the kingdom. "His knowledge of the names and faces of those belonging to his court," she adds, "and the anecdotes peculiar to each, extended to all persons who had come into prominence during the Revolution; no subject could be mentioned to him on which he had not some opinion founded on certain facts.

At first, the sessions of the ministry went off very tranquilly. The King, with an accent of candour, protested his attachment to the Constitution and his desire to see it solidly established. Often he left his ministers to chat among themselves without taking any part in their conversation. During such times he read his French and English journals, or wrote letters. If a decree was presented for his sanction, he deferred his decision until the next meeting, to which he came with a settled opinion, concealing it carefully, none the less, and appearing to decide only in accordance with the will of the majority. He frequently evaded irritating questions by turning the conversation to other subjects. If war were the topic, he spoke of travels; *apropos* of diplomacy, he described the manners of the country in question; to Roland he spoke of his works, to Dumouriez of his adventures. The Minister of

Foreign Affairs, who was a first-class story-teller, and whose freedom of speech was welcomed by the King, to use Madame Roland's expression, amused both his colleagues and his sovereign by his jests and anecdotes.

But all this was far from agreeable to the spiteful companion of the Minister of the Interior. Indignant at the accord which seemed to exist between Louis XVI. and his counsellors, she dreamed of nothing but discussions and conflicts. All that wore the appearance of reconciliation was repugnant to her. She made her obedient spouse recount to her the smallest details of the sessions of the Council, meddling with and criticising all. During the first three weeks, Roland and Clavière, enchanted with the King's dispositions, flattered themselves that the Revolution was at an end. Madame Roland scoffed at their confidence. "*Bon Dieu*," she said to them, "every time I see you start for the Council with this charming confidence, it seems to me you are ready to commit some folly."

"I assure you," replied Clavière, "that the King is perfectly aware that his interests are bound up with the observance of the laws just established; he reasons too pertinently not to be convinced of this truth."

"Well," added Roland, "if he is not an honest man, he is the greatest rascal in the kingdom; nobody can dissimulate like that."

Madame Roland rejoined that she could not believe in love for the Constitution on the part of a man nourished in the prejudices and accustomed to the use of despotic power. She, who doubtless thought herself the only person capable of presiding well at the council of ministers, treated it as a "*café* where they amused themselves with idle gossip."

"There was no record of their deliberations," says she, "nor a secretary to take them down; after sitting three or four hours, they went away without having accomplished anything but a few signatures; it was like this three times a week."

"This is pitiable!" she would exclaim impatiently when, on his return, she asked her husband what had passed. "You are all in very good humour because there have been no disputes or vexations, and you have even been treated with civility; each of you seems to be doing pretty much as he pleases in his own department. I am afraid you are being made game of."

"Nevertheless, business is getting on."

"Yes, and time is wasted, for in the torrent that is carrying you away, I should be much better pleased to have you employ three hours in solid meditation on great combinations than to see you spend them in useless chatter."

It must needs be said that no person contributed more to the downfall of royalty than Madame Roland. At the moment when the good temper and gentleness of Louis XVI. began to gain upon his ministers, when Dumouriez was softened by the royal kindness, when minds experienced a relaxation, and honest people, worn out by so many political shocks, were sincerely desirous of repose, it was she who nourished discord, made the Gironde irreconcilable, inspired the subversive pamphlets of Louvet, embittered her husband's heart, and invented the provocations against which the conscience of the unfortunate monarch rebelled. This part, which would have been a sorry one for a man to play, seems still worse in a woman. Count Beugnot has said very justly:

> I have seen that a woman can preserve only the faults of her sex in the midst of such a frightful catastrophe, not its virtues. The gentle, amiable, sensitive qualities grow and develop in the shelter of peaceful domestic joys; they are lost and obliterated in the heat of debates, the bitterness of parties, and the shock of passions. The soft and tender foot of woman cannot tread unharmed in paths bristling with steel and red with blood. To do so with safety she must become a man; but to me, a man-woman seems a monster. Ah! let them leave to us, whom nature has granted the pitiful advantage of strength, the field of contention and the fate of war; we are adequate to this cruel destiny; but let them keep to the easier and sweeter part of pouring balm into wounds and staunching tears.

Roland's character was tranquil; it was his wife who made him ambitious, haughty, and inflexible. She should have pacified her husband, but instead of that she excited him. Never was he malevolent and spiteful enough to suit her. She would not pardon him a single movement of compassion or respect towards the august unfortunates. Led by her, Roland no longer dared entertain a generous thought. He returned shamefaced to the Ministry of the Interior if he had felt a humane sentiment while at the Tuileries. It is sad to find tenderness and pity in the heart of a man, Dumouriez, and in the heart of a woman, Madame Roland, nothing but malevolence and hatred. Dumouriez wanted to put out the fire; Madame Roland, to stir it up.

Dumouriez sincerely desired the King's safety; Madame Roland swore that he should perish. If a germ of pity woke to life in the hearts of the ministers, Madame Roland hastened to stifle it. Her hostility towards the royal family was more than deliberate; there was something like ferocity in it. Her *Memoirs* and those of Dumouriez display two very different minds. Sadness dominates in his; anger in hers. Even on the steps of the scaffold, Madame Roland will not feel her hatred lessen. Dumouriez, on the contrary, will cast a glance of melancholy respect upon the unfortunate sovereign whose sorrows and whose resignation, whose gentleness and uprightness, had touched him so profoundly.

11.

The Fête of the Swiss
of Chateauvieux

Dumouriez, at the beginning of his ministry, was still the slave of the Jacobins, his allies and protectors. His elevation to the ministry was in great part due to them, and even while despising them, he felt unable to shake off their yoke. Little by little, they inspired him with horror, and before many weeks were over, his only idea was to free himself from their control. But at first he treated them like a power with which he was obliged to reckon. What proves this is his passive attitude at the time of the celebrated *fête* of the Swiss of Chateauvieux. The prologue of the bloody tragedies that were in course of preparation, this *fête* shows what headway the revolutionary ideas had made. The sinister days of the Convention were approaching, the Terror existed in germ, and already many representatives who, on a secret ballot, would have voted in accordance with right and honour, were cowardly enough to do so against their conscience when they had to answer to their names.

Things had travelled fast since the close of the Constituent Assembly. In 1790, that Assembly, as the faithful guardian of discipline, had congratulated the Marquis de Bouillé on the energy with which he repressed the military rebellion that broke out at Nancy, August 31. The soldiers garrisoned at this town were guilty of the greatest crimes. They pillaged the military chests, arrested the officers, and fired on the troops who remained faithful. M. Desilles, an officer of the King's regiment, conducted himself at the time in a heroic manner. When the insurgents were about to discharge the cannon opposite the Stainville gate, he sprang towards it, and covering it with his body, cried: "It is your friends, your brothers, who are coming! The National Assembly sends them. Do you mean to fire on them? Will you disgrace your flags?" It was useless to try to hold Desilles back. He broke away from his friends and threw himself again in front of the rebels, falling under four wounds at the moment when the fight began.

The Constituent Assembly passed a decree by which it thanked the Marquis de Bouillé and his troops "for having gloriously fulfilled their duty" in repressing the military insurrection of Nancy. Its president wrote an official letter to Desilles, soon to die in consequence of his wounds:

> The National Assembly has learned with just admiration, mingled with profound sorrow, the danger to which your heroic devotion has exposed you; in trying to describe it, I should weaken the emotion by which the Assembly was penetrated. So sublime an example of courage and civic virtue is above all praise. It has secured you a sweeter recompense and one more worthy of you; you will find it in your own heart, and the eternal memory of the French people.

The Swiss regiment of Chateauvieux had taken part in the rebellion at Nancy. Switzerland had reserved, by treaty, its federal jurisdiction over such of its troops as had taken service under the King of France. By virtue of this special jurisdiction the soldiers of the regiment of Chateauvieux, taken arms in hand, were tried before a council of war composed of Swiss officers. Twenty-two were condemned to death and shot. Fifty were condemned to the galleys and sent to the convict prison at Brest. It was in vain that Louis XVI. attempted to negotiate their pardon with the Swiss Confederacy. It remained inflexible, and the guilty were still undergoing their penalty when the Jacobins resolved to release them from prison in defiance of the treaties uniting Switzerland and France.

"To deliver these condemned prisoners," says Dumouriez in his *Memoirs*, "was to insult the Cantons, attack their treaty rights, and judge their criminals. We had enemies enough already without seeking new ones among an allied people who were behaving wisely towards us, especially a free and republican people."

But revolutionary passions do not reason. Collot d'Herbois, a wretched actor who had passed from the theatrical stage to that of politics, and who, not content with having bored people, wished to terrorize them also, made himself the champion of the galley-slaves of the regiment of Chateauvieux. He was the principal *impresario* of the lugubrious *fête* which disgraced Paris on April 15, 1792.

The programme was not arranged without some opposition. Public opinion was not yet ripe for saturnalia. There were still a few honest and courageous publicists who, like André Chénier, boldly lifted their voices to stigmatize certain infamies. In the tribune of the Assembly some orators were to be found who expressed their minds freely and held their own against the tempests of demagogy. There were generals and soldiers in the army for whom discipline was not an idle word; and if the *fête* of the Swiss of Chateauvieux made the future Septembrists and furies of the guillotine utter shouts of joy, it drew from honest men a long cry of grief and indignation.

Intimidated by the menaces of the Jacobins, the Assembly voted the release of the Swiss incarcerated in the prison of Brest. But merely to deliver them was not enough: the Jacobins wanted to give them an ovation. Their march from Brest to Paris was a triumph, and Collot d'Herbois organized a gigantic *fête* in their honour.

André Chénier was at this time writing weekly letters for the *Journal de Paris*, in which he eloquently supported the principles of order and liberty. As M. de Lamartine has said, he was the Tyrtæus of good sense and moderation. He was indignant at the threatened scandal, and, in concert with his collaborator on the *Journal de Paris*, Roucher, the poet of *Les Mois*, he criticised in most energetic terms the revolutionary manifestation then organizing. At the Jacobin Club, on April 4, Collot d'Herbois freed his mind against him.

"This is not Chénier-Gracchus," said the comedian; "it is another person, quite another." He spoke of André as a "sterile prose writer," and pointed him out to popular vengeance. The two brothers were in opposing camps. While André Chénier stigmatized the *fête* of anarchy, his brother Joseph was diligently manufacturing scraps of poetry, inscriptions, and devices which were to figure in the programme.

"What!" cried André, "must we invent extravagances capable of destroying any form of government, recompense rebellion against the laws, and crown foreign satellites for having shot French citizens in a riot? People say that the statues will be veiled in every place through which this procession is to pass. Oh! if this odious orgy takes place, it will be well to veil the whole city; but it is not the images of despots that should be wrapt in funeral crape, but the faces of honest men. How is it that you do not blush when a turbulent handful, who seem numerous because they are united and make a noise, oblige you to do their will, telling you that it is your own, and amusing your childish curiosity meanwhile with unworthy spectacles? In a city which re-spected itself such a *fête* would meet nothing but solitude and silence." The controversy waxed furious. The walls were covered with posters for and against the *fête*. Roucher thus flagellated Collot d'Herbois: "This character out of a comic novel, who skipped from Polichinello's booth to the platform of the Jacobins, has sprung at me as if he were going to strike me with the oar the Swiss brought back from the gal-leys!"

Pétion, then mayor of Paris, far from opposing the *fête*, approved and encouraged it. "I think it my duty," he wrote, April 6, 1792, "to explain myself briefly concerning the *fête* which is being arranged to celebrate the arrival of the soldiers of Chateauvieux. Minds are heated, passions are in ferment, and citizens hold different opinions; everything seems to betoken disorder. It is sought to change a day of rejoicing into a day of mourning. . . . What is it all about? Some soldiers, leaders with the French guards, who have broken our chains and afterwards been overloaded with them, are about to enter within our walls; some citizens propose to meet and offer them a fraternal welcome; these citizens are obeying a natural impulse and using a right which belongs to all. The magistrates see nothing but what is simple and innocent in all this; they see certain citizens abandoning themselves to joy and mirth; everyone is at liberty to participate or not to participate in the *fête*. Public spirit rises and assumes a new degree of energy amidst civic amusements."

The municipality ordered this letter of Pétion's to be printed, post-ed on the walls, and sent to the forty-eight sectional committees and the sixty battalions of the National Guard.

Not all the members of the National Assembly shared the opti-mism of the mayor of Paris. The preparations for the *fête*, which was announced for April 15, occasioned, on the 9th, a session as affecting as it was stormy. The whole debate should be read in the *Moniteur*. The question was put whether the Swiss of Chateauvieux, then waiting outside the doors, should be introduced and admitted to the honours of the session. M. de Gouvion, who had been major-general of the National Guard under Lafayette, gravely ascended the tribune.

"Gentlemen," said he, "I had a brother, a good patriot, who, through the favourable opinion of your fellow-citizens, had been successively a commander of the National Guard and a member from the Depart-ment. Always ready to sacrifice himself for the Revolution and the law, it was in the name of the Revolution and the law that he was required to march to Nancy with the brave National Guards. There he fell, pierced by fifty bayonets in the hands of those who. . . . I ask if I am condemned to look on tranquilly while the assassins of my brother enter here?"

A voice rising from the midst of the Assembly cried: "Very well, sir, go out!" The galleries applauded. Gouvion attempted to continue. The murmurs redoubled. Several persons in the galleries cried: "Down! down!"

The Assembly, revolutionary though it was, felt indignant at the scandal, and called the galleries to order. The president reiterated the injunction to keep silence. Gouvion began anew: "I treat with all the contempt he merits, and with . . . I would say the word if I did not respect the Assembly—the coward who has been base enough to outrage a brother's grief." The question was then put whether the Swiss of Chateauvieux should be admitted to the honours of the session. Out of 546 votes, 288 were in the affirmative, and 265 in the negative. Consequently, the president announced that the soldiers of Chateauvieux, who had asked to present themselves to the Assembly, should be admitted to the honours of the session. Gouvion went out by one door, indignant, and swearing that he would never re-enter an Assembly which received his brother's assassins as conquerors. By another door, Collot d'Herbois made his entry with his *protégés*, the ex-galley slaves.

The party of the left and the spectators in the galleries burst into transports of joy, and gave three rounds of applause. The soldiers entered the hall to the beating of drums and cries of "Long live the nation!" They were followed by a large procession of men and women carrying pikes and banners. Collot d'Herbois, the showman of the Swiss, pronounced an emphatic address in praise of the pretended martyrs of liberty, which the Assembly ordered to be printed. One Goachon, speaking for the Faubourg Saint-Antoine, and holding a pike ornamented with a red liberty cap, exclaimed:

The citizens of the Faubourg Saint-Antoine, the victors of the Bastille, the men of July 14, have charged me to warn you that they are going to make ten thousand more pikes after the model which you see.

The *fête* took place on Sunday, April 15. It was the triumph of anarchy, the glorification of indiscipline and revolt. On that day the galley slaves were treated like heroes. The emblems adopted were a colossal galley, ornamented with flowers, and the convicts' head gear, that hideous red bonnet in which Dumouriez had already played the buffoon, and which was presently to be set on the august head of Louis XVI. The soldier galley slaves, whose chains were kissed with transports by a swarm of harlots, came forward wearing civic crowns. What a difference between the Constituent Assembly and the Legislative Assembly! Under the one, a grand expiatory ceremony on the Champ-de-Mars had honoured the soldiers slain at Nancy, and the National Guards had worn mourning for these martyrs of duty.

Under the other, it was not the victims who were lauded, but their assassins. A goddess of Liberty in a Phrygian cap was borne in a state chariot. The procession halted at the Bastille, the Hôtel de Ville, and the Champ-de-Mars. The mayor and municipality of Paris were present in their official capacity. The *Ça ira* was sung in a frenzy of enthusiasm. Soldiers and public women embraced each other. It was David who had designed the costumes, planned the chariot, and organized the whole performance,—David, the revolutionary artist who was destined by a change of fortune to paint the portrait of a Pope and the coronation of an Emperor.

In 1791, André Chénier and David, then friends, and saluting together the dawn of the Revolution, had celebrated with lyre and pencil the "*Serment du Jeu de Paumé*"[1] Consecrating an ode to the painter's magnificent tableau, the poet exclaimed:—

Resume thy golden robe, bind on thy chaplet rich,
Divine and youthful Poesy!
To David's lips, King of the skilful brush,
Bear the ambrosial cup.

How he repented his enthusiasm now! What ill-will he bore the artist who placed his art, that sacred gift, at the service of anarchical passions! With what irony the same pen passed from dithyramb to satire!

Arts worthy of our eyes, pomp and magnificence
Worthy of our liberty,
Worthy of the vile tyrants who are devouring France,
Worthy of the atrocious dementia
Of that stupid David whom in other days I sang!

On the very day of the *fête* the young poet had the courage to

1. The oath taken by the deputies of the third estate in the tennis-court of Versailles, in 1789.

publish in the *Journal de Paris* an avenging satire, which branded the shoulders of the ex-galley slaves as with a new hot iron. The sweet and pathetic elegiast, the Catullus, the Tibullus of France, added a bronze chord to his lyre:—

Hail, divine triumph! Enter within our walls!
Bring us these warriors so famed
For Desilles' blood, and for the obsequies
Of many Frenchmen massacred...
One day alone could win so much renown,
And this fair day will shine upon us soon!
When thou shalt lead Jourdan to our army,
And Lafayette to the scaffold!

Jourdan was the slaughterer, the headsman, the torturer of the Glacier of Avignon, who, coming under the provisions of the amnesty, had arrived to take part in the triumph of the Swiss of Chateauvieux. The acclamations were lugubrious. The lanterns and torches shed a funereal glare. Nothing is more doleful than enthusiasm for ignominy. The applause accorded to disgrace and crime sounds like sinister derision. Outraged public conscience extinguishes the fires of apotheoses such as these. Madame Elisabeth, in a letter of April 18, speaks with a sort of pity of this odious but ridiculous *fête*: "The people have been to see Dame Liberty waggling about on her triumphal car, but they shrugged their shoulders. Three or four hundred *sans-culottes* followed, crying 'Long live the nation! Long live liberty! Long live the *sans-culottes*! to the devil with Lafayette!' All this was noisy but sad. The National Guards took no part in it; on the contrary, they were indignant, and Pétion, they say, is ashamed of his conduct. The next day a pike surmounted by a red bonnet was carried noiselessly through the garden, and did not remain there long." The Princess de Lamballe, who was living at the Tuileries in the Pavilion of Flora, could see the pike thus carried by a passer. It may, perhaps, have been that belonging to one of the Septembrists,—that on which her own head was to be placed.

The *Moniteur*, however, grew ecstatic over the *fête*. "There are plenty of others," it said, "who will describe the march of the triumphal *cortège*, the groups composing it, the car of Liberty, conducted by Fame, drawn by twenty superb horses, preceded by ravishing music which was sometimes listened to in religious silence and sometimes interrupted by wild, irregular dances whose very disorder was ren-

dered more piquant by the fraternal union reigning in all hearts. . . .
The people were there in all their might, and did not abuse it. There
was not a weapon to repress excesses, and not an excess to be repressed." It concluded thus: "We say to the administration: Give such
festivals as these often. Repeat this one every year on April 15; let the
feast of Liberty be our spring festival; and let other civic solemnities
signalize the return of the other seasons. In former days the people
had none but those of their masters, and all that was accomplished by
them was their depravity and abasement. Give them some that shall be
their own, and that will elevate their souls, develop their sensibilities,
and fortify their courage. They will create, or, better, they have already
created, a new people. Popular festivals are the best education for the
people."

Optimists, how will your illusions terminate? You who see nothing but an idyll in all this, cannot you perceive that such ceremonies
are the prelude to massacres, and that an odour of blood mingles with
their perfumes? All who took part on either side of the heated controversy which preceded the ovation to the Swiss of Chateauvieux,
will be pursued by fate. Gouvion, who had sworn never again to set
foot within the precincts of the Assembly where the murderers of his
brother triumphed, kept his word. On the very day of that shameful session he asked to be sent to the Army of the North, and three
months later was to be carried off by a cannon-ball. Still more melancholy was to be the fate of Pétion, who showed such complaisance
toward the Swiss on this occasion.

He, once so popular that in 1791 he was asked to allow the ninth
child, which a citizeness had just presented to her country, "to be
baptized in his name, revered almost as much as that of the Divinity";
he of whom someone said at that time, "For the same reason which
would have made Jesus a suitable mayor of Jerusalem, Pétion is a suitable mayor of Paris; there is too striking a resemblance between them
to be overlooked," was sadly to exclaim some months later: "I am one
of the most notable examples of popular inconsistency. . . . For a long
time I have said to myself and to my friends: The people will hate
me still more than they have loved me. I can no longer either enter
or depart from the place where we hold our sessions without being
exposed to the grossest insults and the most seditious threats. How
often have I not heard them say as I was passing: 'Scoundrel! we will
have your head!'"

Proscribed with the Girondins, May 31, 1793, he fled at first to

Normandy, and afterwards into the Gironde, wandering from town to town, from field to field, and hiding for several months thirty feet underground, in a sort of well; the poor people who showed him hospitality paid for it with their heads. Ah! how disenchanted he must have been with that revolutionary policy of which he had been the enthusiastic promoter! How sad was the farewell to life signed by him and Buzot:

> Now that it has been demonstrated that liberty is hopelessly lost; that the principles of morality and justice are trodden under foot; that there is nothing to choose between two despotisms,—that of the brigands who are tearing the vitals of France and that of foreign powers; that the nation has lost all its energy; that it lies at the feet of the tyrants by whom it is oppressed; that we can render no further service to our country; that, far from being able to give happiness to the beings we hold most dear, we shall bring down hatred, vengeance, and misfortune upon them, so long as we live,—we have resolved to quit life and be no longer witnesses of the slavery which is about to desolate our unhappy country.

After ending with this cry of grief and indignation: "We devote the vile scoundrels who have destroyed liberty and plunged France into an abyss of evils to the scorn and indignation of all time," the two proscripts were found dead in a wheat-field about a league from Saint-Emilion. Their bodies were half devoured by wolves.

And how will André Chénier end? On the day of the Swiss *fête*, the city where such a scandal took place seemed to him insupportable. For several days he sought refuge in the country where he could breathe a purer air beneath the blossoming trees. But contemplation of nature did not soothe him. Running to meet danger, he returned and threw himself into the furnace, more ardent and indignant than before. With manly enthusiasm he exclaimed: "It is above all when the sacrifices which must be made to truth, liberty, and country are dangerous and difficult, that they are accompanied by inexpressible delights. It is in the midst of spying accusations, outrages, and proscriptions, it is in dungeons and on scaffolds, that virtue, probity, and constancy taste the pleasures of a proud and pure conscience." André had a presentiment of his fate.

He was to die on the same day and the same scaffold as his friend Roucher, a few hours earlier than the moment when Robespierre's condemnation would have saved them. It is thus that he was to pay with his life for his opposition to the *fête* of the Swiss of Chateauvieux, and Collot d'Herbois was avenged. But after the turn of the victims came that of the headsmen. The unlucky comedian who, pursuing even his comrades with his hatred, asked that "the head of the *Comédie Française* should be guillotined and the rest transported," the impresario of the *fête* of the Swiss galley slaves, the organizer of the Lyons massacres, Collot d'Herbois, cursed by friends and enemies, was transported to Guiana and died there in 1796, just as he had lived, in an access of burning fever.

12

The Declaration of War

The wave of anarchy constantly rose higher, but the optimists, sheltering themselves, like Pétion, in a beatific calm, obstinately closed their eyes and would not see it. Abroad and at home there was such a series of shocks and agitations, of struggles and emotions, perils and troubles; things hurried on so fast, and the scenes of the drama were so varied and so violent, that what happened today was forgotten by the morrow. The noise of the *fête* of the Swiss of Chateauvieux had hardly ceased when the shouts of the multitude were heard saluting Louis XVI., who had just declared war on Austria.

In reality, the King did not desire war, but the bellicose current had become irresistible. The court of Vienna had shown itself intractable. It forbade the princes who owned possessions in Lorraine and Alsace to receive the indemnities offered by France in exchange for their feudal rights, and threatened to have the Diet of Ratisbonne annul any private treaties they might conclude concerning them. The electors of Trèves, Cologne, and Mayence undisguisedly favoured the levying of troops by the emigrant princes, and even paid subsidies toward their support. They refused to recognize the official ambassadors of Louis XVI., while recognizing the plenipotentiaries of these princes. There was talk of holding a Congress at Aix-la-Chapelle for the purpose of intimidating the National Assembly.

The successor of the Emperor Leopold, Francis II., who, before his election to the Empire, had assumed the title of King of Hungary and Bohemia, displayed extremely martial sentiments. Austria, which had sent forty thousand men to the Low Countries and twenty thousand to the Rhine, had just signed a treaty of alliance with Prussia, "to put an end to the troubles in France." Dumouriez urgently demanded the court of Vienna to explain itself. It finally sent the French Ambassador, Marquis de Noailles, a dry, curt, and formal note, naming the only conditions on which peace could be preserved. These were: the re-establishment of the French monarchy on the bases of the royal declaration of June 23, 1789, and, consequently, the restoration of the nobility and clergy as orders; the restitution of Church property; the return of Alsace to the German princes, with all their sovereign and feudal rights; and, finally, the surrender of Avignon and the county of Venaisson to the Holy See.

"In truth," says Dumouriez in his *Memoirs*, "if the Viennese minister had slept through the entire thirty-three months that had elapsed since the royal séance, and had dictated this note on awaking without knowledge of what had happened, he could not have proposed conditions more incongruous with the progress of the Revolution. . . . The new social compact was founded on the abolition of the orders and the equality of all citizens. The financial system, which alone could prevent bankruptcy, was founded on the creation of *assignats*. The *assignats* were hypothecated on the property of the clergy, now become the property of the nation, and the greater part of which had been already sold. The nation, therefore, could not accept these conditions except by violating its Constitution, destroying property, ruining its purchasers, annulling its *assignats*, and declaring bankruptcy. Could so humiliating an obedience be expected from a great nation, proud of having conquered its liberty? and that for the sake of placing itself once more under the yoke of nobles who, having abandoned their King himself, now threatened to re-enter their country with sword and flame and every scourge of vengeance?"

The entire National Assembly reasoned in the same way as Dumouriez. A cry for war arose on all sides. The Girondins saw in it the indispensable consecration of the Revolution. The Feuillants hoped that besides proving creditable to the government, it would accomplish the additional end of drawing away from Paris and other great cities a multitude of turbulent men who, for lack of anything else to do, were disturbing public order. Certain reactionists, stifling the sentiment of patriotism in their hearts, were equally anxious for war, in the secret hope that it would prove disastrous for the French army, and result in the re-establishment of the old *régime*. On the other hand, there were good citizens, inclined to optimism and judging others by themselves, who thought that when confronted with an enemy, all intestine dissensions would vanish as by enchantment, and that the new

Constitution, hallowed by victory and glory, would ensure the country a most brilliant destiny. Ministers were unanimous, and enthusiasm universal. Even if he had so desired, Louis XVI. could no longer resist it. On April 20, 1792, he went to the Assembly. The hall was filled with a crowd which comprehended the importance and solemnity of the act about to be accomplished.

According to Dumouriez, the King was very majestic: "I come," he said, "in accordance with the terms of the Constitution, formally to propose war against the King of Hungary and Bohemia." He afterwards paid the greatest attention to the report of the Minister of Foreign Affairs, and seemed, by the motions of his head and hands, to approve it in every respect. He returned to the Tuileries amidst general acclamations. War was unanimously decided on, and Dumouriez went to the diplomatic committee in order to draw up the declaration. At ten in the evening the decree was brought in and carried to the King, who sanctioned it at once.

Thus commenced that gigantic war which France was to wage against all Europe, and which ended, twenty-three years later, in the disaster of Waterloo. How many battles, what suffering, and what a prodigious shedding of blood! And to attain what end? Simply the point of departure; that is to say, in the political order, to constitutional monarchy, and in territory, to the boundaries of 1792. What! to have filled Europe with noise and renown; to have carried the standards of France from east to west, from north to south; to have camped victoriously in Brussels, Milan, Venice, Rome, Naples, Cairo, Berlin, Madrid, Vienna, Moscow; to have enlarged the borders of valour, heroism, and self-sacrifice in order to arrive, after so many efforts, just at the spot where the strife began?

Ah! how short-sighted is human wisdom, how deceitful the previsions of mortal man, how sterile the agitations of republics and monarchs! "Assuredly!" says Dumouriez, "if the Emperor and the King of Prussia could have foreseen that France was able to withstand all Europe, they would not have meddled with her domestic quarrels; they would have treated the *émigrés* not with confidence, but compassion; they would have responded frankly and without trickery to the minister's negotiation; the Revolution would have been accomplished without cruelties; Europe would have remained at peace, and France would be happy." What sadness underlies all history, and what disproportion there is between man's sacrifices and their results! The Revolution was achieved. All necessary liberties had been conquered. Privileges existed no longer.

Animated by excellent intentions, Louis XVI. would have been the best of constitutional sovereigns, had his subjects possessed wisdom. Why this long misunderstanding between him and his people? Why, on one side, the insensate attitude of the *émigrés*, whose task seemed to be to justify the revolutionists; and why, on the other, those savage passions which seemed trying to justify the wrathful recriminations of Coblentz? Why that untimely intervention of Austria which irritated French national sentiment and gave a political pretext to inexcusable violence, cruelty, and crime? Inextricable confusion of false situations! Multitudes asked themselves in what direction right and duty lay. A large contingent of the French nobility heartily desired the success of foreign armies. At Coblentz a gathering of twenty-two thousand gentlemen hastened to the side of the seven Bourbon princes: the Comte de Provence, the Comte d'Artois, the Duc de Berry, the Duc d'Angoulême, the Prince de Conde, the Duc de Bourbon, and the Duc d'Enghien.

As M. de Lamartine has said:

Infidelity to the country called itself fidelity to the King. Desertion called itself honour. Fealty to the throne was the religion of the French nobility. To them the sovereignty of the people seemed an insolent dogma against which it was necessary to draw the sword under penalty of sharing the crime. There was real devotion in the act by which these men, young and old, abandoned their rank in the army, and the ties of country and family, and rushed into a foreign land to defend the white flag as common soldiers. . . . Their country symbolized duty for the patriots; to the *émigrés*, duty meant the throne. One of these parties deceived itself concerning its duty, but both of them believed they were performing it.

As to the unfortunate Louis XVI., he suffered cruelly. It was like death to him to declare war against his nephew, and at certain moments he felt that this Austrian army against which his troops contended might yet be his last resource. He could not even flatter himself that the sacrifice he had made of his sympathies and family feelings would be repaid by the love and confidence of his people.

"We have no difficulty nowadays in comprehending," says M. Geffroy very justly, "what pure patriotism there was in that young army of 1792, which represented new France. But this army, formed in independence of the old regiments, was none the less, in the eyes of the

Queen, a veritable army of sedition. She thought of it as composed of the victors of the Bastille, those whom Mirabeau styled the greatest scoundrels of Paris; the very rabble who came to Versailles on the 6th of October. She believed they could be crushed by the first attack at the frontier, and that France and Paris would be rid of them." The following reflection by M. Geffroy is very judicious:

Marie Antoinette committed a double error, but honest men who had not the same overpowering motives as she, have committed it likewise. I do not allude merely to those Frenchmen who, after April 20, remained in the ranks of the Emigration, and who, apparently, did not suppose themselves to be betraying the true interests of their country. But look at M. de Bouillé. He even accepted a command in the foreign army under Gustavus III. And yet M. de Bouillé is an honest man who knows France and loves her ardently. Observe, in his *Memoirs*, his involuntary pride in our success, and how he shrugs his shoulders at the bluster of the Prussian officers.

It is not yet well understood what vigour, enthusiasm, and martial ardour animated that brave national army, which, according to the foreigners, was but a band of rioters, but which was suddenly to appear on the battlefield as a people of heroes. Honour took refuge in the camps. It was there that men whom the Jacobin Club enraged, and who had no consolation for their patriotic grief but the virile emotions of combat, went to fight and die. Why did not Louis XVI. call to mind that he was the commander-in-chief of the army? Ah! had he been a soldier, had he been accustomed to wear a uniform, to command, and, above all, to speak to his troops, how quickly he would have come to the end of his difficulties! Count de Vaublanc had good reason to say:

Anything can be done with Frenchmen if one knows how to animate and impress them with vehement ardour; otherwise, nothing need be expected. . . . Never did a prince merit better the eternal rewards promised by religion to the true Christian; and yet his example should forever teach kings that their conduct must be totally different from his. Lacking the courage which acts, the most virtuous king cannot achieve his own safety.

Why did not Louis XVI. go amongst his soldiers? Victory would have given him a sceptre and a crown. While he still retained his sword, why did he leave it in the scabbard? Why did he not remember that it might launch thunderbolts?

On the contrary, Louis XVI. hesitates, fumbles, temporizes. Count de Vaublanc says again:

> This wretched time proves thoroughly that finesse is the most detestable means of conducting great affairs. Nothing but finesse was opposed to the impetuous attacks of the Jacobins. All was dissimulation; conversations, writings, measures; authority acted only by crooked ways. With a thousand means of safety, people were lost because they pushed prudence to excess, and extreme prudence always degenerates into despicable means. I was in every great crisis of the Revolution, and I have always seen the same faults produce the same misfortunes. It is the same thing in revolution as in war; no matter how prudent a general may be, he must take some risk. Otherwise it would be impossible to gain a single battle.

Ah! how true and how striking is that great saying of Bossuet: "*When God wills to overthrow empires, all is feeble and irregular in their designs.*" Undecided and fickle, Louis XVI. does not even know whether to desire the success or the failure of the Austrian army. He has no plan, no steadiness of purpose. The secret mission he gives to Mallet du Pan is a fresh proof of the irresolution of his character and his policy. What is it he asks? To have the Powers declare that they are making war against an anti-social faction, and not the French nation; that they are undertaking the defence of legitimate governments and of peoples against anarchy; that they will treat only with the King; that they shall demand perfect liberty for him; that they convoke a congress to which the *émigrés* may be admitted as complainants, and where the general scheme of claims and reclamations shall be negotiated under the auspices and the guarantee of the great courts of Europe.

Hesitating between Austria and his own kingdom, the unhappy monarch attempts to continue that equivocal system, that see-saw policy in which he has succeeded so ill, and which constrains him to dissimulation, that last resource of the feeble. Sent to Germany with instructions written by Louis XVI., with his own hand, Mallet du Pan recommends the sovereigns to be cautious in advancing into France, to observe the greatest prudence in dealing with the inhabitants of the invaded provinces, and to precede their arrival by a manifesto in which they declare conciliatory and pacific intentions. It follows that official ministers of the King did not possess his confidence and were not the interpreters of his mind. A sort of occult and mysterious government existed, with a diplomacy, secret funds, and agents abroad and at home. Such a system, lacking all grandeur and sincerity, could accomplish nothing but catastrophes.

Meanwhile, the war had begun under the most painful conditions. The invasion of Belgium, arranged for the end of April, failed miserably. Near Mons, Biron's troops took to flight, threatening to fire on their officers, and crying: "We are betrayed!" At Lille, General Theobald Dillon was massacred by his own soldiers. Such news caused indescribable emotion in Paris. Popular mistrust and irritation reached their height. The different parties hurled reproaches and accusations in each other's face. The Girondins, finding the National Guard too conservative, demanded pikes for the men of the *faubourgs* who had no guns. The *sans-culottes* enlisted. The army of assassins was organized. The only thing left to do before giving the signal for a riot was to obtain from the King a last concession,—the disbanding of his guard.

13

The Disbanding of the Constitutional Guard

Louis XVI. had still some defenders, some heroes resolved to shed the last drop of their blood for their King. Hence it was necessary to remove them from his person. What means of doing so could be found? Calumny. Fable on fable was spread among an always credulous public, imaginary conspiracies invented, and the wretched monarch constrained to deprive himself of his last resource, in order to deliver him, weak and disarmed, into the hands of his enemies.

The Constitution provided a guard for Louis XVI. One third of it was composed of soldiers of the line, and the remainder of National Guards, chosen by the Departments themselves from among their best-formed, richest, and best-bred citizens. It was commanded by one of the greatest lords of the old *régime*, the Duke de Cossé-Brissac. Born in 1734, the son of a marshal of France, the Duke had been governor of Paris, grand steward of France, and colonel of the Hundred-Switzers. He had never been willing to leave the King since the beginning of the Revolution. When his regiment was disbanded he might have fled, and Louis XVI. begged him to do so; but the heart of a subject so faithful had been deaf to the entreaties of the unfortunate sovereign.

"Sire," he had answered, "if I fly, they will say that I am guilty, and you will be considered my accomplice: my flight would be your accusation; I would rather die." And, in fact, he did die. He had a real devotion to the former mistress of Louis XV., the Countess du Barry, and this latest conquest is not the least important of the favorite's adventures. Probably Count d'Allonville exaggerates when, in his Memoirs, he extols in Madame du Barry "that decency of tone, that nobility of manners, that bearing equally removed from pride and humility, from license and from prudery, that countenance which was enough to refute all the pamphlets." Nevertheless, it is certain that the society of the Duke de Brissac inspired the former favourite with generous sentiments. After the October Days, she took the wounded body-guards into her own house, and when the Queen sent to thank her for it, she replied:

> These wounded young men regret nothing except not having died for a princess so worthy of all homage as Your Majesty. . . . Luciennes [1] is yours, *Madame*; did not your benevolence give it back to me? . .. The late King, by a sort of presentiment, forced me to accept a thousand precious objects before sending me away from his person. I already had the honour of offering you this treasure in the time of the Notables; I offer it again, Madame, with eagerness. You have so many expenses to provide for, and so many favours to confer. Permit me, I entreat you, to render to Cæsar that which belongs to Cæsar.

An enthusiastic royalist, a gentleman of the old nobility, chivalrous and full of courtesy, bred in notions of romantic susceptibility like those of *Clélie* and *Astrée*, the Duke de Brissac, like a knight-errant of former times, represented at the court of Louis XVI. a whole past which was crumbling to decay. If the unhappy monarch had been a man of action, he would have turned to good advantage a guard commanded by such a champion. He could have made it the nucleus of resistance by grouping the Swiss regiments and the well-inclined battalions of the National Guard around it. Unfortunately, there was nothing warlike in Louis XVI.

"Among the deplorable causes which ruined him," says the Count de Vaublanc in his *Memoirs*, "must be counted the wretched education which kept him apart from every sort of military action. I remember that in the early days of the Consulate, after a review held on the Place of the Tuileries by Bonaparte, when talking about this to M. Suard, of the French Academy, I said that Bonaparte walked as if he were always ready to defend himself sword in hand. 'Ah, well!' responded M. Suard, *naïvely*, 'we used to think differently; we wanted the King to have nothing military about him, and never to wear a uniform.'"

To this anecdote, M. de Vaublanc adds another. "We had in 1792,"

---

1. The magnificent mansion built for Madame du Barry by Louis XV., and restored to her after her banishment to Meaux by Marie Antoinette.

he says, "a forcible proof of the despondency under which a royal soul, spoiled by a detestable education, can labour. M. de Narbonne, the Minister of War, with great difficulty induced the King to review three excellent battalions of the Paris National Guard. He was on foot, in silk breeches and white silk stockings, and wearing his hair in a black bag. After the review a notary, named Chandon, I think, left the ranks and said to the King: 'Sire, the National Guard would be greatly honoured to see Your Majesty in its uniform.' 'Sire,' said M. de Narbonne, at once, 'have the goodness to promise to do so. At the head of these three battalions of heroes you could destroy the Jacobins' den.' After a minute's reflection, the King replied: 'I will inquire of my Council whether the Constitution permits me to wear the uniform of the National Guard.'"

Louis XVI. allowed the last resources accorded by fortune to slip away, and elements which in other hands would have produced notable results, remained sterile in his.

The Constitutional Guard, which according to regulation should have numbered eighteen hundred men, really amounted, says Dumouriez, to six thousand fit for duty. The royalist element predominated in it. But a certain number of "false brethren" had found their way into the ranks, who managed by the aid of bribery to spy upon their officers, and made reports to the committee of public safety. Undoubtedly the King's guards did not approve of all that was going on. But how could devoted royalists and men accustomed to discipline be expected to approve the *fête* of the Swiss of Chateauvieux, for example? How could they help being indignant when, while on duty at the Tuileries, they heard the populace insult the royal family under the very windows of the palace?

When they returned to their barracks at the Military School, they expressed this indignation too forcibly, and their words, hawked about in all quarters by ill-will, were represented as the preliminary symptoms of a reactionary plot. A guard commanded by a Duke de Brissac was intolerable to the Jacobins. Their sole idea was to drive it from the Tuileries, where its presence appeared to insure order,—a thing they held in utmost horror. A 20th of June would not have been possible with a constitutional guard, and ever since May, the 20th of June had been in course of preparation.

Its organizers had their plan completely laid already. An adroit rumour was started of a so-called plot, some Saint-Bartholomew or other, which they pretended was on foot against the patriots, and of which the École Militaire was the centre. The white flag, which was to be the signal for the assassins to assemble, was said to be hidden there. Pétion, the mayor of Paris, under pretext of preventing troubles, sent municipal officers to make a search. They could not lay their hands on the white flag which was the pretended object of their visit, but they did find monarchical hymns and ballads, and counter-revolutionary writings.

An unlucky incident still further increased suspicion. The famous Countess de La Motte had just published in London some new particulars concerning the affair of the necklace. In order to avert scandal, the Queen had caused Laporte, intendant of the civil list, to buy up the whole edition, and he had burned every copy of it at the manufactory of Sèvres. That very evening the committee of surveillance were in possession of the fact that Laporte had gone to Sèvres with three unknown persons, and that thirty bales of paper had been put into the fire in his presence. There was at this time a great deal of talk concerning a pretended Austrian committee, in which a complete plan of restoration by foreign aid was being elaborated. It was claimed that the papers burned at the manufactory were the archives of this committee, with which popular imagination was extremely busy.

Denunciations fell in showers. Laporte and several others were summoned before the committee of surveillance. Pétion declared that the people were surrounded by conspiracies. Bazire demanded the disbanding of the King's guard, which, according to him, was made up of servants of the *émigrés*, and refractory priests. It was claimed that the soldiers, to whom the Duke de Brissac had given sabres with hilts representing a cock surmounted by a royal crown, used insulting language concerning the Assembly and the nation in their barracks. They were said to rejoice in the reverses which the French troops had just sustained on the northern frontier, and it was added that they meant to march twenty leagues under a white flag to meet the Austrians. The masses, always so easily deceived, were convinced that the conspiracy was on the brink of discovery.

The National Assembly took up the question, and a stormy debate on it occupied the evening session of May 29. "What will become of the individual liberty of citizens," cried M. Daverhouté, "if the dominant party, merely by alleging suspicions, can decree the impeachment of all who displease it, and if the different parties, coming successively into power, overthrow, by means of this unchecked right of impeachment, both ministers and all functionaries by the torrent of their intrigues? In that case you would see proscriptions like those of Marius and Sylla." In fact, this was what the near future was about to show. Vergniaud responded by evoking a souvenir of the prætorian guards of Caligula and Nero. At the close of his speech the Assembly passed the following decree:—

Article 1. The existing hired guard of the King is disbanded, and will be replaced immediately in conformity with the laws.

Art. 2. Until the formation of the new guard, the National Guard of Paris will be on duty near the King's person, in the same manner as before the establishment of the King's guard.

A discussion ensued on the subject of Brissac's impeachment. The struggle between the two opposing parties was of unheard-of vivacity. One of the most courageous members of the right, M. Calvet, gave free vent to his indignation. "The informer," said he, "is a scoundrel who makes a thrust with a poniard and hides himself; he was unknown at Rome until the times of Sejanus and Tiberius; times, gentlemen, of which you remind me often." "To the Abbey! to the Abbey!" retorted the left, with fury.

Said Guadet:

I demand that M. Calvet should be sent to the Abbey for three days, for having dared to say that the representatives of the French people remind him of the Roman Tiberius and Sejanus.

The motion was adopted, and the Assembly decided that M. Calvet should pass three days in prison. M. de Jaucourt threatened to cudgel Chabot, and the ex-friar, ascending the tribune, said: "I think it was very cowardly on the part of a colonel to offer to cane a Capuchin." The Assembly, having passed an order of the day concerning this incident, decreed that "there was reason for an accusation against M. Cossé, styled Brissac, and that his papers should be sealed up at once."

The King and Queen, awakened in the middle of the night by these tidings, besought Brissac to make his escape, and provided him with the means. The Duke refused, and instead of trying to assure his safety, sat down to write a long letter to Madame du Barry. At first Louis XVI. wished to veto this decree, as was his duty, but his ministers dissuaded him. They reminded him of the October Days, and the weak monarch, alarmed on account of his family, if not on his own, sacrificed his Constitutional Guard and also the brave servitor who commanded it. Speaking to M. d'Aubier, one of the ordinary gentlemen of the King's bedchamber, the Queen said: "I tremble lest the King's guard should think the honour of the corps compromised by their disarmament."

"Doubtless, *Madame*, that corps would have preferred to die at the feet of Your Majesties."

"Yes," replied the Queen, "but the few partisans who still adhere to the King in the Assembly counsel him to sanction the decree disbanding them, and to disregard their advice is to run the risk of losing them." While the Queen was yet speaking, a man approached under pretence of asking alms. "You see," said she to M. d'Aubier, "there is no place and no time when I am free from spies."

The Constitutional Guard were sent as prisoners to the École Militaire between a double file of National Guards, and forced to surrender their weapons. By a sort of fatality Louis XVI. was led to disarm himself, to spike his cannons, tear down his flags, and dismantle his fortresses. By dint of approaching too near the fatal declivity of concessions, he ended by losing even his dignity as man and King. He was paralyzed, annihilated by the Assembly, which treated him like a hostage, a conquered man, and which struck down, one after another, the last defenders of the monarchy and of public order.

The fate of the Constitutional Guard might well discourage honest men who only sought to devote themselves. How was it possible to remain faithful to a chief who was false to himself, who was more like a victim than a king? Finding themselves unsupported by the Tuileries, the royalists began to look across the frontier, and many men who would have flocked around an energetic monarch, fled from a feeble king and sorrowfully went to swell the ranks of the emigration.

In spite of the advice of Dumouriez, Louis XVI. would not make use of his right to form another guard. He preferred to put himself in the hands of the National Guard, who were his jailors rather than his servants. As to the Duke de Brissac, even the formality of an interrogatory was dispensed with, and he was sent before the Superior Court of Orleans. When he bade *adieu* to Louis XVI., the King said to him: "You are going to prison; I should be much more afflicted if you were not leaving me there myself."

What was to be the fate of the loyal and devoted servant, thus sacrificed to his master's inexcusable weakness? He left the dungeons of Orleans only to be transferred to Versailles by the Marseillais, and there, on September 9, 1792, was assaulted by a furious throng surrounding the carriages containing the prisoners. The brave old man struggled long against the assassins, but, after losing two fingers and receiving several other wounds, he was killed by a sabre-thrust which broke his jaw, and his head was set on one of the spikes of the palace gate.

14

The Sufferings of Louis XVI

Dissatisfied with men and things, dissatisfied with others and himself, the mind and heart of Louis XVI. were the prey of moral tortures which left him no repose. He began to be ashamed of his concessions, and to repent of having accepted pusillanimous advice. Why had he not succeeded in being a king? Why had he garrisoned Paris insufficiently ever since the outbreak of the Revolution? Why had he suffered the Bastille to be taken, encouraged the emigration, and disbanded his bodyguards? Why had he not opposed the first persecutions aimed at the Church? Why had he pretended to approve acts and ideas which horrified him? Why, by resorting to deplorable equivocations which cast a shadow over his policy and his character, had he reduced his most devoted followers to doubt and despair?

Such thoughts as these assailed him like so many stings of conscience. The sentiments of monarchy and of military honour awoke in him once more, and he sounded with bitterness the whole depth of the abyss into which his irresolution had plunged him. In seeing what he was, he recalled sorrowfully what he had been, and comprehended by cruel experience what feebleness could make of a Most Christian King and eldest son of the Church, an heir of Louis XIV. He thought of the many brave men, victims of his political errors, who on his account had suffered exile and ruin; of the faithful royalists menaced, because of him, with prison and death.

He thought of the incessantly repeated crimes, the massacres of the Glacière, the impunity of the brigands of "headsman" Jourdan, of Brissac's incarceration. This is what it is, he said within himself, to have suffered religion to be persecuted and to have believed that, were the altar once overthrown, the throne might rest secure. He reproached himself bitterly for having sanctioned the civil organization of the clergy at the close of 1790, and thus drawn upon himself the censure of the Sovereign Pontiff. He wanted to be done with concessions, but he understood perfectly that it was too late now to resist, and that he was irrevocably lost in consequence of events undesired and unforeseen.

What was to be done? How could he sail against the stream? Where find a point of vantage? Ought he to take violent measures? If the unhappy King had been alone, perhaps he might have tried to do so. But he feared to endanger his wife and children by thus acting.

As if to push the wretched monarch to extremities, the National Assembly passed two decrees which struck him to the heart. According to the first of these, voted May 19, any ecclesiastic having refused the oath to the civil constitution of the clergy, could be transported at the simple request of twenty citizens of the canton in which he resided. According to the second, voted June 8, a camp of twenty thousand federates, recruited from every canton of the realm, were to be assembled before Paris, in order, as was said in one of the preambles, "to take every hope from the enemies of the common weal who are scheming in the interior."

They had counted too much on the King's patience. He could not resolve to sanction the two decrees, and banish the ecclesiastics whose behaviour he honoured. Dumouriez afflicted him still further, when, in entreating him to yield, he asked why he had sanctioned, at the close of 1790, the decree obliging the clergy to take oath to the civil constitution of the clergy. "Sire," said he, "you sanctioned the decree for the priests' oath, and it is to that your *veto* must be applied. If I had been one of your counsellors at the time, I would, at the risk of my life, have advised you to refuse your sanction. Now my opinion is that having, as I dare to say, committed the fault of approving this decree, which has produced enormous evils, your *veto*, if you apply it to the second decree, which may arrest the deluge of blood ready to flow, will burden your conscience with all the crimes to which the people are tending."

Never had a sovereign's conscience been a prey to similar perplexities. Louis XVI. seemed crushed beneath an irresistible fatality. The Tuileries, haunted night and day by the spectre of Charles I., assumed a dismal air. At this period a sort of stupor characterized the countenance, the gait, and even the silence of the future victim of January 21. He no longer spoke; one might say he no longer thought. He seemed prostrated, petrified.

A rumour got about that he had become almost imbecile through care and trouble, so much so that he did not recognize his son, but on seeing him approach, had asked: "What child is that?"

It was added that while out walking he caught sight of the steeple of Saint Denis from the top of the hill, and cried out: "That is where I shall be on my birthday." He had been so calumniated, so misunderstood, so outraged, that not merely his crown but his existence had become an intolerable burden to him. His throne and his life alike disgusted him. He was no longer a King, but only the ghost of one.

Madame Campan thus describes him: "At this period the King fell into a discouragement amounting to physical prostration. For ten days together he never uttered a word, even in the bosom of his family, except when the game of backgammon, which he played with Madame Elisabeth after dinner, obliged him to pronounce some indispensable words. The Queen drew him out of this condition, so fatal at a critical time when every minute may necessitate action, by throwing herself at his feet and addressing him sometimes in words intended only to frighten him, and at others expressing her affection for him. She demanded, also, what he owed to his family, and went so far as to say that if they must perish, it ought to be with honour, and without waiting to be strangled one after another on the floor of their apartment."

While Louis XVI. assisted unmoved, not merely like Charles V. at his own obsequies, but at those of royalty, the blood of Maria Theresa was boiling in the veins of Marie Antoinette. The scenes she had witnessed sometimes extorted sobs and cries of anguish from her. Her pride revolted at seeing the royal mantle, crown, and sceptre dragged through the mire. She wanted to struggle to the last, to hope against all hope, to cling to the last chances of safety like a shipwrecked sailor to the fragments of his ship. Who could say? She might find defenders where she least expected them. It was for this reason that she wished to meet Dumouriez, as she had met Mirabeau and Barnave. Dumouriez has preserved the details of this interview in his Memoirs.

How times had changed! Secrecy was almost necessary if one sought the honour of speaking with the Queen of France. Even to salute her was to expose one's self to the suspicion of belonging to the pretended Austrian committee which was the perpetual object of popular invective. When Louis XVI. told Dumouriez that the Queen desired a private interview with him, the minister was not at all well pleased. He thought it a useless step which might be misinterpreted by all parties. However, he must needs obey. He had received an order to go down to the Queen an hour before the meeting of the Council.

That it might be the sooner over, he took the precaution of going half an hour late to this perilous rendezvous. He had been presented to Marie Antoinette on the day of his nomination as minister. She had then addressed him several words, asking him to serve the King well, and he had replied with a respectful phrase. Since then he had not seen her. When he entered her room, he found the Queen alone, very much flushed, and pacing to and fro in an agitation which promised a lively interview. She approached him with an air of majestic irritation: "Sir!" she exclaimed, "you are all-powerful at this moment, but it is by the favour of the people, who soon break their idols. Your existence depends upon your conduct." Dumouriez insisted on the necessity of scrupulously respecting the Constitution, which Marie Antoinette was unwilling to do.

"It will not last," she said, raising her voice; "take care of yourself!"

"*Madame*," replied the minister, "I am past fifty; I have encountered many perils during my life, and in entering the ministry, I thoroughly understood that responsibility was not the greatest of my dangers."

"Nothing was wanting but to calumniate me," cried the Queen, tears flowing from her eyes; "you seem to think me capable of having you assassinated."

Agitated as greatly as the sovereign, "God preserve me," said Dumouriez, "from offering you so grievous an offence! Your Majesty's character is great and noble. You have given proofs of it which I admire and which have attached me to you."

Marie Antoinette grew calmer. "Believe me, *Madame*," went on the minister; "I have no interest in deceiving you, and I abhor anarchy and crime as much as you do. . . . This is not, as you seem to think, a popular and transitory movement. It is the almost unanimous insurrection of a great nation against inveterate abuses. The conflagration is stirred up by great parties, and there are scoundrels and fools in all of them. I behold nothing in the Revolution but the King and the nation as a whole; all that tends to separate them leads to their mutual ruin; I am doing all I can to reunite them, and it is your part to aid me. If I am an obstacle to your designs, say so, and I will at once offer my resignation to the King, and go into a corner to bewail the fate of my country and your own."

The interview ended amicably. The Queen and the minister talked over the different factions. Dumouriez spoke to Marie Antoinette of the faults and crimes of each; he tried to convince her that she was misled by those who surrounded her, and the Queen appeared to be convinced. When he was obliged to call her attention to the clock, as the hour for the Council had arrived, she dismissed him most affably.

If we may credit Madame Campan, who has also given an account of this interview, the impression Marie Antoinette received from it was scarcely a good one.

"One day," says Madame Campan, "I found the Queen extremely troubled. She said she no longer knew where she stood; whether the Jacobin chiefs were making overtures to her through Dumouriez, or Dumouriez, abandoning the Jacobins, was acting on his own account; that she had given him an audience; that, when alone with her, he had fallen at her feet and said that although he had pulled the red bonnet down to his ears, yet he was not and could not be a Jacobin; that the Revolution had been allowed to fall into the hands of a rabble of disorganizers who, seeking only for pillage, were capable of everything, and could furnish the Assembly with a formidable army, ready to undermine the support of a throne already too much shaken. While speaking with extreme warmth, he had seized the Queen's hand, and, kissing it with transport, cried, 'Permit yourself to be saved!' The Queen said to me that the protestations of a traitor could not be believed, and that his entire conduct was so well known that undoubtedly the wisest thing would be not to trust him."

Meantime, the danger constantly increased. Even the gates of the Tuileries were no longer fastened. Hawkers of vile pamphlets and sanguinary satires on the Queen cried their infamous wares under the very windows of the palace; and the National Assembly, sitting close beside, and hearing them—the National Assembly, terrorized by Jacobins and pikemen—dared not even censure such baseness. On June 4, a deputy named Ribes, till then unknown, cited from the tribune the titles of the following articles in Fréron's journal, *l'Orateur du Peuple*: "The crowned porcupine, a constitutional animal who behaves unconstitutionally."—"Crimes of M. Capet since the Revolution."—"Decree to be passed forbidding the Queen to sleep with the King."—"The royal tigress, separated from her worthy spouse, to serve as a hostage." "Rouse up!" cried the indignant deputy. "There is still time. Join with me in proclaiming war on traitors and justice for the seditious, and the country is safe!" Ribes preached in the desert. The Assembly shrugged their shoulders and treated him as a fool.

June 11, another deputy, M. Delsaux, said from the tribune:

"Last evening, at half-past seven, passing through the Tuileries, I saw an orator standing on a chair and speaking with great vehemence. Mixing with the crowd, I heard him read a libel strongly inciting to the King's assassination. This libel is called, 'The Fall of the Idol of the French,' and these sentences occur in it: 'This monster employs his power and his treasures to hinder our regeneration. A new Charles IX., he wishes to bring desolation and death to France. Go, cruel wretch; thy crimes shall have an end. Damiens was less guilty. He was punished by most horrible tortures for having desired to deliver France from a monster. And thou, whose offences are twenty-five million times greater, art left unpunished! But tremble, tyrant; there is a Scævola amongst us.'

The Assembly listened, but took no measures. No further restraint was placed either on moral or material disorder. Anarchy showed a nameless epileptic ferocity. Never had the press been more furious or licentious. It was a torrent of mud and gall and blood. The limits of invective and insult were driven further back.

"You see that I am annoyed," said the Queen to Dumouriez in Louis XVI.'s presence; "I dare not go to the window looking into the garden. Last evening, needing a breath of air, I showed myself at the window facing the courtyard. A gunner belonging to the guard apostrophized me in an insulting way, and added: 'What pleasure it would give me to have your head on the end of my bayonet!' In that frightful garden a man standing on a chair reads out horrors against us on one side, and on the other may be seen a soldier or a priest whom they are dragging through a pond, and crushing with blows and insults. Meantime, others are flying balloons or quietly strolling about. Ah! what a place! what a people!"

15

Roland's Dismissal From Office

In the ministry, as elsewhere, discord reigned. At first, the ministers had seemed to be of one mind. They dined at each other's houses four times a week, on the days when there was a meeting of the Council. Friday was Roland's day for receiving his colleagues at his table, where his wife presided and perorated. "These dinners," says Etienne Dumont, "were often remarkable for their gaiety, of which no situation can deprive Frenchmen when they meet in society, and which was natural to men contented with themselves and flattered by their elevation. The future was hidden from them by the present. The cares of the ministry were forgotten. They seated themselves in their dwellings as if they were to abide there forever."

This sort of political honeymoon could not last very long. Things presently began to change for the worse. Dumouriez tired very soon of Madame Roland's pretensions; she wanted to know, see, and direct everything, and he persisted in refusing to transform himself into a puppet whose strings were to be pulled by this woman and the Girondins. Madame Roland, who posed as a puritan, caused remonstrances to be addressed to Dumouriez on the subject of some more or less suspicious affairs, said to have been negotiated by Bonne-Carrère, the director at the Ministry of Foreign Affairs, by which Madame de Beauvert was supposed to have gained large sums. The wife of the Minister of the Interior had a grudge against the favourite of the Minister of Foreign Affairs.

"She is Dumouriez's mistress," said she; "she lives in his house and does the honours at his table, to the great scandal of sensible men, who are friendly to good morals and liberty. For this license on the part of a public man charged with State affairs marks too plainly his contempt for decorum; and Madame de Beauvert, Rivarol's sister, very well and very unfavorably known, is surrounded by the tools of aristocracy, unworthy in all respects." One evening, after dinner, Roland, "with the gravity belonging to his age and character," as his wife says, gave a lecture on morality to the Minister of Foreign Affairs *apropos* of this matter. At first Dumouriez made jesting replies, but afterwards showed temper and appeared displeased with his entertainers. Thereafter he seldom visited the Ministry of the Interior.

Reflecting on this, Madame Roland said to her husband:

Though not a good judge of intrigue, I think worldly wisdom would dictate that the hour has come for getting rid of Dumouriez, if we wish to avoid being ruined by him. I know very well that you would be unwilling to lower yourself to such an action; and yet it is plain that Dumouriez must be seeking to disembarrass himself of those whose censure has offended him. When one undertakes to preach, and does so in vain, he must either punish or expect to be molested.

Thenceforward, Madame Roland formed a distinct group within the ministry, composed of her husband, Clavière, and Servan, who had just replaced De Grave as Minister of War. While Dumouriez, Lacoste, and Duranton (whom Louis XVI. called "the good Duranton") allowed themselves to be affected by the King's goodness, and sincerely wished to save him, their three colleagues, inspired by the spiteful Madame Roland, had but one idea: to destroy him. "Roland, Clavière, and Servan," says Dumouriez in his *Memoirs*, "no longer observed any moderation, not merely with their colleagues, but with the King himself. At every meeting of the Council they abused the mildness of this prince, in order to mortify and kill him with pin-pricks."

It was Servan who proposed forming a camp of twenty thousand federates around Paris. He thought it would be a sort of central revolutionary army, analogous to that English parliamentary army under command of Cromwell, which had brought Charles I. to the scaffold. "Servan, a very wicked man and most inimical to the King," says Dumouriez again, "took the notion to write to the President of the Assembly, without consulting his colleagues, and propose a decree for assembling an army of twenty thousand men around Paris. This was at the time when the Girondin faction was at the height of its power, having the Jacobins at their command, and governing Paris through Pétion. They wanted to destroy the Feuillants, perhaps at the sword's point, to put down the court, and probably to begin putting their republican projects into execution.

Thus it was this faction which brought to Paris the federates who ended by causing every one of them to perish on the scaffold after making Louis XVI. ascend it." Dumouriez was indignant that the Minister of War should have taken it on himself to propose such a decree without even mentioning it to the sovereign. The dispute on this matter was so violent that, but for the presence of the King, the meeting of the Council might have come to a bloody close. Louis XVI., deeply grieved by such scandals, resolved to dismiss the three ministers, who, instead of supporting him, were merely conspirators who had sworn his ruin.

The anguish of the unhappy monarch had reached its height. Four councils were held without his returning the decrees submitted to him for consideration. The National Assembly grew impatient. The Jacobins were in a rage. At last the King concluded to take up in the Council the decree relative to the camp of twenty thousand federates.

"I think," said Dumouriez, "that the decree is dangerous to the nation, the King, the National Assembly, and above all to its authors, whose chastisement it will turn out to be; and yet, Sire, it is my opinion that you cannot refuse it. It was proposed by profound malice, debated with fury, and decreed with enthusiasm; everybody is blinded. If you *veto* it, it will none the less be passed."

The hesitation of Louis XVI. redoubled. As to the decree concerning the clergy, he declared that he would never sanction it. This was the only time that Dumouriez ever saw "the character of this gentle soul somewhat changed for the worse."

Meanwhile, Madame Roland, more impatient and vindictive than ever, wrote the famous letter supposed to issue from her husband, which was to echo in the ears of royalty like a funeral knell. She says of it:—

> The letter was written at one stroke, like nearly all matters of the sort which I have done; for, to feel the necessity, the fitness of a thing, to apprehend its good effect, to desire to produce it, and to give form to the object from which this effect should result, was to me but a single operation.

This letter, a veritable arraignment of the King, was much more like a club speech or a newspaper article than a letter from a minister of state to his sovereign. Such sentences as these occur in it:

Sire, the existing state of things in France cannot long continue; it is a crisis whose violence is attaining its highest point; it must end by an outbreak which should interest Your Majesty as seriously as it affects the entire kingdom. . . . It is no longer possible to draw back. The Revolution is accomplished in men's minds; it will end in blood and be cemented by blood if wisdom does not avert the evils which it is still possible to prevent. . . . Yet a little more delay, and the afflicted people will behold in their King the friend and accomplice of conspirators. Just Heaven! hast Thou stricken with blindness the powerful of this earth, and will they never heed other counsels than those which drag them to destruction! I know that the austere language of truth is rarely welcomed near the throne; I know, also, that it is because it so rarely obtains a hearing there that revolutions become necessary; I know, above all, that I am bound to employ it to Your Majesty, not merely as a citizen submissive to the law, but as a minister honoured with your confidence, or vested with functions which imply this.

The letter also contained a defence of the two decrees, and plainly threatened Louis XVI., should he *veto* them, with the horrors of a civil war which would develop "that sombre energy, mother of virtues and of crimes, which is always fatal to those who have evoked it!" Was not Madame Roland here announcing the September massacres, and the heinous crimes of which she herself was speedily to become one of the most celebrated victims?

At first Roland sent this letter to the King, with a promise that it should always remain a secret between them. But, incited by the vanity of his wife, who was incessantly urging him on to notoriety and display, Roland did not keep this promise. He read the letter at the next meeting of the Council, June 11.

"The King," says Dumouriez, "listened to this impudent diatribe with admirable patience, and said with the greatest coolness: 'M. Roland, you had already sent me your letter; it was unnecessary to read it to the Council, as it was to remain a secret between ourselves.'" Dumouriez was summoned to the palace the following morning, June 12. He found the King in his own room, accompanied by the Queen. "Do you think, *Monsieur*," said Marie Antoinette, "that the King ought to submit any longer to the threats and insolence of Roland and the knavery of Servan and Clavière?"

"No, *Madame*," he replied; "I am indignant at them; I admire the

King's patience, and I venture to ask him to make an entire change in his ministry. Let him dismiss us on the spot, and appoint men belonging to neither party."—

"That is not my intention," said Louis XVI. "I wish you to remain, as well as Lacoste and that good man, Duranton. Do me the service of ridding me of these three factious and insolent persons, for my patience is exhausted."

"It is a dangerous matter, Sire, but I will do it."

As a condition of remaining in the ministry, Dumouriez exacted the sanction of the two decrees. There was another ministerial council the same evening. Roland, Servan, and Clavière were more insolent and acrimonious than usual. Louis XVI. closed the session with mingled dissatisfaction and dignity.

At eight o'clock that evening (June 12), Servan, the Minister of War, went to Madame Roland and said: "Congratulate me! I have been turned out."

"I am much piqued," replied she, "that you should be the first to receive that honour, but I hope it will not be long before it will be decreed to my husband also." Madame Roland's prayer was granted. The virtuous Minister of the Interior received his letters of dismissal the next morning. As Duranton, who delivered it at the Ministry of Justice, was slowly drawing it from his pocket,—

"You make us wait for our liberty," said Roland; and, taking the letter, he added, "In reality that is what it is." Then he went home to his wife to announce to her that he was no longer minister.

Madame Roland, with the instinct of hatred, saw at once how to obtain revenge. "One thing remains to be done," she cried; "we must be the first to communicate the news to the Assembly, sending them at the same time a copy of the letter to the King which must have caused it." This idea pleased the ex-minister highly, and he put it instantly into execution.

"I was conscious," says the irascible Egeria of the Girondins in her *Memoirs*, "of all the effects this might produce, and I was not deceived; my double object was attained, and both utility and glory attended the retirement of my husband. I had not been proud of his entering the ministry, but I was of his leaving it." Thenceforward Madame Roland was to be the most indefatigable cause of the Revolution, and Louis XVI. was to learn by experience what the vengeance of a woman can accomplish.

16

A Three Days' Ministry

Dumouriez had taken the portfolio of war. He kept it three days only. But during those three days what activity! what excitement! More than fifteen hundred signatures affixed, instructions sent to all the generals, a most tumultuous session of the National Assembly, a last effort to induce Louis XVI. to make further concessions, a resignation which was to be the signal for catastrophes. How the scenes of the drama multiply! How the *dénouement* is accelerated!

The session at which Dumouriez was to appear for the first time as Minister of War could not fail to be singular. It took place June 13, 1792, and from ten o'clock in the morning all the galleries had been crowded. The Jacobins had filled them with their satellites. The Girondins had prepared a dramatic surprise. The three ex-ministers were to be brought into the chamber under pretext of explaining the causes of their dismissal. It was agreed that they should be received as victims of the aristocracy and martyrs of the Revolution. Roland's letter—say, rather, his wife's letter—to Louis XVI. was read to the Assembly and frequently interrupted by loud bursts of applause. Just as it was finished, and someone was demanding that it should be sent to all the eighty-three departments, Dumouriez entered the hall.

Murmurs and hisses arose on all sides. The Assembly voted the despatch of the letter to the departments. A deputy exclaimed: "It will be a famous document in the history of the Revolution and of the ministers." The Assembly went on to declare that Roland was followed by the regrets of the nation. Then Dumouriez ascended the tribune and read a message in which M. Lafayette announced the death of M. de Gouvion. He had been major-general of the National Guard, and, having quitted the Assembly rather than be present at the triumph of the Swiss of Chateauvieux, had met his death bravely in the Army

113

of the North. "A cannon-ball," said the message, "has terminated a virtuous life." The Assembly was affected, and voted complimentary condolences to the father of the heroic officer.

Afterwards, Dumouriez read his report on military affairs. It was a long criticism on the legislators who had ordered a new levy of troops before providing the existing corps with their full complements; on the muster-masters, the standing committees, and the market-contractors, who were piling up abuses. Dumouriez complained of everything; he reproached the factions, and insisted on the consideration due to ministers. Guadet thundered out: "Do you hear him? He already thinks himself so sure of power that he takes it on him to give us advice."—"And why not?" resumed the minister, turning toward the side of the Mountain.[1] This bold response astonished the most furious. Someone said: "The document is not signed. Let him sign it! Let him sign it!"

Dumouriez called for pen and ink, signed his memoir, and went to lay it on the desk. Then he slowly crossed the hall and went quietly out by the door beneath the Mountain, with a haughty glance at his adversaries. His martial attitude disconcerted them. The shouts and hootings ceased, and complete silence ensued. On leaving the Assembly, Dumouriez was surrounded by a group of persons before the door of the Feuillants, but their faces displayed no signs of anger toward him. As soon as he quitted the Assembly, his enemies, no longer intimidated by his presence, redoubled their attacks.

Three or four deputies left the Chamber, and making their way to him through the crowd, said: "They are raising the devil inside; they would like to send you to Orleans." (It was there the Duke de Brissac was imprisoned and the Superior Court held its sessions.) "So much the better," replied Dumouriez; "I would take the baths, drink buttermilk, and rest myself." This sally amused the crowd, and the minister as he entered the Tuileries garden, said to the deputies who followed him: "It will be a mistake for my enemies to have my memoir printed, for it will bring all good citizens back to me. At present, being drunk and crazy, you have just extolled Roland's infamous perfidy to the skies." Then he went to the palace. Louis XVI. complimented him on his firmness, but absolutely refused to sanction the decree against the priests.

Far from ameliorating, the situation continued to grow worse. Pétion's emissaries stirred up the inhabitants of the *faubourgs*. That

---

1. The Advanced Republican party in the Assembly.

evening Dumouriez sent a letter to the King announcing that a riot was apprehended. Louis XVI. suspected that the minister was lying, and wrote to him:

"Do not believe, *Monsieur,* that anyone can succeed in frightening me by threats; my resolution is taken."

Dumouriez had based his entire scheme on the hypothesis that the decree concerning the priests would be accepted by the King. From the moment that Louis XVI. rejected it, Dumouriez no longer hoped to remain in the ministry. He wrote again, imploring the sovereign to give it his sanction, and announcing that, in case of his refusal, the ministers would all feel obliged to retire. The next day, June 15, the King received them in his chamber. "Are you still," said he to Dumouriez, "in the same sentiments expressed in your letter last evening?"

"Yes, Sire, if Your Majesty will not permit yourself to be moved by our fidelity and attachment."

"Very well," replied Louis XVI., with a gloomy air, "since your decision is made, I accept your resignation and will provide for it." Dumouriez was no longer a minister. In his *Memoirs* he describes himself as much affected, "not on account of quitting a dangerous post, which simply made his existence disturbed and painful, but because he saw all his trouble thrown away, and the King handed over to the fury of cruel enemies and the criminal indiscretion of false friends."

At bottom, Dumouriez inspired nobody with confidence. He belonged to no party, and no one knew his opinions. He had leaned on both Jacobins and Girondins, while at the same time he was inspiring certain hopes in the Feuillants, and flattering the King, to whom he promised signs and wonders. Too revolutionary for the conservatives and too conservative for the revolutionists, he had tried a see-saw policy which would no longer answer. It became indispensable to make a choice. It was impossible to please both the Jacobins and the court.

And yet Dumouriez was a man of resources, and it is much to be regretted, on the King's account, that no better understanding could be arrived at between them. More successfully than anyone else, Dumouriez might have resorted to bold measures and called in at this time the intervention of the army, as he did several years later. He loved money and rank; royalty still excited a great prestige over him, and he had used the Revolution as a means, not as an end.

Could Louis XVI. have pretended patience for a few days longer, perhaps he might have extricated himself from difficulties which, though grave, were still not insoluble. He did not choose his hour for resistance wisely. It was either too late or too soon. The dismission of Dumouriez was a blunder. At what moment did Louis XVI. elect to deprive himself of his minister's aid? That very one when, attacked by the Girondins, exasperated by Roland's conduct, and disgusted with the progress of anarchy, the force of circumstances was about to toss Dumouriez back to the side of the reactionists. The camp of twenty thousand men, if confided to safe hands, and secret service money judiciously employed, might have become the nucleus of a monarchical resistance.

Lafayette and his partisans were becoming conservative, and between him and Dumouriez agreement was not impossible. Louis XVI. was in too great a hurry. His conscience revolted at an unfortunate moment. Why, if he was bent on this *veto*, so just, so honest, but so ill-timed, had he freely made so many concessions which thus became inexplicable? In rejecting the offers of Dumouriez, the Queen possibly deprived herself of her only remaining support. He who saved France in the Passes of Argonne might, had he gained the entire confidence of Louis XVI. and Marie Antoinette, have saved the King and royalty.

Dumouriez had a final interview with Louis XVI., June 18. The King received him in his chamber. He had resumed his kindly air, and when the ex-minister had shown him the accounts of the last fortnight, he complimented him on their clearness. Afterwards, the following conversation took place: "Then you are going to join Luckner's army?"

"Yes, Sire, I leave this frightful city with delight; I have but one regret; you are in danger here."

"Yes, that is certain."

"Well, Sire, you can no longer fancy that I have any personal interest to consult in talking with you; once having left your Council, I shall never again approach you; it is through fidelity and the purest attachment that I dare once more entreat you, by your love for your country, your safety and that of your crown, by your august spouse and your interesting children, not to persist in the fatal resolution of vetoing the two decrees. This persistence will do no good, and you will ruin yourself by it."

"Don't say any more about it; my decision is made."

"Ah! Sire, you said the same thing when, in this very room, and in presence of the Queen, you gave me your word to sanction them."

"I was wrong, and I repent of it."

"Sire, I shall never see you again; pardon my frankness; I am fifty-three, and I have some experience. It was not then that you were wrong, but now. Your conscience is abused concerning this decree against the priests; you are being forced into civil war; you are helpless, and you will be overthrown, and history, though it may pity you, will reproach you with having caused all the misfortunes of France. On your account, I fear your friends still more than your enemies."

"God is my witness that I wish for nothing but the welfare of France."

"I do not doubt it, Sire; but you will have to account to God, not solely for the purity but also for the enlightened execution of your intentions. You expect to save religion, and you destroy it. The priests will be massacred and your crown torn from you. Perhaps even your wife, your children. . ."

Emotion prevented Dumouriez from going on. Tears stood in his eyes. He kissed the hand of Louis XVI. respectfully. The King wept also, and for a moment both were silent. "Sire," resumed Dumouriez, "if all Frenchmen knew you as well as I do, our woes would soon be ended. Do you desire the welfare of France? Very well! That demands the sacrifice of your scruples . . . You are still master of your fate. Your soul is guiltless; believe a man exempt from passion and prejudice, and who has always told you the truth."

"I expect my death," replied Louis XVI. sadly, "and I forgive them for it in advance. I thank you for your sensibility. You have served me well; I esteem you, and if a happier time shall ever come, I will prove it to you." With these words the King rose sadly, and went to a window at the end of the apartment.

Dumouriez gathered up his papers slowly, in order to gain time to compose his features; he was unwilling to let his emotion become evident to the persons at the door as he went out. "*Adieu*," said the King kindly, "and be happy!"

As he was leaving, he met his friend Laporte, intendant of the civil list. The two, who were meeting for the last time, went into another room and closed the door. "You advised me to resign," said Laporte, "and I meant to do so, but I have changed my mind. My master is in danger, and I will share his fate."

"If I were in the personal service of the King, as you are," replied Dumouriez, "I would think and act the same; I esteem your devotion, and love you the more for it; each of us is faithful in his own way; you, to Louis; I, to the King of the French. May both of us felicitate him some day on his happiness!" Then the two friends separated, after embracing each other with tears.

The sole thought of Dumouriez now was to escape from the city where he had witnessed so many intrigues and been so often deceived. He was very sorrowful at heart. Ordinarily so gay, so brilliant, so full of Gallic and *Rabelaisian* wit, power had made him melancholy. His ministerial life left on him an abiding impression of bitterness and repugnance. "One needs," he has said, "either a patriotism equal to any test, or else an insatiable ambition, to aspire in any way whatever after those difficult positions where one is surrounded with snares and calumnies. One learns only too soon that men are not worth the trouble one takes to govern them." June 19, he wrote to the Assembly, asking an authorization to repair to the Army of the North.

"I have spent thirty-six years in military and diplomatic service, and have twenty-two wounds," said he in this letter; "I envy the fate of the virtuous Gouvion, and should esteem myself happy if a cannon-ball could put an end to all differences concerning me." He never again returned either to the palace, the Assembly, or any other place where he might encounter either ministers, deputies, or persons belonging to the court. He started for the army, June 26, regarding it as "the only asylum where an honest man might still be safe. At least, death presents itself there under the attractive aspect of glory." He left in the capital "consternation, suspicion, hatred, which pierced through the frivolity of the wretched Parisians."

With an intuition worthy of a man of genius, he foresaw the vicious circle about to be described by French history, and divined that by plunging into license men return inevitably to servitude, because "it is impossible to sustain liberty with an absurd government, founded on barbarity, terror, and the subversion of every principle necessary to the maintenance of human society." Two years later, in 1794, he wrote in his Memoirs: "The serpent will recoil upon itself. His tail, which is anarchy, will re-enter his throat, which is despotism."

17

The Prologue to June Twentieth

On retiring from the ministry, Dumouriez left his successors a burden far too heavy for their shoulders, and under which they were to succumb. The new ministers, Lajard, Terrier de Montciel, and Chambonas, were almost unknown men who had no definite, decided opinions, and offered no resistance to disorder: for that matter, they had no means of doing so. The political system then in power had left Paris a helpless prey to sedition. By the new laws, the executive power could take no direct action looking to the preservation of public order in any French commune. Any minister or departmental administration that should adopt a police regulation or give a commander to armed forces, would be guilty of betraying a trust.

The power to prevent or repress disorder belonged exclusively to the municipal authority, which, in Paris, was composed of a mayor, sixteen administrators, thirty-two municipal councillors, a council-general of ninety-six notables, an attorney-general and his two substitutes. This body of 148 members was the redoubtable power known as the Commune of Paris. It was not composed entirely of seditious persons, and in the National Guard, also, there were still battalions fervently devoted to the constitutional monarchy. But Pétion was mayor of Paris; Manuel, the attorney-general, and Danton his substitute. Seditious movements were sure to find instigators and accomplices in these three men.

Moreover, the insurrection was regularly organized. It had its muster-rolls, its officers, sergeants, soldiers; its strategy and plans of battle. It utilized wineshops as guard-houses, the *faubourgs* as barracks, the red bonnet and the *carmagnole*, or revolutionary jacket, as a uniform. Its agitators distributed wine, beer, and brandy gratuitously. The Jacobins or the Cordeliers had but to give the signal for a riot, and a riot sprang out of the ground. The mine was loaded; the only question was when to fire the train. The Girondins were of one mind with the Jacobins. Exasperated by the dismissal of three ministers who shared their opinions, they wanted to intimidate the court by means of a popular tumult, and thus force the unhappy sovereign to sanction the two decrees, concerning the deportation of priests and the camp of twenty thousand men. The populace already manifested their restlessness by threats and strange rumours.

At the Jacobin Club the most violent propositions were mooted. Some wanted to establish a minority, on the ground of the King's mental alienation; some, to send the Queen back to Austria; the more moderate talked of suppressing the army, dismissing the staff-officers of the National Guard, depriving the King of the right of veto, and electing a Constituent Assembly. Revolutionary conventicles multiplied beyond all measure. The division of Paris into forty-eight sections became an exhaustless source of confusion. The assembly of each section transformed itself into a club.

Meanwhile, the moderate party rested all its hopes on Lafayette, who was friendly not only to liberty, but to order. He considered himself the founder of the new monarchy, of constitutional royalty; but, for that very reason, he felt that he had duties toward the King. Despising the reactionists, whose hopes were more or less enlisted on behalf of the foreign armies, he also detested the Jacobins who were dishonouring and compromising the new order of things. He expresses both sentiments in a letter addressed to the National Assembly, and written from the intrenched camp of Maubeuge, June 16, 1792, the Fourth Year of Liberty:

"Can you conceal from yourselves," he says in it, "that a faction, and to use plain terms, the Jacobin faction, has caused all these disorders? I make the accusation boldly. Organized like a separate empire, with its capital and its affiliations blindly directed by certain ambitious chiefs, this sect forms a distinct body in the midst of the French people, whose powers it usurps by subjugating its representatives and agents. In its public meetings, attachment to the laws is named aristocracy, and disobedience to them patriotism; there the assassins of Desilles are received in triumph, and Jourdan's insensate clamour finds panegyrists; there the story of the assassinations which defiled the city of Metz is still greeted with infernal applause."

Lafayette puts himself courageously forward in his letter:

As to me, gentlemen, who espoused the American cause at the

very time when the ambassadors assured me it was lost; who, from that period, devoted myself to a persistent defence of the liberty and sovereignty of peoples; who, on June 11, 1789, in presenting a declaration of rights to my country, dared to say, 'For a nation to be free, all that is necessary is that it shall will to be so,' I come today, full of confidence in the justice of our cause, of scorn for the cowards who desert it, and of indignation against the traitors who would sully it; I come to declare that the French nation, if it be not the vilest in the universe, can and ought to resist the conspiracy of kings which has been leagued against it." At the same time, the general enthusiastically praised his soldiers: "Doubtless it is not within the bosom of my brave army that sentiments of timidity are permissible. Patriotism, energy, discipline, patience, mutual confidence, all civic and military virtues, I find here. Here the principles of liberty and equality are cherished, the laws respected, and property held sacred; here, neither calumnies nor seditions are known.

Including both revolutionists and reactionists in the same accusation, Lafayette makes this reflection:

What a remarkable conformity of language exists, gentlemen, between those seditious persons acknowledged by the aristocracy, and those who usurp the name of patriots! All are alike ready to repeal our laws, to rejoice in disorders, to rebel against the authorities granted by the people, to detest the National Guard, to preach indiscipline to the army, and almost to disseminate distrust and discouragement.

Lafayette concludes in these words:

Let the royal power be intact, for it is guaranteed by the Constitution; let it be independent, for this independence is one of the forces of our liberty; let the King be revered, for he is invested with the national majesty; let him choose a ministry unhampered by the yoke of any faction; if conspirators exist, let them perish only by the sword of law; finally, let the reign of clubs, brought to nothing by you, give place to the reign of law; their disorganizing maxims to the true principles of liberty; their delirious fury to the calm courage of a nation which knows its rights and which defends them!

Lafayette's letter was read to the Assembly at the session of June 18. The noble thoughts it expresses produced at first a favourable impression, and it was greeted with much applause. For an instant the Girondins were disconcerted; but, feeling themselves supported by the Jacobins who lined the galleries, they soon resumed the offensive. "What does the advice of the general of the army amount to," said Vergniaud, "if it is not law?"

Guadet maintained that the letter must be apocryphal. "When Cromwell used such language," said he, "liberty was at an end in England, and I cannot persuade myself that the emulator of Washington desires to imitate the conduct of the Protector. We no longer have a constitution if a general can give us laws." The allusion to Cromwell produced its effect. The letter, instead of being published and copies sent to the eighty-three departments, was merely referred to a committee.

Nevertheless, public opinion was aroused. A reactionary sentiment against the Jacobins began to show itself. The King might have profited by it, and found his account in relying upon Lafayette, the army, and the National Guard. But Louis XVI. was in too much haste. His resistance, like his concessions, was maladroit and inopportune. Without having combined his means of defence, consulted with Lafayette, or having any troops at his disposal, he vetoed the two famous decrees, June 19, and thus threw himself headlong into the snare. The Revolution, which had lain in wait for him, would not let its prey escape. It gave Lafayette no time to arrive, but, without losing a minute, organized an insurrection for the next day. The royal tree had been so violently shaken, that it needed, or so they thought, but one more shock to lay it low and root it out.

On June 16, a request had been presented to the Council-General of the Commune, asking them to authorize the citizens of the Faubourg Saint-Antoine to assemble in arms on June 20, the anniversary of the oath of the Jeu de Paume, and present a petition to the Assembly and the King. The Council had passed to the order of the day, but the petitioners declared that they would assemble notwithstanding. On the 19th, the Directory of the department, which on all occasions had shown itself inimical to agitators, and which was presided over by the Duke de La Rochefoucauld, issued an order forbidding all armed gatherings, and enjoining the commandant-general and the mayor to take all necessary measures for dispersing them. This order was communicated to the National Assembly by the Minister of the Interior at the evening session.

"It is important," said a deputy, "that the Assembly should know the decrees of the administrative bodies when they tend to assure public tranquillity. Nobody is ignorant that at this moment the people are greatly agitated. Nobody is ignorant that tomorrow threatens to be a day of violence." Vergniaud replied: "I do not know whether or not tomorrow is to be a day of troubles, but I cannot understand how M. Becquet, who is always so constitutional" (here there was laughter and applause), "how M. Becquet, by an inversion of law and order, desires the National Assembly to occupy itself with police regulations." The decree of the Directory was read, nevertheless. But the Assembly, far from supporting it, passed to the order of the day. The rioters had nothing to fear.

During the same session, a deputation of citizens from Marseilles had been presented at the bar of the Assembly. The orator of this deputation thus expressed himself: "French liberty is in danger. The free men of the South are ready to march in its defence. The day of the people's wrath has come at last. The people, whom they have always sought to ruin or enslave, are tired of parrying blows. They want to inflict them, and to annihilate conspiracies. It is time for the people to rise. This lion, generous but enraged, is about to quit his repose, and spring upon the pack of conspirators." Here the galleries applauded furiously. The orator continued: "The popular force is your force; employ it. No quarter, since you can expect none."

The applause and enthusiastic cries of the galleries redoubled. Somebody demanded that the speech should be sent to the eighty-three departments of France. A deputy, M. Rouher, was courageous enough to exclaim: "It is not by the harangues of seditious persons that the departments should be instructed!"

Another deputy, M. Lecointre-Puyravaux, responded: "Is it surprising that men born under a burning sun should have a more ardent imagination and a patriotism more energetic than ours?" The question whether the discourse should be sent to the departments was put to vote, and the president and secretaries declared that the Assembly had decided against it. This did not suit the public in the galleries. They howled, they vociferated. They claimed that the result was doubtful. They demanded a *viva voce* count. This demand alarmed those deputies who never dared to look the Revolution in the face. A new vote was taken, and this time, the sending of the address to the eighty-three departments was decreed. With such an Assembly, why should the insurrectionists have hesitated?

The rioters of the next day did not hesitate a moment. The order of the Directory had somewhat intimidated them. But Chabot, the deputy so celebrated for his violence at the Jacobin Club, hastened to reassure them. "Tomorrow," said he, "you will be received with open arms by the National Assembly. People count on you." The Faubourg Saint-Antoine was in commotion.

Condorcet said, in speaking of the anxieties expressed by the ministers: "Is it not fine to see the Executive asking legislators to provide means of action! Let them save themselves; that is their business!"

The Most Christian King is treated like the Divine Master. Pétion, mayor of Paris, is to play the *rôle* of Pontius Pilate. He washes his hands of all that is to happen. He orders the battalions of National Guards under arms for the following day, not in order to oppose the march of the columns of the people, but to fraternize with the petitioners, and act as escort to the insurrection. This equivocal measure, he thinks, will set him right with both the Directory and the populace. To one he says: "I am watching," and to the other, "I am with you." The rioters count on Pétion as anarchy counts on weakness. He is precisely the magistrate that suits the *faubourgs* when they resort to violent measures.

A last conventicle was held at the house of Santerre the brewer, chief of battalion of the National Guard of the Faubourg Saint-Antoine, on the night of June 19-20. It broke up at midnight. All was ready. The leaders of the insurrection repaired each to his post. They summoned their loyal adherents, and sent them about in small detachments to assemble and mass together the working classes, as soon as they should leave their houses in the morning. Santerre had declared that the National Guard could offer no opposition to the rioters. "Rest easy," said he to the conspirators; "Pétion will be there."

Louis XVI. no longer feigned not to notice the danger. "Who knows," said he during the night to M. de Malesherbes, with a melancholy smile, "who knows if I shall see the sun set tomorrow?"

18

The Morning of June Twentieth

It is Wednesday, June 20, 1792, the anniversary of the oath of the Jeu de Paume. The signal is given. The *faubourgs* assemble. It is five in the morning. Santerre, on horseback, is at the Place de la Bastille, at the head of a popular staff. The army of rioters forms slowly. Some anxiety is shown at first. The departmental decree forbidding armed gatherings had been posted, and occasioned some reflection in the timid. But Santerre reassures them. He tells them that the National Guard will not be ordered to oppose their march, and that they may count on Pétion's complicity.

When the march toward the National Assembly begins, hardly more than fifteen hundred are in line. But the little band increases as it goes. The route lies through rues Saint-Antoine, de la Verrerie, des Lombards, de la Ferronnerie, and Saint-Honoré. The procession is headed by soldiers, after whom comes a great poplar stretched upon a wagon. It is the Liberty tree. According to some, it is to be planted in the courtyard of the Riding School, opposite the Assembly chamber; according to others, on the terrace of the Tuileries, before the principal door of the palace. A military band plays the *Ça ira*, which is chanted in chorus by the insurrectionary troop. No obstacle impedes their march. The torrent swells incessantly. The inquisitive mingle with the bandits. Some are in uniform, some in rags; there are soldiers, active and disabled, National Guards, workmen, and beggars. Harlots in dirty silk gowns join the contingent from studios, garrets, and robbers' dens, and gangs of ragpickers unite with butchers from the slaughter-houses. Pikes, lances, spits, masons' hammers, *paviors'* crowbars, kitchen utensils,—their equipment is oddity itself.

It is noon. The session of the Assembly has just been opened. At this hour the throng, now numbering some twenty thousand persons, enters the rue Saint-Honoré. The Directory of the Department of Paris demands admission to the bar on pressing business, and the municipal attorney-general, Roederer, begins to speak. Heeding neither the murmurs of the galleries, the disapprobation of part of the Assembly, nor the clamour sure to be raised against him that evening in the Jacobin and *Cordelier* clubs, he boldly announces what is going on. He reminds them of the law, and the decrees forbidding armed gatherings which have been issued by the Commune and the Department. He adds that, without such prohibitions, neither the authorities nor private individuals have any security for their lives. "We demand," cried he, "to be invested with complete responsibility; we demand that our obligation to die for the maintenance of public tranquillity shall in nowise be diminished."

Vergniaud ascends the platform. He owns that, in principle, the Assembly is wrong in admitting armed gatherings within its precincts, but he declares that he thinks it impossible to refuse a permission accorded to so many others to that which now presents itself. He believes, moreover, that it could not be dispersed without a resort to martial law and a renewal of the massacre of the Champ-de-Mars. "It would be insulting to the citizens who are now asking to pay their respects to you," said he, "to suspect them of bad intentions... The assemblage doubtless does not claim to accompany the citizens who desire to present a petition to the King. Nevertheless, as a precaution, I propose that sixty members of the Assembly shall be commissioned to go to the King and remain near him until this gathering shall have been dispersed."

The discussion continues. M. Ramond follows Vergniaud. What is going to happen? What will the insurrectionary column do? Glance for an instant at the topography of the Assembly and its environs. The session-chamber is the Hall of the Riding School, which extends to the terrace of the Feuillants, and occupies the site where the rue de Rivoli was opened later on, almost at the corner of the future rue de Castiglione. It is a building about one hundred and fifty feet long. In front of it is a long and narrow courtyard beginning very near the rue de *Dauphin*. It is entered through this courtyard, which a wall, afterwards replaced by a grating, separates from the terrace of the Feuillants. It may be entered at the other extremity, also, at the spot where the flight of steps facing the Place Vendôme was afterwards built.

From the side of the courtyard it can be approached by carriages, but from the other, only by pedestrians who cross the narrow passage of the Feuillants, which starts from the rue Saint-Honoré, opposite the Place Vendôme, and leads to the garden of the Tuileries. This passage is bordered on the right by the convent of the Capuchins; on the left is the Riding School, almost at the spot where the passage opens into the Tuileries Garden by a door which had just been closed, and before which had been placed a cannon and a battalion of National Guards.

On reaching the rue Saint-Honoré, the crowd had taken good care not to enter the court of the Riding School, where they might have been arrested and disarmed. They preferred to follow the rue Saint-Honoré and take the passage conducting thence to the Assembly and the terrace of the Feuillants. Three municipal officers who had gone to the Tuileries Garden, passed through this passage before the crowd, and met the advancing column at the door of the Assembly, just as M. Ramond was in the tribune discussing Vergniaud's proposition. While the head of the column was awaiting the issue of this discussion, the rank and file were constantly advancing.

The passage became so thronged that people were in danger of stifling. Part of them withdrew from the crowd and went into the garden of the Capuchin convent, where they amused themselves by planting the Liberty tree in the classic ground of monkish ignorance and idleness, as was said in those days. The remainder, which was in front of the door and the grating of the terrace of the Feuillants, became exasperated. The sight of the glittering bayonets, and the cannon placed in front of this grating, roused them to fury.

Meanwhile, a letter from Santerre reached the president of the National Assembly: "Gentlemen," said he, "I have received a letter from the commandant of the National Guard, which announces that the gathering amounts to eight thousand men, and that they demand admission to the bar of the chamber."

"Since there are eight thousand of them," cried a deputy, "and since we are only seven hundred and forty-five, I move that we adjourn the session and go away."

Santerre's letter is thus expressed:

Mr. President, the inhabitants of the Faubourg Saint-Antoine are celebrating today the anniversary of the oath of the *Jeu de Paume*. They have been calumniated before you; they ask to be admitted to the bar; they will confound their cowardly detractors for the second time, and prove that they are still the men of July 14.

It was applauded by a large number of the Assembly. On the other side murmurs rose against it. M. Ramond went on with his speech:

Eight thousand men, they say, are awaiting your decision. You owe it to twenty-five millions of other men who await it with no less interest. . . . Certainly, I shall never fear to see the citizens of Paris in our midst, nor the entire French people around us. No one could behold with greater pleasure than I the weapons which are a terror to the enemies of liberty; but the law and the authorities have spoken. Let the petitioners, therefore, lay down at the entrance of the sanctuary the arms they are forbidden to bear within it. You ought to insist on this. They ought to obey.

M. Ramond's courage did not last long. Passing to Vergniaud's proposal to send sixty members of the Assembly to the Tuileries, he said: "I applaud the motive which prompted this proposition. But, convinced that there is nothing to be feared by any person from the citizens of Paris, I regard the motion as insulting to them."

Meanwhile, the noise at the door redoubles; the petitioners are growing impatient. Guadet rises to demand that they shall come in with their arms. It is plain that the Gironde has taken the riot under its patronage. After some disorderly and violent debate, it is resolved that the president shall put the question: Are the petitioners to be admitted to the bar? They do not yet decide this other: Shall the armed citizens defile before the Assembly after they have been heard? The first question is answered in the affirmative. The delegates of the crowd are admitted to the bar. They make their entry into the Assembly between one and two in the afternoon.

Their orator is a person named Huguenin, who will preside a few weeks later at the Council of the Commune during the September massacres. In his declamatory harangue he includes every tirade, threat, and insult current in the streets. "We demand," said he, "that you should find out why our armies are inactive. If the executive power is the cause, let it be abolished. The blood of patriots must not flow to satisfy the pride and ambition of the perfidious palace of the Tuileries." Here the galleries burst into enthusiastic applause.

The orator goes on:

We complain of the delays of the Superior National Court. Why is it so slow in bringing down the sword of the law upon the heads of the guilty? . . . Do the enemies of the country imagine that the men of July 14 are sleeping? If they appear to be so, their awakening will be terrible. . . . There is no time to dissimulate; the hour is come, blood will flow, and the tree of Liberty we are about to plant will flourish in peace.

The applause from the galleries redoubles. Huguenin excites himself to fury: "The image of the country," he shouts, "is the sole divinity which it shall be permitted to adore. Ought this divinity, so dear to Frenchmen, to find in its own temple those who rebel against its worship? Are there any such? Let them show themselves, these friends of arbitrary power; let them make themselves known! This is not their place! Let them depart from the land of liberty! Let them go to Coblentz and rejoin the *émigrés*. There, their hearts will expand, they will distil their venom, they will machinate, they will conspire against their country." The orator concludes by demanding that the armed citizens shall be passed in review by the Assembly.

It was in vain that Stanislas de Girardin cries, "Do the laws exist no longer, then?" The Assembly capitulates. Armed citizens are introduced. Twenty thousand men are about to pass through the session hall. The march is opened by a dozen musicians, who stop in front of the president's armchair. Then the two leaders of the manifestation make their appearance: Santerre, king of the fish markets, idol of the *faubourgs*, and Saint-Huruge, the deserter from the aristocracy, the marquis demagogue; Saint-Huruge, cast into the Bastille for his debts and scandalous behaviour, and liberated by the Revolution; Saint-Huruge, the man of gigantic stature and the strength of a Hercules, who is the rioter *par excellence*, and whose stentorian voice rises above the bellowing of the crowd.

The spectators in the galleries tremble with joy; they stamp on perceiving both Santerre and Saint-Huruge, sabre in hand and pistols at the belt. The band plays the *Ça ira*, the national hymn of the red caps. Is this an orgy, a masquerade? Look at these rags, these bizarre costumes, these butcher-boys brandishing their knives, these tattered women, these drunken harlots who dance and shout; inhale this odour of wine and *eau-de-vie;* behold the ensigns, the banners of insurrection, the ambulating trophies, the stone table on which are inscribed the Rights of Man; the placards wherein one reads: "Down with the *veto*!" "The people are tired of suffering!" "Liberty or Death!" "Tremble, tyrant!"; the gibbet from which hangs a doll representing Marie Antoinette; the ragged breeches surmounting the fashionable motto: "Live the *Sans-Culottes*!"; the bleeding heart set upon a pike, with the inscription, "Heart of an aristocrat!"

The procession, which began about two in the afternoon, is not over until nearly four o'clock. At this time Santerre repairs to the bar, where he says:

> The citizens of the Faubourg Saint-Antoine came here to express to you their ardent wishes for the welfare of the country. They beg you to accept this flag in gratitude for the good will you have shown towards them.

The president responds:

> The National Assembly receives your offering; it invites you to continue to march under the protection of the law, the safeguard of the country.

And then, heedless of the dangers the King was about to incur, he adjourns the session at half-past four in the afternoon.

What is going to happen? Will the armed citizens return peaceably to their homes? Or, not content with their promenade to the Assembly, will they make another to the palace of the Tuileries? What preparations have been made for its defence? Ten battalions line the terrace facing the palace. Two others are on the terrace at the water side, four on the side of the Carrousel. There are two companies of *gendarmes* before the door of the Royal Court; four on the Place Louis XVI., to guard the passage of the Orangery, opposite rue Saint-Florentin. Here, there might have been serious means of defence. But Louis XVI. is a sovereign who does not defend himself. Two municipal officers, MM. Boucher-Saint-Sauveur and Mouchet, had just approached him:

"My colleagues and myself," said M. Mouchet to him, "have observed with pain that the Tuileries were closed the very instant the *cortège* made its appearance. The people, crowded into the passage of the Feuillants, were all the more dissatisfied because they could see through the wicket that there were persons in the garden. We ourselves, Sire, were very much affected at seeing cannon pointed at the people. It is urgent that Your Majesty should order the gates of the Tuileries to be opened."

After hesitating slightly, Louis XVI. ended by replying: "I consent that the door of the Feuillants shall be opened; but on condition that you make the procession march across the length of the terrace and go out by the courtyard gate of the Riding School, without descending into the garden."

This was one of the King's illusions. While he was parleying with the two municipal officers the armed citizens had passed in review before the Assembly. They had just left the session hall by a door leading into the courtyard. Once in this courtyard, the intervention of some municipal officers caused the entrance known as the *Dauphin's* door, opposite the street of the same name, to be opened for them. It was by this that they entered the Tuileries Garden, while it was the wish of Louis XVI. that they should pass out through it from the terrace of the Feuillants. There they are, then, in the garden, having made an irruption there instead of continuing their route through rue Saint-Honoré. Here they come along the terrace in front of the palace, on which several battalions of the National Guard are stationed.

The crowd passes quickly before these battalions. Some of the guards unfix their bayonets; others present arms, as if to do honour to the riot. Having passed through the garden, the columns of the people go out through the gate before the Pont-Royal. They pass up the quay, and through the Louvre wickets, and so into the Place Carrousel, which is cut up by a multitude of streets, a sort of covered ways very suitable to facilitate the attack.

Certain municipal officers make some slight efforts to quiet the assailants; others, on the contrary, do what they can to embolden and excite them. The four battalions at the entrance of the Carrousel, and the two companies of *gendarmes* posted before the door of the Royal Court, make no resistance. The rioters, who have invaded the Carrousel, find their march obstructed by the closing of this door. Santerre and Saint-Huruge, who had been the last to leave the National Assembly, make their appearance, raging with anger. They rail at the people for not having penetrated into the palace. "That is all we came for," say they. Santerre, before the door of the Royal Court—one of the three courtyards in front of the palace, opposite the Carrousel—summons his cannoneers. "I am going," he cries, "to open the doors with cannon-balls."

Some royalist officers of the National Guard seek vainly to defend the palace. No one heeds them. The door of the Royal Court opens its two leaves. The crowd presses through. No more dike to the torrent; the *gendarmes* set their caps on the ends of their sabres, and cry: "Live the nation!" The thing is done; the palace is invaded.

19

The Invasion of the Tuileries

It is nearly four o'clock in the afternoon. The invasion of the Tuileries is beginning. Let us glance at the palace and get a notion of the apartments through which the crowd are about to rush. On approaching it by way of the Carrousel, one comes first to three courtyards: that of the Princes, in front of the Pavilion of Flora; the Royal Court, before the Pavilion of the Horloge; and the Swiss Court, before the Pavilion of Marsan. The assailants enter by the Royal Court, pass into the palace through the vestibule of the Horloge Pavilion, and climb the great staircase. On the left of this are the large apartments of the first storey:—

1. The Hall of the Hundred Swiss (the future Hall of the Marshals);

2. The Hall of the Guards (the future Hall of the First Consul);

3. The King's Antechamber (the future *Salon d'Apollon*);

4. The State Bedchamber (the future Throne-room);

5. The King's Grand Cabinet (called later the *Salon* of Louis XIV.);

6. The Gallery of Diana.

There are a battalion and two companies of *gendarmes* in the palace, as well as the guards then on duty and those they had relieved. But as no orders are given to these troops, they either break their ranks or fraternize with the enemy. No obstacle, no resistance, is offered, and nobody defends the apartments. The assailants, who have taken a cannon as far as the first story, enter the Hall of the Hundred Swiss, whose doors are neither locked nor barricaded. They penetrate into the Hall of the Guards with the same ease. But when they try to make their way into the Œil-de-Boeuf, or King's Antechamber, the locked door of this apartment arrests their progress. This exasperates them, and one of the panels is soon broken.

Where is Louis XVI. when the invasion begins? In his bedroom with his family. It communicates with the Grand Cabinet, and has windows commanding a view of the garden. M. Acloque, chief of the Second Legion of the National Guard, and a faithful royalist, hastens to the King by way of the little staircase leading from the Princes' Court to the royal chamber, in order to tell him what has happened. He finds the door locked; he knocks, gives his name, urgently demands admittance, and obtains it. He advises Louis XVI. to show himself to the people. The King, whom no peril has ever frightened, does not hesitate to follow this advice. The Queen wishes to accompany her husband; but she is opposed in this and forcibly drawn into the *Dauphin's* chamber, which is near that of Louis XVI. Happier than the Queen,—these are her own words,—Madame Elisabeth finds nobody to tear her from the King. She takes hold of the skirts of her brother's coat. Nothing could separate them.

Louis XVI. passes into the Great Cabinet, thence into the State Bedchamber, and through it into the Œil-de-Boeuf, where he will presently receive the crowd. He is surrounded at this moment by Madame Elisabeth, three of his ministers (MM. de Beaulieu, de Lajard, and Terrier de Montciel), the old Marshal de Mouchy, Chevalier de Canolle, M. d'Hervilly, M. Guinguerlet, lieutenant-colonel of the unmounted *gendarmes*, and M. de Vainfrais, also an officer of *gendarmes*. Some grenadiers of the National Guard afterwards arrive through the Great Cabinet and the State Bedchamber. "Come here! four grenadiers of the National Guard!" cries the King.

One of them says, "Sire, do not be afraid."

"I am not afraid," replies the King; "put your hand on my heart; it is pure and tranquil." And taking the grenadier's hand he presses it forcibly against his breast. The grenadier is a tailor named Jean Lalanne. Later, under the Terror, by a decree of the 12th Messidor, Year II., he will be condemned to death for having—so runs the sentence—"displayed the character of a cringing valet of the tyrant, in boasting before several citizens that Capet, taking his hand and laying it on his heart, had said to him, 'Feel, my friend, whether it palpitates.'"

"Gentlemen, save the King!" cries Madame Elisabeth. Meanwhile, the crowd is still in the next apartment, the Hall of the Guards. They are battering away with hatchets and gun-stocks at the door which opens into the King's Antechamber. Nothing but a partition separates Louis XVI. from the assailants. He orders the door to be opened. The crowd rush in. "Here I am," says Louis XVI. calmly; "I have never deviated from the Constitution."

"Citizens," says Acloque, "recognize your King and respect him; the law commands you to do so. We will all perish rather than suffer him to receive the slightest harm."

M. de Canolle cries: "Long live the nation! Long live the King!"

This cry is not repeated. Someone begs Madame Elisabeth to retire. "I will not leave the King," she replies, "I will not leave him." Those who surround Louis XVI. make a rampart for him of their bodies. The crowd becomes immense. It is proposed to the King that he stand on a bench in the embrasure of the central window, from which there is a view of the courtyard. Other benches and a table are placed in front of him. Madame Elisabeth takes a bench in the next window with M. de Marsilly. The hall is full. Groans, atrocious threats, and gross insults resound on every side. Someone shouts: "Down with the *veto*! To the devil with the *veto*! Recall the patriot ministers! Let him sign, or we will not go out of here!"

The butcher Legendre comes forward. He asks permission to speak. Silence is obtained, and, addressing the King, he says: "*Monsieur.*" At this unusual title, Louis XVI. make a gesture of surprise. "Yes, *Monsieur*," goes on Legendre, "listen to us; it is your duty to listen to us. . . . You are a traitor. You have always deceived us, and you deceive us still; the measure is full, and the people are tired of being made your laughing-stock."

The insolent butcher, who calls himself the agent of the people, then reads a pretended petition which is a mere tissue of recriminations and threats. Louis XVI. listens with imperturbable *sang-froid*. He answers simply: "I will do what the Constitution and the decrees ordain that I shall do." The noise begins anew. It is a rain, a hail of insults.

Some individuals mistake Madame Elisabeth for Marie Antoinette. Her equerry, M. de Saint-Pardoux, throws himself between her and the furious wretches, who cry: "Ah! there is the Austrian woman; we must have the Austrian!" and undeceives them by naming her.

"Why did you not allow them to believe I am the Queen?" says the courageous Princess; "perhaps you might have averted a greater crime."

And, putting aside a bayonet which almost touches her breast,

"Take care, *Monsieur*," she says gently, "you might hurt somebody, and I am sure you would be sorry to do that." The shouts redouble. The confusion becomes terrible. It is with great difficulty that some grenadiers of the National Guard defend the embrasure of the window where Louis XVI. still stands immovable on his bench. Mingled with the crowd there are inoffensive persons, who have come merely out of curiosity, and even honest men who sincerely pity the King. But there are tigers and assassins as well.

One of them, armed with a club ending in a sword-blade, tries to thrust it into the King's heart. The grenadiers parry the blow with their bayonets. A market porter struggles long to reach Louis XVI., against whom he brandishes a sabre. Several times the wretched monarch seeks to address the crowd. His voice is lost in the uproar. A municipal official, M. Mouchet, hoisting himself on the shoulders of two persons, demands by voice and gesture a moment's silence for the King and for himself. Vain efforts. The vociferations of the crowd only increase. Here comes a long pole on the end of which is a Phrygian cap, a *bonnet rouge*. The pole is inclined towards M. Mouchet. M. Mouchet takes the cap and presents it to the King, who, to please the crowd, puts it on his head.

Is it possible? That man on a bench, with the ignoble cap of a galley-slave on his head, surrounded by a drunken and tattered rabble who vomit filthy language, that man the King of France and Navarre, the most Christian King, Louis XVI.? Go back to the day of the coronation, June 11, 1775. It is just seventeen years and nine days ago! Do you remember the Cathedral of Rheims, luminous, glittering; the cardinals, ministers, and marshals of France, the red ribbons, the blue ribbons, the lay peers with their vests of cloth-of-gold, their violet ducal mantles lined with ermine; the clerical peers with cope and cross?

Do you remember the King taking Charlemagne's sword in his hand, and then prostrating himself before the altar on a great kneeling-cushion of velvet sown with golden lilies? Do you see him vested by the grand-chamberlain with the tunic, the *dalmatica*, and the ermine-lined mantle which represent the vestments of a sub-deacon, deacon, and priest, because the King is not merely a sovereign, but a pontiff? Do you see him seizing the royal sceptre, that golden sceptre set with oriental pearls, and carvings representing the great Carlovingian Emperor on a throne adorned with lions and eagles? Do you remember the pealing of the bells, the chords of the organ, the blare of trumpets, the clouds of incense, the birds flying in the nave?

And now, instead of the coronation the pillory; instead of the crown the hideous red cap; instead of hymns and murmurs of admiration and respect,—insults, the buffoonery of the fish-market, shouts of contempt and hatred, threats of murder. Ah! the time is not far distant when a Conventionist will break the vial containing the sacred oil on the pavement of the Abbey of Saint Remi. How slippery is the swift descent, the fatal descent by which a sovereign who disarms himself glides down from the heights of power and glory to the depths of opprobrium and sorrow! There he is! Not content with putting the red bonnet on his head, he keeps it there, and mumming in the Jacobin coiffure, he cries: "Long live the nation!" The crowd find the spectacle amusing. A National Guard, to whom someone has passed a bottle of wine, offers the complaisant King a drink. Perhaps the wine is poisoned. No matter; Louis XVI. takes a glass of it.

While all this is going on, two deputies, Isnard and Vergniaud, present themselves. "Citizens," says the first, "I am Isnard, a deputy. If what you demand were at once granted, it might be thought you extorted it by force. In the name of the law and the National Assembly, I ask you to respect the constituted authorities and retire. The National Assembly will do justice; I will aid thereto with all my power. You shall obtain satisfaction; I answer for it with my head; but go away." Vergniaud follows him with similar remarks. Neither is listened to. Nobody departs.

It is six in the evening. For two hours, one man, exposed to every insult, has held his own against a multitude. At last Pétion arrives wearing his mayor's scarf. The crowd draws back. "Sire," says he, "I have just this instant learned the situation you were in."

"That is very astonishing," returns Louis XVI.; "for it has lasted two hours."

"Sire, truly, I was ignorant that there was trouble at the palace. As soon as I was informed, I hastened to your side. But you have nothing to fear; I answer for it that the people will respect you."

"I fear nothing," replies the King. "Moreover, I have not been in any danger, since I was surrounded by the National Guard."

Pétion, like Pontius Pilate, pretends indifference. A municipal officer, M. Champion, reminds him of his duties, and says with firmness: "Order the people to retire; order them in the name of the law; we are threatened with great danger, and you must speak."

At last Pétion decides to intervene. "Citizens," he says, "all you who are listening to me, came to present legally your petition to the hereditary representative of the nation, and you have done so with the dignity and majesty of a free people; return now to your homes, for you can desire nothing further. Your demand will doubtless be reiterated by all the eighty-three departments, and the King will grant your prayer. Retire, and do not, by remaining longer, give occasion to the public enemies to impugn your worthy intentions."

At first this discourse of the mayor of Paris produces but slight effect. The cries and threats continue. But, after a while, the crowd, worn out with shouting, and hungry and thirsty as well, begin to quiet down a little. The most excited cry: "We are waiting for an answer from the King. Nothing has been asked of him yet."

Others say: "Listen to the mayor, he is going to speak again; we will hear him."

Pétion repeats what he said before: "If you do not wish your magistrates to be unjustly accused, withdraw."

M. Sergent, administrator of police, who had come with the mayor, asked if anyone has ordered the doors leading from the Grand Cabinet to the Gallery of Diana to be opened, so as to allow the crowd to pass out by the small staircase into the Court of the Princes. Louis XVI. overheard this question. "I have had the apartments opened," said he; "the people, marching out on the gallery side, will like to see them." A sentiment of curiosity hastened the movements of the crowd. In order to go out, they had to pass through the State Bedchamber, the Grand Cabinet, and the Gallery of Diana. Sergent, standing in front of the door, leading from the Œil-de-Boeuf to the State Bedchamber, unfastens his scarf and waving it over his head, cries: "Citizens, this is the badge of the law; in its name we invite you to retire and follow us."

Pétion says: "The people have done what they ought to do. You have acted with the pride and dignity of freemen. But there has been enough of it; let all retire." A double row of National Guards is formed, and the people pass between them. The return march begins.

A few recalcitrants want to remain, and keep up a cry of "Down with the *veto*! Recall the ministers!" But they are swept on by the stream, and follow the march like all the rest. While they are going out through the door between the Œil-de-Boeuf and the State Bedchamber, the National Guard prevents any one from entering on the other side, through the door connecting the Œil-de-Boeuf with the Hall of the Guards.

At this moment, a deputation of twenty-four members of the Assembly present themselves. Roused by the public clamour announcing that the King's life is in danger, the National Assembly has called an extraordinary evening session. The president of the deputation, M. Brunk, says to the King: "Sire, the National Assembly sends us to assure ourselves of your situation, to protect the constitutional liberty you should enjoy, and to share your danger."

Louis XVI. replies: "I am grateful for the solicitude of the Assembly; I am undisturbed in the midst of Frenchmen."

At the same time, Pétion goes to turn back the crowd, who are constantly ascending the great staircase, and who threaten another invasion. The sentry at the doorway of the Œil-de-Boeuf is replaced, and the crowd ceases to flock thither. The circle of National Guards about the sovereign is increased. A space is formed, and he is surrounded by the deputation from the Assembly. Acloque, seeing that the tumult is lessening and the room no longer encumbered by the crowd, proposes to the King that he should retire, and Louis XVI. decides to do so. Surrounded by deputies and National Guards, he passes into the State Bedchamber, and notwithstanding the throng, he manages to reach a secret door at the right of the bed, near the chimney, which communicates with his bedroom. He goes through this little door, and someone closes it behind him.

It is not far from eight o'clock in the evening. The peril and humiliation of Louis XVI. have lasted nearly four hours, and the unhappy King is not yet at the end of his sufferings, for he does not know what has become of his wife and children. While these sad scenes had been enacting in the palace, a furious populace had been in incessant commotion beneath the windows, in the garden and the courtyards. People desiring to establish communication between those down stairs and those above, had been heard to cry: "Have they been struck down? Are they dead? Throw us down their heads!"

A slender young man, with the profile of a Roman medal, a pale complexion, and flashing eyes, was looking at all this from the upper part of the terrace beside the water. Unable to comprehend the long-suffering of Louis XVI., he said in an indignant tone: "How could they have allowed this rabble to enter? They should have swept out four or five hundred of them with cannon, and the rest would have run." The man who spoke thus, obscure and hidden in the crowd, opposite that palace where he was to play so great a part, was the "straight-haired Corsican," the future Emperor Napoleon.

20

Marie Antoinette on June Twentieth

Louis XVI. had just entered his bedchamber. The crowd, after leaving the hall of the Œil-de-Boeuf, had departed through the State Bedchamber, and the King's Great Cabinet, called also the Council Hall. On entering this last apartment, an unexpected scene had surprised them. Behind the large table they saw the Queen, Madame Elisabeth, the *Dauphin*, and Madame Royale.

How came the Queen to be there? What had happened? At a quarter of four, when Louis XVI. had left his room to go into the hall of the Bull's-Eye and meet the rioters, Marie Antoinette, as we have already said, made desperate efforts to follow him. M. Aubier, placing himself before the door of the King's chamber, prevented the Queen from going out. In vain she cried: "Let me pass; my place is beside the King; I will join him and perish with him if it must be." M. Aubier, through devotion, disobeyed her.

Nevertheless, the Queen, whose courage redoubled her strength, would have borne down this faithful servant if M. Rougeville, a chevalier of Saint-Louis, had not aided him to block up the passage. Imploring Marie Antoinette in the name of her own safety and that of the King, not to expose herself needlessly to poniards, and aided by the Minister of Foreign Affairs, they drew her almost by force into the chamber of the *Dauphin*, which was near the King's. MM. de Choiseul, d'Haussonville, and de Saint-Priest, assisted by several grenadiers of the National Guard, afterwards induced her to go with her children into the Grand Cabinet of the King, called also the Council Hall, because the ministers were accustomed to assemble there.

The Princess de Lamballe, the Princess of Tarento, the Marchioness de Tourzel, the Duchesses de Luynes, de Duras, de Maillé, the Marchioness de Laroche-Aymon, Madame de Soucy, the Baroness de Mackau, the Countess de Ginestous, remained with the Queen. So also did the Minister Chambonas, the Duke de Choiseul, Counts d'Haussonville and de Montmorin, Viscount de Saint-Priest, Marquis de Champcenetz, and General de Wittenghoff, commander of the 17th military division. The Queen and her children occupied the embrasure of a window, and the large and heavy table used by the ministerial council was placed in front of them as a sort of barricade.

Meanwhile, Marie Antoinette's apartments and her bedroom on the ground-floor were invaded. Some National Guards tried vainly to defend them. "You are cutting your own throats!" shouted the people. Overwhelmed by numbers, they saw the door of the first apartment broken down by hatchets. It contained the beds of the Queen's servants, ranged behind screens. Afterwards they saw the invaders go into Marie Antoinette's sleeping-room, tear the clothes off her bed, and loll upon it, crying as they did so, "We will have the Austrian woman, dead or alive!"

The Queen, however, remained in the Council Hall, where she could hear the echo of the cries resounding in that of the Œil-de-Boeuf, where Louis XVI. was, and from which she was separated only by the State Bedchamber. Toward seven in the evening she beheld Madame Elisabeth, who, after heroically sharing the dangers of the King, had now found means to rejoin her.

"The deputies who came to us," she wrote to Madame de Raigecourt, July 3, "had come out of good will. A veritable deputation arrived and persuaded the King to go back to his own apartments. As I was told this, and as I was unwilling to be left in the crowd, I went away about an hour before he did, and rejoined the Queen: you can imagine with what pleasure I embraced her." In their perils, therefore, Madame Elisabeth was near both Louis XVI. and Marie Antoinette.

After having voluntarily exposed herself to all the anguish of the invasion of the Œil-de-Boeuf, the courageous Princess was with the Queen in the Council Hall, when the crowd, coming through the State Bed-chamber, arrived there. The horde marched through it, carrying their barbarous inscriptions like so many ferocious standards. "One of these," says Madame Campan in her *Memoirs*, "represented a gibbet from which an ugly doll was hanging; below it was written: 'Marie Antoinette to the lamp-post!' Another was a plank to which a bullock's heart had been fastened, surrounded by the words: 'Heart of Louis XVI.' Finally, a third presented a pair of bullock's horns with an indecent motto."

Some royalist grenadiers belonging to the battalion called the *Filles-Saint-Thomas*, were near the council-table and protected the Queen. Marie Antoinette was standing, and held her daughter's hand. The *Dauphin* sat on the table in front of her. At the moment when the march began, a woman threw a red cap on this table and cried out that it must be placed on the Queen's head. M. de Wittenghoff, his hand trembling with indignation, took the cap and after holding it for a moment over Marie Antoinette's head, put it back on the table. Then a cry was raised: "The red cap for the Prince Royal! Tri-coloured ribbons for little *Veto!*" Ribbons were thrown down beside the Phrygian cap.

Someone shouted: "If you love the nation, set the red cap on your son's head." The Queen made an affirmative sign, and the revolutionary *coiffure* was set on the child's fair head.

What humiliations were these for the unhappy mother! What anguish for so haughty, so magnanimous a queen! The galley-slave's cap has touched the head of the daughter of Cæsars, and now soils the forehead of her son! The slang of the fish-markets resounds beneath the venerable arches of the palace. How bitterly the unfortunate sovereign expiates her former triumphs! Where are the ovations and the apotheoses, the carriages of gold and crystal, the solemn entries into the city in its gala dress, to the sound of bells and trumpets? What trace remains of those brilliant days when, more goddess than woman, the Queen of France and Navarre appeared through a cloud of incense, in the midst of flowers and light?

This good and beautiful sovereign, whose least smile, or glance, or nod, had been regarded as a precious recompense, a supreme favour by the noble lords and ladies who bent respectfully before her, behold how she is treated now! Consider the costumes and the language of her new courtiers! And yet, Marie Antoinette is majestic still. Even in this horrible scene, in presence of these drunken women and ragged suburbans, she does not lose that gift of pleasing which is her special dower. At a distance they curse her; but when they come near they are subjugated by her spell. Her most ferocious enemies are touched in their own despite. A young girl had just called her "*Autrichienné.*"

"You call me an Austrian woman," replied she, "but I am the wife of the King of France, I am the mother of the *Dauphin*; I am a French-woman by my sentiments as wife and mother. I shall never again see the land where I was born. I can be happy or unhappy nowhere but in France. I was happy when you loved me."

Confused by this gentle reproach, the young girl softened. "Pardon me," she said; "it was because I did not know you; I see very well now that you are not wicked." A woman, passing, stopped before the Queen and began to sob.

"What is the matter with her?" asked Santerre; "what is she crying about?" And he shook her by the arm, saying: "Make her pass on, she is drunk."

Even Santerre himself felt Marie Antoinette's influence. "*Madame*," he said to her, "the people wish you no harm. Your friends deceive you; you have nothing to fear, and I am going to prove it by serving as your shield." It was he who took pity on the *Dauphin* whom the heat was stifling, and said: "Take the red cap off the child; he is too hot." He too, it was, that hastened the march of the procession and pointed out to the people the different members of the royal family by name, saying: "This is the Queen, this is her son, this her daughter, this Madame Elisabeth."

At last the crowd is gone. The hall is empty. It is eight o'clock. The Queen and her children enter the King's chamber. Louis XVI., who finds them once more after so many perils and emotions, covers them with kisses. In the midst of this pathetic scene some deputies arrive. Marie Antoinette shows them the traces of violence which the people have left behind them,—locks broken, hinges forced off, wainscoting burst through, furniture ruined. She speaks of the dangers that have threatened the King and the insults offered to herself. Perceiving that Merlin de Thionville, an ardent Jacobin, has tears in his eyes, she says: "You are weeping to see the King and his family so cruelly treated by people whom he has always desired to render happy."

The republican answered: "Yes, *Madame*, I weep, but it is for the misfortunes of the mother of a family, not for the King and Queen; I hate kings and queens."

A deputy accosted Marie Antoinette, saying in a familiar tone: "You were very much afraid, *Madame*, you must admit."

"No, *Monsieur*," she replied, "I was not at all afraid; but I suffered much in being separated from the King at a moment when his life was in danger. At least, I had the consolation of being with my children and performing one of my duties."

"Without pretending to excuse everything, agree, *Madame*, that the people showed themselves very good-natured."

"The King and I, *Monsieur*, are convinced of the natural goodness of the people; it is only when they are misled that they are wicked."

"How old is *Mademoiselle*?" went on the deputy, pointing to Madame Royale.

"She is at that age, *Monsieur*, when one feels only too great a horror of such scenes."

Other deputies surround the *Dauphin*. They question him on different subjects, especially concerning the geography of France and its new territorial division into departments and districts, and are enchanted by the correctness of his replies.

An officer of *Chasseurs* of the National Guard enters the King's chamber. This officer had shown the utmost zeal in protecting his sovereign and had had the honour of being wounded at his side. He is congratulated. The *Dauphin* perceives him. "What is the name of that guard who defended my father so bravely?" he asks.

"*Monseigneur*," replies M. Hue, "I do not know; he will be flattered if you ask him." The Prince runs to put his question to the officer, but the latter, in respectful terms, declines to answer. Then M. Hue insists. "I beg you," he cries, "tell us your name."

"I ought to conceal my name," replies the officer; "unfortunately for me, it is the same as that of an execrable man."

The faithful royalist bore the same name as the man who had caused the arrest of the royal family at Varennes the previous year. He was called Drouot.

The hour for repose has come at last. It is ten o'clock. Certain individuals still complain: "They took us there for nothing; but we will go back and have what we want." Still, the storm is over. The crowd has evacuated the palace, the courtyards, and the garden. The Assembly closes its sessions at half-past ten.

Pétion said there: "The King has no cause of complaint against the citizens who marched before him. He has said as much to the deputies and magistrates."

Finally, as the deputies were about to separate after this exciting day, one of them, M. Guyton-Morveau, remarked: "The deputation which preceded us, has doubtless announced to you that all is now tranquil. We remained with the King for some time, and saw nothing which could inspire the least alarm. We invited the King to seek some repose. He sent an officer of the National Guard to visit the posts, and the officer reported that there was nobody in the palace. His Majesty assured us that he desired to remain alone; we left him; and we can certify to you that all is quiet."

21

The Morrow of June Twentieth

In the morning of June 21 there were still some disorderly gatherings in front of the Tuileries. On awaking, the *Dauphin* put this artless question to the Queen: "Mamma, is it yesterday still?" Alas! yes, it was still yesterday, it was always to be yesterday until the catastrophes at the end of the drama. It was just a year to a day since the royal family had furtively quitted Paris to begin the fatal journey which terminated at Varennes. This souvenir occurred to Marie Antoinette, and, recalling the first stations of her Calvary, the unfortunate sovereign told herself that her humiliations had but just begun. Her lips had touched only the brim of the chalice, and it must be drained to the dregs.

Meanwhile, visitors were arriving at the Tuileries one after another to condole with and protest their fidelity to the King and his family. When Marshal de Mouchy made his appearance, the worthy old man was received with the honours due to his noble conduct on the previous day. When the invasion began, Louis XVI., in order not to irritate the rabble, had given his gentlemen a formal order to withdraw, but the old marshal, hoping that his great age (he was seventy-seven) would excuse his presence in the palace, had refused to leave his master. More than once, with a strength rejuvenated by devotion, he had succeeded in repulsing persons whose violence made him tremble for the King's life.

As soon as she saw the marshal, Marie Antoinette made haste to say: "I have learned from the King how courageously you defended him yesterday. I share his gratitude."

"*Madame*," he replied, alluding to those of his relatives who had figured among the promoters of the Revolution, "I did very little in comparison with the injuries I should like to repair. They were not mine, but they touch me very nearly."

"My son," said the Queen, calling the *Dauphin*, "repeat before the marshal, the prayer you addressed to God this morning for the King."

The child, kneeling down, put his hands together, and looking up to heaven, began to sing this refrain from the opera of *Pierre le Grand*:—

Ciel, entends la prière
Qu'ici je fais:
Conserve un si bon père
A ses sujets. [1]

After the Marshal de Mouchy came M. de Malesherbes. Contrary to his usual custom, the ex-first president wore his sword. "It is a long time," someone said to him, "since you have worn a sword."

"True," replied the old man, "but who would not arm when the King's life is in danger?" Then, looking with emotion at the little Prince, he said to Marie Antoinette: "I hope, *Madame*, that at least our children will see better days!"

And yet, even for the present there still remained a glimmer of hope. Hardly had the invaders left the palace than invectives against them rose from all classes of society. The calmness and courage of the King and his family found admirers on every side. The departments sent addresses demanding the punishment of those who had been guilty. Royalist sentiments woke to life anew. One might almost believe that the indignation caused by the recent scandals would produce an immediate reaction in favour of Louis XVI. Possibly, with an energetic sovereign, something might have been attempted. On the whole, the insurrection had obtained nothing.

Even the Girondins perceived the dangerous character of revolutionary passions. Honest men stigmatized the criminal tendencies which had just displayed themselves. It was the moment for the King to show himself and strike a great blow. But Louis XVI. had neither will nor energy. Letting the last chance of safety which fortune offered him escape, he was unable to profit by the turn in public opinion. Nothing could shake him out of that easy patience which was the chief cause of his ruin.

Marie Antoinette herself was opposed to vigorous measures. She still desired to try the effects of kindness. Learning that a legal inquiry

1. Listen, heaven, to the prayer
That here I make
Preserve so good a father
To his subjects.

was proposed into the events of June 20, and foreseeing that M. Hue would be called as a witness, she said to this loyal servant: "Say as little in your deposition as truth will permit. I recommend you, on the King's part and my own, to forget that we were the objects of these popular movements. Every suspicion that either the King or myself feel the least resentment for what happened must be avoided; it is not the people who are guilty, and even if it were, they would always obtain pardon and forgetfulness of their errors from us."

During this time the Assembly maintained an attitude more than equivocal. It contained a great number of honest men. But, terrorized already, it no longer possessed the courage of indignation. It grew pale before the menaces of the public. By cringing to the rabble it had attained that hypocritical optimism which is the distinctive mark of moderate revolutionists, and which makes them in turn the dupes and the victims of those who are more zealous.

If the majority of the deputies had said openly what they silently thought, they would not have hesitated to stigmatize the invasion of the Tuileries as it deserved. But in that case, what would have become of their popularity with the pikemen? And then, must they not take into account the ambitions of the Girondins, the hatreds of the Mountain party, and the rancour of Madame Roland and her friends? Was it not, moreover, a real satisfaction to the *bourgeoisie* to give power a lesson and humiliate a sovereign? Ah! how cruelly this pleasure will be expiated by those who take delight in it, and how they will repent some day for having permitted justice, law, and authority to be trampled underfoot!

When the session of June 21 opened, Deputy Daverhoult denounced in energetic terms the violence of the previous day. Thuriot exclaimed: "Are we expected to press an inquiry against forty thousand men?" Duranton, the Minister of Justice, then read a letter from the King, dated that day, and worded thus:

Gentlemen, the National Assembly is already acquainted with the events of yesterday. Paris is doubtless in consternation; France will hear the news with astonishment and grief. I was much affected by the zeal shown for me by the National Assembly on this occasion. I leave to its prudence the task of investigating the causes of this event, weighing its circumstances, and taking the necessary measures to maintain the Constitution and assure the inviolability and constitutional liberty of the hereditary representative of the nation. For my part, nothing can prevent me, at all times and under all circumstances, from performing the duties imposed on me by the Constitution, which I have accepted in the true interests of the French nation.

A few moments after this letter had been read, the session was disturbed by a warning from the municipal agent of the department, to the effect that an armed crowd were marching towards the palace. This was soon followed by tidings that Pétion had hindered their further advance, and the mayor himself came to the Assembly to receive the laudations of his friends. "Order reigns everywhere," said he; "all precautions have been taken. The magistrates have done their duty; they will always do so, and the hour approaches when justice will be rendered them."

Pétion then went to the Tuileries, where he addressed the King nearly in these terms:—

Sire, we learn that you have been warned of the arrival of a crowd at the palace. We come to announce that this crowd is composed of unarmed citizens who wish to set up a Maypole. I know, Sire, that the municipality has been calumniated; but its conduct will be understood by you.

"It ought to be by all France," responded Louis XVI.; "I accuse no one in particular, I saw everything."

"It will be," returned the mayor; "and but for the prudent measures taken by the municipality, much more disagreeable events might have occurred."

The King attempted to reply, but Pétion, without listening to him, went on: "Not to your own person; you may well understand that it will always be respected."

The King, unaccustomed to interruption when speaking, said in a loud voice: "Be silent!" There was silence for an instant, and then Louis XVI. added: "Is it what you call respecting my person to enter my house in arms, break down my doors and use force to my guards?"

"Sire," answered Pétion, "I know the extent of my duties and of my responsibility."

"Do your duty!" replied Louis XVI.; "You are answerable for the tranquillity of Paris. *Adieu!*" And the King turned his back on the mayor.

Pétion revenged himself that very evening, by circulating a rumour that the royal family were preparing to escape; in consequence, he requested the commanders of the National Guard to re-enforce the sentries and redouble their vigilance. The revolutionists, who had been disconcerted for a moment by popular indignation, raised their heads again. Prudhomme wrote in the *Révolutions de Paris*:

> The Parisian people—yes, the people, not the aristocratic class of citizens—have just set a grand example to France. The King, at the instigation of Lafayette, discharged his patriotic ministers; he paralyzed by his *veto* the decree relative to the camp of twenty thousand men, and that on the banishment of priests. Very well! the people rose and signified to him their sovereign will that the ministers should be reinstated and these two murderous vetoes recalled. . . . Doubtless it will not be long before Europe will be full of a caricature representing Louis XVI. of the big paunch, covered with orders, crowned with a red cap, and drinking out of the same bottle with the *sans-culottes*, who are crying: 'The King is drinking, the King has drunk. He has the liberty cap on his head.' Would he might have it in his heart!

Apropos of this red bonnet which remained for three hours on the sovereign's head, Bertrand de Molleville ventured to put some questions to Louis XVI. on the evening of June 21. According to the *Memoirs* of the former Minister of Marine, this is what the King replied:

> The cries of 'Long live the Nation' increasing in violence and seeming to be addressed to me, I answered that the nation had no better friend than I. Then an ill-looking man, thrusting himself through the crowd, came close to me and said in a rude tone: 'Very well! if you are telling the truth, prove it to us by putting on this red cap.' 'I consent,' said I. Instantly one or two of these people advanced and placed the cap on my hair, for it was too small for my head to enter it. I was convinced, I don't know why, that their intention was simply to place this cap on my head and then retire, and I was so preoccupied with what was going on before my eyes, that I did not notice whether it was there or not. So little did I feel it that after I had returned to my chamber I did not observe that I still wore it until I was told. I was greatly astonished to find it on my head, and was all the more displeased because I could have taken it off at once without the least difficulty. But I am convinced that if I had hesitated to receive it, the drunken man by whom it was presented would have thrust his pike into my stomach.

During the same interview Bertrand de Molleville congratulated the King upon his almost miraculous escape from the dangers of the previous day. Louis XVI. replied: "All my anxieties were for the Queen, my children and my sister; because I feared nothing for myself."

"But it seems to me," rejoined his interlocutor, "that this insurrection was aimed chiefly against Your Majesty."

"I know it very well," returned Louis XVI.; "I saw clearly that they wanted to assassinate me, and I don't know why they did not do it; but I shall not escape them another day. So I have gained nothing; it is all the same whether I am assassinated now or two months from now!"

"Great God!" cried Bertrand de Molleville, "does Your Majesty believe that you will be assassinated?"

"I am convinced of it," replied the King; "I have expected it for a long time and have accustomed myself to the thought. Do you think I am afraid of death?"

"Certainly not, but I would desire Your Majesty to take vigorous measures to protect yourself from danger."

"It is possible," went on the King after a moment of reflection, "that I may escape. There are many odds against me, and I am not lucky. If I were alone I would risk one more attempt. Ah! if my wife and children were not with me, people should see that I am not so weak as they fancy. What would be their fate if the measures you propose to me did not succeed?"

"But if they assassinate Your Majesty, do you think that the Queen and her children would be in less danger?"

"Yes, I think so, and even were it otherwise, I should not have to reproach myself with being the cause."

A sort of Christian fanaticism had taken possession of the King's soul. Resigned to his fate, he ceased to struggle, and wrote to his confessor: "Come to see me today; I have done with men; I want nothing now but heaven."

22

Lafayette in Paris

One of the greatest griefs of a political career is disenchantment. To pass from devout optimism to profound discouragement; to have treated as alarmists or cowards whoever perceived the least cloud on the horizon, and then to see the most formidable tempests unchained; to be obliged to recognize at one's proper cost that one has carried illusion to the verge of simplicity and has judged neither men nor things aright; to have heard distressed passengers saying that a pilot without experience or prudence is responsible for the shipwreck; to have promised the age of gold and suddenly found one's self in the age of iron, is a veritable torture for the pride and the conscience of a statesman. And this torture is still more cruel when to disappointment is added the loss of a popularity laboriously acquired; when, having been accustomed to excite nothing but enthusiasm and applause, one is all at once greeted with criticism, howls, and curses, and when, having long strutted about triumphantly on the summits of the Capitol, one sees yawning before him the gulf at the foot of the Tarpeian rock.

Such was the fate of Lafayette. A few months had sufficed to throw down the popular idol from his pedestal, and the same persons who had once almost burned incense before him, now thought of nothing but flinging him into the gutter. Stunned by his fall, Lafayette could not believe it. To familiarize himself with the fickleness, the caprices, and the inconsequence of the multitude was impossible. For him the Constitution was the sacred ark, and he did not believe that the very men who had constructed this edifice at such a cost had now nothing so much at heart as to destroy it. He would not admit that the predictions of the royalists were about to be accomplished in every point, and still desired to hold aloof from the complicities into which revolutions drag the most upright minds and the most honest characters.

He who, in July, 1789, had not been able to prevent the assassination of Foulon and Berthier; who, on October 5, had marched, despite himself, against Versailles; who, on April 18, 1791, had been unable to protect the departure of the royal family to Saint Cloud; who, on the following June 21, had thought himself obliged to say to the Jacobins in their club: "I have come to rejoin you, because I think the true patriots are here," nevertheless imagined that just a year later, all that was necessary to vanquish the same Jacobins was for him to show himself and say like Cæsar: "*Veni, vidi, vici.*"

It was only a later illusion of the generous but imprudent man who had already dreamed many dreams. He thought the popular tiger could be muzzled by persuasion. He was going to make a *coup d'état*, not in deeds, but in words, forgetting that the Revolution neither esteems nor fears anything but force. As M. de Larmartime has said: "One gets from factions only what one snatches." Instead of striking, Lafayette was going to speak and write. The Jacobins might have feared his sword; they despised his words and pen. But though it was not very wise, the noble audacity with which the hero of America came spontaneously to throw himself into the heat of the struggle and utter his protest in the name of right and honour, was none the less an act of courage. While with the army, that asylum of generous ideas, the sentiments on which his ancestors had prided themselves rekindled in his heart.

Memories of his early youth revived anew. Doubtless he also recalled his personal obligations to Louis XVI. On his return from the United States, had he not been created major-general over the heads of a multitude of older officers? Had not the Queen accorded him at that epoch the most flattering eulogies? Had he not been received at the great receptions of May 29, 1785, when any other officer unless highly born would have remained in the Œil-de-Boeuf or paid his court in the passage of the chapel? Had he not accepted the rank of lieutenant-general from the King, on June 30, 1791? The gentleman reappeared beneath the revolutionist. The humiliation of a throne for which his ancestors had so often shed their blood caused him a real grief, and it is perhaps regrettable that Louis XVI. should have refused the hand which his recent adversary extended loyally though late.

Lafayette was encamped near Bavay with the Army of the North when the first tidings of June 20 reached him. His soul was roused to indignation, and he wanted to start at once for Paris to lift his voice against the Jacobins. Old Marshal Luckner tried in vain to restrain him by saying that the *sans-culottes* would have his head. Nothing could stop him. Placing his army in safety under the cannon of Maubeuge, he started with no companion but an *aide-de-camp*. At Soissons some persons tried to dissuade him from going further by painting a doleful picture of the dangers to which he would expose himself. He listened to nobody and went on his way.

Reaching Paris in the night of June 27–28, he alighted at the house of his intimate friend, the Duke de La Rochefoucauld, who was about to play so honourable a part. As soon as morning came, Lafayette was at the door of the National Assembly, asking permission to offer the homage of his respect. This authorization having been granted, he entered the hall. The right applauded; the left kept silence. Being allowed to speak, he declared that he was the author of the letter to the Assembly of June 16, whose authenticity had been denied, and that he openly avowed responsibility for it. He then expressed himself in the sincerest terms concerning the outrages committed in the palace of the Tuileries on June 20. He said he had received from the officers, subalterns, and soldiers of his army a great number of addresses expressive of their love for the Constitution, their respect for the authorities, and their patriotic hatred against seditious men of all parties.

He ended by imploring the Assembly to punish the authors or instigators of the violences committed on June 20, as guilty of treason against the nation, and to destroy a sect which encroached upon National Sovereignty, and terrorized citizens, and by their public debates removed all doubts concerning the atrocity of their projects. "In my own name and that of all honest men in the kingdom," said he in conclusion, "I entreat you to take efficacious measures to make all constitutional authorities respected, particularly your own and that of the King, and to assure the army that the Constitution will receive no injury from within, while so many brave Frenchmen are lavishing their blood to defend it on the frontiers."

Applause from the right and from some of those in the galleries began anew. The president said:

The National Assembly has sworn to maintain the Constitution. Faithful to its oath, it will be able to guarantee it against all attacks. It accords to you the honours of the session.

The general went to take his seat on the right. Deputy Kersaint observed that his place was on the petitioners' bench. The general obeyed this hint and sat down modestly on the bench assigned him. Renewed applause ensued. Thereupon Guadet ascended the tribune and said in an ironic tone:

At the moment when M. Lafayette's presence in Paris was announced to me, a most consoling idea presented itself. So we have no more external enemies, thought I; the Austrians are conquered. This illusion did not last long. Our enemies remain the same. Our exterior situation is not altered, and yet M. Lafayette is in Paris! What powerful motives have brought him hither? Our internal troubles? Does he fear, then, that the National Assembly is not strong enough to repress them? He constitutes himself the organ of his army and of honest men. Where are these honest men? How has the army been able to deliberate?

Guadet concluded thus:

I demand that the Minister of War be asked whether he gave leave of absence to M. Lafayette, and that the extraordinary Committee of Twelve make a report tomorrow on the danger of granting the right of petition to generals.

Ramond, one of the most courageous members of the right, was the next speaker:

"Four days ago," said he, "an armed multitude asked to appear before you. Positive laws forbade such a thing, and a proclamation made by the department on the previous day recalled this law and demanded that it should be put into execution. You paid no attention, but admitted armed men into your midst. Today M. Lafayette presents himself; he is known only by reason of his love of liberty; his life is a series of combats against despotisms of every sort; he has sacrificed his life and fortune to the Revolution. It is against this man that pretended suspicions are directed and every passion unchained. Has the National Assembly two weights and measures, then? Certainly, if respect is to be had to persons, it should be shown to this eldest son of French liberty."

This eulogy exasperated the left. Deputy Saladin exclaimed: "I ask M. Ramond if he is making M. Lafayette's funeral oration?" However, the right was still in the majority. After a long tumult Guadet's motion against Lafayette was rejected by 339 votes against 234. The general left the Assembly surrounded by a numerous *cortège* of deputies and National Guards, and went directly to the palace of the Tuileries.

It is the decisive moment. The vote just taken may serve as the starting-point of a conservative reaction if the King will trust himself to Lafayette. But how will he receive him? The sovereign's greeting will be polite, but not cordial. The King and Queen say they are persuaded that there is no safety but in the Constitution. Louis XVI. adds that he would consider it a very fortunate thing if the Austrians were beaten without delay. Lafayette is treated with a courtesy through which suspicion pierces. When he leaves the palace, a large crowd accompany him to his house and plant a Maypole before the door. On the next day Louis XVI. was to review four thousand men of the National Guard. Lafayette had proposed to appear at this review beside the King and make a speech in favour of order. But the court does not desire the general's aid, and takes what measures it can to defeat this project. Pétion, whom it had preferred to Lafayette as mayor of Paris, countermands the review an hour before daybreak.

Perhaps Louis XVI. might have succeeded in overcoming his repugnance to Lafayette and submitted to be rescued by him. But the Queen absolutely refused to trust the man whom she considered her evil genius. She had seen him rise like a spectre at every hapless hour. He had brought her back to Paris a prisoner on the 6th of October. He had been her jailer. His apparition amid the glare of torches in the Court of the Carrousel had frozen her with terror when she was flying from her prison, the Tuileries, to begin the fatal journey to Varennes. His *aides-de-camp* had pursued her. He was responsible for her arrest; he was present at her humiliating and sorrowful return; the sight of his face, the sound of his voice, made her tremble; she could not hear his name without a shudder.

In vain Madame Elisabeth exclaimed: "Let us forget the past and throw ourselves into the arms of the only man who can save the King and his family!" Marie Antoinette's pride revolted at the thought of owing anything to her former persecutor.

Moreover, in his latest confidential communications with her, Mirabeau had said: "*Madame*, be on your guard against Lafayette; if ever he commands the army, he would like to keep the King in his tent." In the Queen's opinion, to rely on Lafayette would be to accept him as regent of the palace under a sluggard King. Protector for protector, she preferred Danton. Danton, who, subsidized from the civil list, accepts money without knowing whether he will fairly earn it; Danton, who, while awaiting events, had made the cynical remark that he would "save the King or kill him."

Strange that the orator of the *faubourgs* inspired the daughter of Cæsars with less repugnance than the gentleman, the marquis. "They propose M. de Lafayette as a resource," she said to Madame Campan; "but it would be better to perish than owe our safety to the man who has done us most harm."

However, Lafayette was not yet discouraged. He wished to save the royal family in spite of themselves. He assembled several officers of the National Guard at his house. He represented to them the dangers into which the apathy of each plunged the affairs of all; he showed the urgent necessity of combining against the avowed enterprises of the anarchists, of inspiring the National Assembly with the firmness required to repress the intended attacks, and foretold the inevitable calamities which would result from the weakness and disunion of honest men. He wanted to march against the Jacobin Club and close it. But, in consequence of the instructions issued by the court, the royalists of the National Guard were indisposed to second him in this measure. Lafayette, having no one on his side but the constitutionals, an honest but scanty group who were suspected by both of the extreme parties, gave up the struggle.

The next day, June 30, he beat a hasty retreat to the army, after writing to the Assembly another letter which was merely an echo of the first one. A moment since, the Jacobins were trembling. Now, they are reassured, they triumph. In his *Chronique des Cinquante Jours*, Roederer says:

> If M. de Lafayette had had the will and ability to make a bold stroke and seize the dictatorship, reserving the power to relinquish it after the re-establishment of order, one could comprehend his coming to the Assembly with the sword of a dictator at his side; but, to show it only, without resolving to draw it from the scabbard, was a fatal imprudence. In civil commotions it will not answer to dare by halves.

23

The Lamourette Kiss

France had still its moments of enthusiasm and illusion before plunging into the abyss of woes. It seemed under an hallucination, or suffering from a sort of vertigo. A nameless frenzy, both in good and evil, agitated and disturbed it beyond measure in 1792, that year so fertile in surprises and dramas of every kind. Strange and bizarre epoch, full of love and hatred, launching itself from one extreme to the other with frightful inconstancy, now weeping with tenderness, and now howling with rage! Society resembled a drunken man who is sometimes amiable in his cups, and sometimes cruel. There were sudden halts on the road of fury, oases in the midst of scorching sands, beneath a sun whose fire consumed. But the caravan does not rest long beneath the shady trees. Quickly it resumes its course as if urged by a mysterious force, and soon the terrible simoom overwhelms and destroys it.

Madame Elisabeth wrote to Madame de Raigecourt, July 8, 1792:

It would need all Madame de Sévigné's eloquence to describe properly what happened yesterday; for it was certainly the most surprising thing, the most extraordinary, the greatest, the smallest, etc., etc. But, fortunately, experience may aid comprehension. In a word, here were Jacobins, Feuillants, republicans, and monarchists, abjuring all their discords and assembling near the tree of the Constitution and of liberty, to promise sincerely that they will act in accordance with law and not depart from it. Luckily, August is coming, the time when, the leaves being well grown, the tree of liberty will afford a more secure shelter.

What had happened on the day before Madame Elisabeth wrote this letter? There had been a very singular session of the Legislative Assembly. In the morning, a woman named Olympe de Gouges, whose mother was a dealer in second-hand clothing at Montauban, being consumed with a desire to be talked about, had caused an emphatic placard to be posted up, in which she preached concord between all parties. This placard was like a prologue to the day's session.

Among the deputies there was a certain Abbé Lamourette, the constitutional bishop of Lyons, who played at religious democracy. He was an ex-Lazarist who had been professor of theology at the Seminary at Toul. Weary of the conventual yoke, he had left his order, and at the beginning of the Revolution was the vicar-general of the diocese of Arras. He had published several works in which he sought to reconcile philosophy and religion. Mirabeau was one of his aco-lytes and adopted him as his theologian in ordinary. Finding him fit to "bishopize" (*à evêquailler*), to use his own expression, the great tribune recommended him to the electors of the Rhone department.

It was thus that the Abbé Lamourette became the constitutional bishop of Lyons. After his consecration, he issued a pastoral instruc-tion in such agreement with current ideas that Mirabeau, his protec-tor, induced the Constituent Assembly to have it sent as a model to every department in France. In 1792, the Abbé Lamourette was fifty years old. Affable, unctuous, his mouth always full of pacific and gentle words, he naïvely preached moderation, concord, and fraternity in conversations which were like so many sermons.

For several days the discussions in the Assembly had been of unpar-alleled violence. Suspicion, hatred, rancor, wrath, were unchained in a fury that bordered on delirium. Right and left emulated each other in outrages and invectives. Lafayette's appearance and the fear of a foreign invasion had disturbed all minds. The National Assembly, sitting both day and night, was like an arena of gladiators fighting without truce or pity. It was this moment which the good Abbé Lamourette chose for delivering his most touching sermon from the tribune.

During the session of July 7, Brissot was about to ascend the trib-une and propose new measures of public safety. Lamourette, getting before him, asked to be heard on a motion of order. He said that of all the means proposed for arresting the divisions which were destroy-ing France, but one had been forgotten, and that the only one which could be efficacious. It was the union of all Frenchmen in one mind, the reconciliation of all the deputies, without exception. What was to prevent this? The only irreconcilable things are crime and virtue. What do all our mistrust and suspicions amount to?

One party in the Assembly attributes to the other a seditious desire to destroy the monarchy. The others attribute to their colleagues a desire to destroy constitutional equality and to establish the aristocratic government known as that of the Two Chambers. These are the disastrous suspicions which divide the empire. "Very well!" cried the *abbé*, "let us crush both the republic and the Two Chambers." The hall rang with unanimous applause from the Assembly and the galleries. From all sides came shouts of "Yes, yes, we want nothing but the Constitution." Lamourette went on: "Let us swear to have but one mind, one sentiment. Let us swear to sink all our differences and become a homogeneous mass of freemen formidable both to the spirit of anarchy and that of feudalism.

The moment when foreigners see that we desire one settled thing, and that we all desire it, will be the moment when liberty will triumph and France be saved. I ask the president to put to vote this simple proposition: That those who equally abjure and execrate the republic and the Two Chambers shall rise." At once, as if moved by the same impulse, the members of the Assembly rose as one man, and swore enthusiastically never to permit, either by the introduction of the republican system or by that of the Two Chambers, any alteration whatsoever in the Constitution.

By a spontaneous movement, the members of the extreme left went towards the deputies of the right. They were received with open arms, and, in their turn, the right advanced toward the ranks of the left. All parties blended. Jaucourt and Merlin, Albite and Ramond, Gensonné and Calvet, Chabot and Genty, men who ordinarily opposed each other relentlessly, could be seen sitting on the same bench. As if by miracle, the Assembly chamber became the temple of Concord. The moved spectators mingled their acclamations with the oaths of the deputies. According to the expressions of the *Moniteur*, serenity and joy were on all faces, and unction in every heart.

M. Emmery was the next speaker. "When the Assembly is reunited," said he, "all the powers ought to be so. I ask, therefore, that the Assembly at once send the King the minutes of its proceedings by a deputation of twenty-four members." The motion was adopted.

A few minutes later, Louis XVI., followed by the deputation and surrounded by his ministers, entered the hall. Cries of "Long live the nation! Long live the King!" resounded from every side. The sovereign placed himself near the president, and in a voice that betrayed emotion, made the following address:

Gentlemen, the spectacle most affecting to my heart is that of the reunion of all wills for the sake of the country's safety. I have long desired this salutary moment; my desire is accomplished. The nation and the King are one. Each of them has the same end in view. Their reunion will save France. The Constitution should be the rallying-point for all Frenchmen. We all ought to defend it. The King will always set the example of so doing." The president replied: "Sire, this memorable moment, when all constituted authorities unite, is a signal of joy to the friends of liberty, and of terror to its enemies. From this union will issue the force necessary to combat the tyrants combined against us. It is a sure warrant of liberty.

After prolonged applause a great silence followed. "I own to you, M. the President," presently said the complaisant Louis XVI., "that I was longing for the deputation to finish, so that I might hasten to the Assembly."

Applause and cries of "Long live the nation! Long live the King!" redoubled. What! this monarch now acclaimed is the same prince against whom Vergniaud hurled invectives a few days ago with the enthusiastic approbation of the same Assembly! He is the sovereign whom the Girondin thus addressed:

O King, who doubtless have believed with Lysander the tyrant that truth is no better than a lie, and that men must be amused with oaths like children with rattles; who have pretended to love the laws only to preserve the power that will enable you to defy them; the Constitution only that it may not cast you from the throne where you must remain in order to destroy it; the nation only to assure the success of your perfidy by inspiring it with confidence,—do you think you can impose upon us today by hypocritical protestations?

What has occurred since the day when Vergniaud, uttering such words as these, was frantically cheered? Nothing. That day, the weather-cock pointed to anger; today to concord. Why? No one knows. Tired of hating, the Assembly doubtless needed an instant of relaxation. Violent sentiments end by wearying the souls that experience them. They must rest and renew their energies in order to hate better tomorrow. And why say tomorrow? This very evening the quarrelling, anger, and fury will begin anew.

At half-past three Louis XVI. left the Hall of the Manège, in the midst of joyful applause from the Assembly and the galleries. During the evening session discord reappeared. The following letter from the King was read: "I have just been handed the departmental decree which provisionally suspends the mayor and the *procureur* of the Commune of Paris. As this decree is based on facts which personally concern me, the first impulse of my heart is to beg the Assembly to decide upon it."

Does anyone believe that the Assembly will have the courage to condemn Pétion and the 20th of June? Not a bit of it. It makes no decision, but passes unanimously from the King's letter to the order of the day. And what occurs at the clubs? Listen to Billaud-Varennes at the Jacobins: "They embrace each other at the Assembly," he exclaims; "it is the kiss of Judas, it is the kiss of Charles IX., extending his hand to Coligny. They were embracing like this while the King was preparing for flight on October 6. They were embracing like this before the massacres of the Champ-de-Mars. They embrace, but are the court conspiracies coming to an end? Have our enemies ceased their advance against our frontiers? Is Lafayette the less a traitor?"

And thereupon the cry broke out: "Pétion or death!" The next day, June 8, at the Assembly, loud applause greeted the orator from a section who said, concerning the department: "It openly serves the sinister projects and disastrous conspiracies of a perfidious court. It is the first link in the immense chain of plots formed against the people. It is an accomplice in the extravagant projects of this general, who, not being able to become the hero of liberty, has preferred to make himself the Don Quixote of the court."

A deputy exclaimed: "The acclamations with which the Assembly has listened to this petition authorize me to ask its publication: I make an express motion to that effect." And the publication was decreed.

O poor Lamourette! humanitarian *abbé*, rose-water revolutionist, of what avail is your democratic holy water? What have you gained by your sentimental jargon? what do your dreams of evangelical philosophy and universal brotherhood amount to? Poor constitutional abbé, people are scoffing already at your sacerdotal unction, your soothing homily! The very men who, to please you, have sworn to destroy the republic, will proclaim it two and a half months later. Your famous reunion of parties, people are already shrugging their shoulders at and calling it the "*baiser d'Amourette, la réconciliation normande*": the calf-love kiss, the pretended reconciliation.

They accuse you of having sold yourself to the court. They ridicule, they flout, and they will kill you. January 11, 1794, Fouquier-Tinville's prosecuting speech will punish you for your moderatism. You will carry your head to the scaffold, and, optimist to the end, you will say: "What is the guillotine? only a rap on the neck."

24

The Féte of the Federation in 1792

The *fête* of the Federation, which was to be celebrated July 14, was awaited with anxiety. The federates came into Paris full of the most revolutionary projects. Anxiety and anguish reigned at the Tuileries. Louis XVI. and Marie Antoinette, who were to be present in the Champ-de-Mars, feared to be assassinated there. The Queen's importunities decided the King to have a plastron made, to ward off a poniard thrust. Composed of fifteen thicknesses of Italian taffeta, this plastron consisted of a vest and a large belt. Madame Campan secretly tried it on the King in the chamber where Marie Antoinette was lying. Pulling Madame Campan by the dress as far as possible from the Queen's bed, Louis XVI. whispered: "It is to satisfy her that I yield; they will not assassinate me; their plan is changed; they will put me to death in another way."

When the King had gone out, the Queen forced Madame Campan to tell her what he had just said. "I had divined it!" she exclaimed. "He has said this long time that all that is going on in France is an imitation of the revolution in England under Charles I. I begin to dread an impeachment for him. As for me, I am a foreigner, and they will assassinate me. What will become of my poor children?" And she fell to weeping.

Madame Campan tried to administer a nervine, but the Queen refused it. "Nervous maladies," said she. "are the ailments of happy women; I no longer have them." Without her knowledge a sort of corset, in the style of her husband's *plastron*, had been made for her. Nothing could induce her to wear it. To those who implored her with tears to put it on, she replied: "If seditious persons assassinate me, so much the better; they will deliver me from a most sorrowful life."

The *fête* of the Federation was celebrated in 1792 amidst extremely tragical preoccupations. Things had changed very greatly since the *fête* which had excited such enthusiasm two years earlier. On July 14, 1790, the Champ-de-Mars was filled at four o'clock in the morning by a crowd delirious with joy. At eight o'clock in the morning of July 14, 1792, it was still empty. The people were said to be at the Bastille witnessing the laying of the first stone of the column to be erected on the ruins of the famous fortress.

On the Champ-de-Mars there was no magnificent altar served by three hundred priests, no side benches covered by an innumerable crowd, none of that sincere and ardent joy which throbbed in every heart two years before. For the *fête* of 1792, eighty-three little tents, representing the departments of the kingdom, had been erected on hillocks of sand. Before each tent stood a poplar, so frail that it seemed as if a breath might blow away the tree and its tri-coloured pendant. In the middle of the Champ-de-Mars were four stretchers covered with canvas painted gray which would have made a miserable decoration for a boulevard theatre. It was a so-called tomb, an honorary monument to those who had died or were about to die on the frontiers. On one side of it was the inscription: "*Tremble, tyrants; we will avenge them!*"

The Altar of the Country could hardly be seen. It was formed of a truncated column placed on the top of the altar steps raised in 1790. Perfumes were burned on the four small corner altars. Two hundred yards farther off, near the Seine, a large tree had been set up and named the Tree of Feudalism. From its branches depended *escutcheons*, helmets, and blue ribbons interwoven with chains. This tree rose out of a wood-pile on which lay a heap of crowns, tiaras, cardinals' hats, Saint Peter's keys, ermine mantles, doctors' caps, and titles of nobility. A royal crown was among them, and beside it the *escutcheons* of the Count de Provence, the Count d'Artois, and the Prince de Condé. The organizers of the *fête* hoped to induce the King himself to set fire to this pile, covered with feudal emblems. A figure representing Liberty, and another representing Law, were placed on casters by the aid of which the two divinities were to be rolled about. Fifty-four pieces of cannon bordered the Champ-de-Mars on the side next the Seine, and the Phrygian cap crowned every tree.

At eleven in the morning the King and his *cortège* arrived at the Military School. A detachment of cavalry opened the march. There were three carriages. In the first were the Prince de Poix, the Marquis de Brézé, and the Count de Saint-Priest; in the second, the Queen's ladies, Mesdames de Tarente, de la Roche-Aymon, de Maillé, and de Mackau; in the third, the King, the Queen, their two children, and Madame Elisabeth. The trumpets sounded and the drums beat a salute. A salvo of artillery announced the arrival of the royal family. The sovereign's countenance was mild and benevolent. Marie Antoinette appeared still more majestic than usual. The dignity of her demeanour, the grace of her children, and the angelic charm of Madame Elisabeth inspired a tender respect. The little *Dauphin* wore the uniform of a National Guard. "He has not deserved the cap yet," said the Queen to the grenadiers.

The royal family took their places on the balcony of the Military School, which was covered with a red velvet carpet embroidered with gold, and watched the popular procession, entering the Champ-de-Mars by the gate of the rue de Grenelle, and marching towards the Altar of the Country. What a strange procession! Men, women, children, armed with pikes, sticks, and hatchets; bands singing the *Ça ira*; drunken harlots, adorned with flowers; people from the *faubourgs* with the inscription, "Long live Pétion!" chalked on their head-gear; six legions of National Guards marching pell-mell with the *sans-culottes*; red caps; placards with devices either ferocious or stupid, like this one: "Long live the heroes who died in the siege of the Bastille!" a plan in relief of the celebrated fortress; a travelling printing-press throwing off copies of the revolutionary manifesto, which the crowd at first mistook for a little guillotine; a great deal of noise and shouting,— and there you have the popular *cortège*. By way of compensation, the troops of the line and the grenadiers of the National Guard displayed extremely royalist sentiments. The 104th regiment of Infantry having halted under the balcony, its band played the air: *Où peut-on être mieux qu'au sein de sa famille?* (Where is one better off than in the bosom of his family?)

The moment when Louis XVI. left the Military School to walk to the Altar of the Country with the National Assembly was not without solemnity. A certain anxiety was felt by all as to what might happen. Would Louis XVI. be struck by a ball or by a poniard? What might not be feared from so many demoniacs, howling like cannibals? The King, the deputies, the soldiers, the crowd, all pressed against each other in a solid mass that left no vacant spaces; all was in continual undulation. Louis XVI. could only advance slowly and with difficulty. The intervention of the troops was necessary to enable him to reach the Altar of the Country, where he was to swear allegiance for the second time to the Constitution whose fragments were to overwhelm his throne.

"It needed the character of Louis XVI.," Madame de Staël has said, "it needed that martyr character which he never belied, to support such a situation as he did. His gait, his countenance, had something peculiar to himself; on other occasions one might have wished he had more grandeur; but at this moment it was enough for him to remain what he was in order to appear sublime. From a distance I watched his powdered head in the midst of all those black ones; his coat, still embroidered as it had been in former days, stood out against the costumes of the common people who pressed around him. When he ascended the steps of the altar, one seemed to behold the sacred victim offering himself in voluntary sacrifice."

The Queen had remained on the balcony of the Military School. From there she watched through a *lorgnette* the dangerous progress of the King. A prey to inexpressible emotion, she remained motionless during an entire hour, hardly able to breathe on account of excessive anguish. She used the *lorgnette* steadily, but at one moment she cried out: "He has come down two steps!" This cry made all those about her shudder. The King could not, in fact, reach the summit of the altar, because a throng of suspicious-looking persons had already taken possession of it.

Deputy Dumas had the presence of mind to cry out: "Attention, Grenadiers! present arms!" The intimidated *sans-culottes* remained quiet, and Louis XVI. took the oath amid the thundering of the cannon ranged beside the Seine.

It was then proposed to the King that he should set fire to the Tree of Feudalism; it was close to the river and the arms of France were hung upon it. Louis XVI. spared himself that shame, exclaiming, "There is no more feudalism!" He returned to the Military School by the way he came. The 6th legion of the National Guard had not yet marched past when the cavalry announced the King's approach. This legion, quickening its pace, was intercepted by the royal escort, and invaded, not to say routed, by the populace, which from all sides pressed into its ranks.

Meanwhile the anguish of Marie Antoinette redoubled. "The expression of the Queen's face," Madame de Staël says again, "will never be effaced from my memory. Her eyes were drowned in tears; the splendour of her *toilette*, the dignity of her demeanour, contrasted with the throng that surrounded her. Nothing separated her from the populace but a few National Guards; the armed men assembled in the Champ-de-Mars seemed more as if they had come together for a riot than for a festival." Pétion, who had been reinstated in his functions as mayor of Paris on the previous day, was the hero of the occasion. They called him King Pétion, and the cheers which resounded in honour of this revolutionist were like a funeral knell in the ears of Marie Antoinette.

At last Louis XVI. appeared in front of the Military School. The Queen experienced a momentary joy in seeing him approach. Rising hastily, she ran down the stairs to meet him. Always calm, the King tenderly clasped his wife's hand. At once royalist sentiment took fire. All who were present—National Guards, troops of the line, Switzers, people in the courts, at the windows, on balconies and gates—all cried: "Long live the King! Long live the Queen!" The royal family regained the Tuileries in the midst of acclamations. At the entrance of the palace enthusiasm deepened. From the Royal Court to the great stairway of the Horloge Pavilion, the grenadiers of the National Guard, who had escorted and saved the King, formed into line with shouts of joy.

"All former souvenirs," says the Count de Vaublanc in his *Memoirs*, "all former habits of respect then awoke. . . . Yes, I saw and observed this multitude; it was animated with the best sentiments; at heart it was faithful to its King and crowned him with sincere benedictions. But do popular love and fidelity afford any support to a tottering throne? He is mad who can think so. The people will be spectators of the latest combat and will applaud the victor. And let no one blame them! What can they do if they are not united, encouraged, and led? The people behold a few seditious individuals attack a throne, and a few courageous men defend it; they fear one party and desire the success of the other. When the struggle is over, they submit and obey. The most honest of them weep in silence, the timid force themselves to display a guilty joy in order to escape the hatred of the victors whom they see bathing themselves in blood. They think about their families, their affairs, their means of support. They were not expected to lead themselves; that duty was imposed on others; have they fulfilled it?"

It is said that during the *fête* those who were friendly to the King, amongst the crowd, were awaiting a signal they expected from him. They hoped that, by the assistance of the Swiss, they could force their way to the royal family during the confusion of a hand-to-hand affray, and get them safely out of Paris. But Louis XVI. neither spoke nor acted. He returned to his palace without having dared anything. And, nevertheless, there were still many chances of safety open. Imagine the effect of a haughty bearing, a commanding gesture in place of the inert attitude habitual to the unfortunate sovereign. Fancy the Most Christian King, the heir of Louis XIV., on horseback, haranguing the people in the style of his witty and valiant ancestor, Henry IV.! He is still King. The troops of the line are faithful. The great majority of the National Guard are well-disposed towards him. Luckner, Lafayette, Dumouriez himself, would ask nothing better than to defend him if he would show a little energy.

The day after the ceremony of July 14, Lafayette was still anxious that Louis XVI. should leave Paris openly and go to Compiègne, so as to show France and Europe that he was free. In case of resistance, the general demanded only fifty loyal cavaliers to take the royal family away. From Compiègne, picked squadrons would conduct them to the midst of the French army, the asylum of devotion and honour. But Louis XVI. refused. The last resources remaining to him were to evaporate between his hands. He will profit neither by the sympathies of all European courts, which ardently desire his safety; by his civil list, which might be such an efficacious means of action; nor by the loyalty of his brave soldiers, who are ready to shed their last drop of blood in his defence.

A large party in the Legislative Assembly would ask nothing but a signal, providing it were seriously given, to rally with vigour to the royal cause. He had intrepid champions there whom no menace could affright, and who on every occasion, no matter how violent or tumultuous the galleries might be, had braved the storm with heroic constancy. Public opinion was changing for the better. The schemes and language of the Jacobins exasperated the mass of honest people. The provinces were sending addresses of fidelity to the King.

What was lacking to the monarch to enable him to combine so many scattered elements into a solid group? A little will, a little of that essential quality, audacity, which, according to Danton, is the last word of politics. But Louis XVI. has a timorous soul. If he makes one step forward, he is in haste to make another back. He is scrupulous, hesitating; he has no confidence in himself or anyone else. This prince, so incontestably courageous, acts as if he were a coward. He has made so many concessions already that the idea of any manner of resistance seems to him chimerical. Does the fate of Charles I. make him dread the beginning of civil war as the supreme danger? Does he fear to imperil the lives of his wife and children by an energetic deed? Is he expecting foreign aid? Does he think to prove his wisdom by his patience, and that success will crown delay? Is he so benevolent, so gentle, that the least thought of repression is repugnant to him? Does he wish to carry to extremes that pardon of injuries which is recommended by the Gospel? What is plain is, that he rejects every firm resolution.

Palliatives, expedients, half-measures, were what suited this honest but feeble nature. Disturbed by contradictory councils, and no longer knowing what to desire or what to hope, he looked on at his own destruction like an unmoved spectator. He was no longer a sovereign full of the sentiment of his power and his rights, but an almost unconscious victim of fatality. Example full of startling lessons for all leaders of state who adopt weakness as a system, and who, under pretext of benevolence or moderation, no longer know how to foresee, to will, or to strike!

25

The Last Days at the Tuileries

During one of the last nights of July, at one o'clock, Madame Campan was alone near the Queen's bed, when she heard someone walking softly in the adjoining corridor, which was ordinarily locked at both ends. Madame Campan summoned the *valet-de-chambre*, who went into the corridor; presently the noise of two men fighting reached the ears of Marie Antoinette. "What a position!" cried the unfortunate Queen. "Insults by day and assassins by night!"

The valet cried: "*Madame*, it is a scoundrel whom I know; I am holding him."

"Let him go," said the Queen. "Open the door for him; he came to assassinate me; he will be carried in triumph by the Jacobins tomorrow."

People were constantly saying that the Faubourg Saint-Antoine was getting ready to march against the palace. Marie Antoinette was so badly guarded, and it was so easy to force an entrance to her apartment on the ground-floor, opposite the garden, that Madame de Tourzel, her children's governess, begged her to sleep in the *Dauphin's* room on the first floor. The Queen was averse to this step, as she was unwilling to have any one suspect her uneasiness. But Madame de Tourzel having shown her that it would be easy to keep the secret of this change by using the *Dauphin's* private staircase, she ended by accepting the proposal so long as the trouble should last. She was so thoughtful of all those in her service that it cost her much to incommode them in the least.

Finally, she consented to use the bed of the governess, and a pallet was laid for the latter every evening. Mademoiselle Pauline de Tourzel slept on a sofa in an adjoining closet. As no one in the house suspected that the Queen might have changed her apartment for the night,

Madame de Tourzel and her daughter took precautionary measures. When the Queen had gone to bed, they rose, and after making sure that the doors were locked, they shot the inside bolts. "The closet I occupied served as a passage for the royal family when they went to supper," says Mademoiselle de Tourzel, afterwards Madame de Béarn, in her *Souvenirs de Quarante Ans:*

> I went to bed early; sometimes I pretended to be asleep when the Princes were passing through, and I saw them approach my sofa, one after another; I heard their expressions of kindness and goodwill toward me, and noticed what care they took not to disturb my slumber.

Poor Marie Antoinette! Could one believe that a Queen of France would be reduced to keeping a little dog in her bedroom to warn her of the least noise in her apartment? The *Dauphin*, delighted to have his mother sleep so near him, used to run to her as soon as he awoke, and clasping her in his little arms would say the most affectionate things. This was the only moment of the day that brought her any consolation.

By the end of July, both the Queen and her children were obliged to give up walking in the garden. She had gone out to take the air with her daughter in the *Dauphin's* small *parterre* at the extreme end of the Tuileries, close to the Place Louis XV. Some federates grossly insulted her. Four Swiss officers made their way through the crowd, and placing the Queen and the young Princess between them, brought them back to the palace. When she reached her apartments, Marie Antoinette thanked her defenders in the most affecting terms, but she never went out again.

After June 20, the garden, excepting the terrace of the Feuillants, which, by a decree of the Assembly, had become a part of its precincts, had been forbidden to the populace. Posters warned the people to remain on the terrace and not go down into the garden. The terrace was called National Ground, and the garden the Land of Coblentz. Inscriptions apprised passers-by of this novel topography. Tri-coloured ribbons had been tied to the banisters of the staircases by way of barriers. Placards were fastened at intervals to the trees bordering the terrace, whereon could be read:

> Citizens, respect yourselves; give the force of bayonets to this feeble barrier. Citizens, do not go into this foreign land, this Coblentz, abode of corruption.

The leaders had such an empire over the crowd that no one disobeyed. And yet it was the height of summer, the trees offered their verdant shade, and the King had withdrawn all his guards and opened every gate. Nobody dared infringe the revolutionary mandate. One young man, paying no attention, went down into the garden. Furious clamours broke out on all sides. "To the lamp-post with him!" cried someone on the terrace. Thereupon the young man, taking off his shoes, drew out his handkerchief and began to wipe the dust from their soles. People cried bravo, and he was carried in triumph.

Marie Antoinette could not become resigned to this hatred. Often she frightened her women by wishing to go out of the palace and address the people. "Yes," she would cry, her voice trembling, as she walked quickly to and fro in her chamber, "yes, I will say to them: Frenchmen, they have had the cruelty to persuade you that I do not love France, I, the wife of its King and the mother of a *Dauphin!*" Then, this brief moment of generous exaltation over, the illusion of being able to move a nation of insulters quickly vanished. Her life was a daily, hourly struggle.

The wife, the mother, the queen, never ceased to contend against destiny. She hardly slept or ate; but from the very excess of danger she drew additional energy, and moral and material force. As she awoke at daybreak, she required that the shutters should not be closed, so that her sleepless nights might be sooner consoled by the light of morning. The most widely diverse sentiments occupied her soul. A captive in her palace, she sometimes believed herself irrevocably condemned by fate, and sometimes hoped for deliverance.

Toward the middle of one of the last nights preceding the 10th of August, the moon shone into her bedchamber. "In a month," she said to Madame Campan, "I shall not see that moon unless I am freed from my chains." But she was not free from anxiety concerning all that might happen before that. "The King is not a poltroon," she added; "he has very great passive courage, but he is crushed by a false shame, a doubt of himself, which arises from his education quite as much as from his character. He is afraid of commanding; he dreads above everything to speak to assemblages of men. He lived uneasily and like a child, under the eyes of Louis XV. until he was twenty, and this constraint has had an effect on his timidity. In our circumstances, a few clearly spoken words addressed to the Parisians who are devoted to us would immensely strengthen our party, but he will not say them."

Then Marie Antoinette explained why she did not put herself forward more: "For my part," said she, "I could act, and mount a horse if need were; but, if I acted, it would put weapons into the hands of King's enemies; a general outcry would be raised in France against the Austrian woman, against female domination; moreover, I should reduce the King to nothingness by showing myself. A queen who is not regent must in such circumstances remain inactive and prepare to die."

The danger constantly increased. At four in the morning of one of the last days of July, warning was given at the palace that the *faubourgs* were threatening, and would doubtless march against the Tuileries. Madame Campan went very softly into the Queen's room. For a wonder, Marie Antoinette was sleeping peacefully and profoundly. Madame Campan did not rouse her.

"You were right," said Louis XVI.; "it is good to see her take a little rest. Oh! her griefs redouble mine!"

At her waking the Queen, on being informed of what had passed, began to weep, and said: "Why was I not called?"

Madame Campan excused herself by saying: "It was only a false alarm. Your Majesty needed to repair your prostrate strength."

"It is not prostrate," quickly replied the courageous sovereign; "misfortune makes it all the greater. Elisabeth was with the King, and I was sleeping! I, who wish to perish beside him! I am his wife; I am not willing that he should incur the least danger without me!"

On Sunday, August 5,—the last Sunday the royal family were to spend at the Tuileries,—as they were going to the chapel to hear Mass, half the National Guards on duty cried: "Long live the King!"

The others said: "No, no; no King, down with the *veto*!"

The same day, at Vespers, the chanters had agreed to swell their tones greatly, and in a menacing way, when reciting this *versicle* of the *Magnificat: Deposuit potentes de sede*—"He hath put down the mighty from their seat."

In their turn the royalists, after the *Dominum salvum fac regem*, cried thrice, turning as they did so toward the Queen: *Et reginam*. There was a continual murmuring all through the divine office. Five days later, the same chapel was to be a pool of blood.

And yet Madame Elisabeth, always calm and always angelic, still had illusions. One morning of this terrible month of August, while in her room in the Pavilion of Flora, she thought she heard someone humming her favourite air, *Pauvre Jacques*, beneath her windows. Attracted by this refrain, which in the midst of sorrow renewed the souvenir of happier times, she half opened her window and listened attentively. The words sung were not those of the ballad she loved, yet they were royalist in sentiment and adapted to the same air. The poor people had been substituted for poor Jack—the poor people who were pitied for having a king no longer and for knowing nothing but wretchedness.

Such marks of attachment consoled the virtuous Princess, and made her hope against all hope. She wrote, August 8, to her friend Madame de Raigecourt:

> They say that the King is going to be turned out of here somewhat forcibly, and made to lodge in the Hôtel-de-Ville. They say that there will be a very strong movement to that effect in Paris. Do you believe it? For my part, I do not. I believe in rumours, but not in their resulting in anything. That is my profession of faith. For the rest, everything is perfectly quiet today. Yesterday passed in the same way, and I think this one will be like it.

On August 9, the eve of the fatal day, Madame Elisabeth again addressed a reassuring letter to one of her friends, Madame de Bombelles. Curiously enough she dated this letter August 10, no doubt by accident, and when Madame de Bombelles received it, she read these lines, which seem like the irony of fate:

> This day of the 10th, which was to have been so exciting, so terrible, is as calm as possible; the Assembly has decreed neither deposition nor suspension.

26

The Prologue to the
Tenth of August

The first rumblings of the storm began. People quarrelled and fought in the Palais Royal, the *cafés*, and the theatres. Half of the National Guard sided with the court, and the other half with the people. To seditious speeches were added songs full of insults to the King and Queen. These songs, sold on every corner, applauded in every tavern, and repeated by the wives and children of the people, propagated revolutionary fury. There was a constant succession of gatherings, brawls, and riots. The Assembly had declared the country in danger. Rumours of every sort excited popular imagination. It was said that priests who refused the oath were in hiding at the Tuileries, which was, moreover, full of arms and munitions. The Duke of Brunswick's manifesto exasperated national sentiment. It was read aloud in every street. The leaders neglected nothing likely to excite the populace, and prepared their last attack on the throne, their afterpiece of June 20, with as much audacity as skill.

In order to subdue the court, it was necessary to destroy its only remaining means of defence. To leave plenty of elbow-room for the riot, the Assembly, on July 15, ordered the troops of the line to be sent some thirty-five miles beyond Paris and kept there. A singular means was devised for breaking up the choice troops of the National Guard, who were royalists. They were told that it was contrary to equality for certain citizens to be more brilliantly equipped than others; that a bearskin cap humiliated those who were entitled only to a felt one; and that there was a something aristocratic about the name of grenadier which was really intolerable to a simple foot-soldier. The choice troops were dissolved in consequence, and the grenadiers came to the

Assembly like good patriots to lay down their epaulettes and bearskin caps and assume the red cap. On July 30, the National Guard was reconstructed, by taking in all the vagabonds and bandits that the clubs could muster.

The famous federates of Marseilles, who were to take such an active part in the coming insurrection, arrived in Paris the same day. The Girondins, having failed to obtain their camp of twenty thousand men before Paris, had devised instead of it a reunion of federate volunteers, summoned from every part of France. The roads were at once thronged by future rioters whom the Assembly allowed thirty cents a day.

The Jacobins of Brest and Marseilles distinguished themselves. Instead of a handful of volunteers they sent two battalions. That of Marseilles, recruited by Barbaroux, comprised five hundred men and two pieces of artillery. Starting July 5, it entered Paris July 30. Excited to fanaticism by the sun and the declamations of the southern clubs, it had run over France, been received under triumphal arches, and chanted in a sort of frenzy the terrible *stanzas* of Rouget de l'Isle's new hymn, the *Marseillaise*. It was at this time that Blanc Gilli, deputy from the Bouches du Rhone department to the Legislative Assembly, wrote:

These pretended Marseillais are the scum of the jails of Genoa, Piedmont, Sicily, and of all Italy, Spain, the Archipelago, and Barbary. I run across them every day.

Rouget de l'Isle received from his old mother, a royalist and Catholic at heart, a letter in which she said: "What is this revolutionary hymn which a horde of brigands are singing as they pass through France, and in which your name is mixed up?" At Paris the accents of that terrible melody sounded like strokes of the tocsin. The men who sang it filled the conservatives with terror. They wore woollen cockades and insulted as aristocrats those who wore silk ones.

There was no longer any dike to the torrent. August 1, Louis XVI. nominated a cabinet composed of loyal men: Joly was Minister of Justice; Champion de Villeneuve, of the Interior; Bigot de Sainte-Croix, of Foreign Affairs; Du Bouchage, of the Marine; Leroux de la Ville, of Public Taxes; and D'Abancourt, of War. But this ministry was to last only ten days. Certain petitioners at the bar of the Assembly asked for the deposition of the King in most violent language.

"This measure," says Barbaroux in his *Memoirs*, "would have carried

Philippe of Orléans to the regency, and therefore his party violently clamoured for it. His creditors, his hirelings, and boon-companions, Marat and his *Cordeliers*, all manner of swindlers and insolvent debtors, thronged public places and incited to this deposition because they were hungry for money and positions under a regent who was their tool and their accomplice."

In vain did Louis XVI. display those sentiments of paternal kindness which had hitherto availed him so little. August 3, he sent a message to the Assembly, in which he said:

I will uphold national independence to my latest breath. Personal dangers are nothing compared to public ones. Oh! what are personal dangers to a King whom men are seeking to deprive of his people's love? This is the real plague-spot in my heart. Perhaps the people will someday know how dear their welfare is to me. How many of my sorrows could be obliterated by the least evidence of a return to right feeling!

How did they respond to this conciliatory language? After it had been read, Pétion, the mayor of Paris, presented himself at the bar, and read an address from the Council General of the Commune, in which these words occur:

The chief of the executive power is the first link of the counter-revolutionary chain. . . . Through a lingering forbearance, we would have desired the power to ask you for the suspension of Louis XVI., but to this the Constitution is opposed. Louis XVI. incessantly invokes the Constitution; we invoke it in our turn, and ask you for his deposition.

The next day the municipality distributed five thousand ball cartridges to the Marseillais, while refusing any to the National Guards.

Nevertheless, the Girondins still hesitated. Guadet, Vergniaud, and Gensonné would have declared themselves satisfied if the three ministers belonging to their party had been reinstated, and on July 29 they secretly despatched a letter to the sovereign, by Thierry, his *valet-de-chambre*, in which they said that, "attached to the interests of the nation, they would never separate them from those of the King except in so far as he separated them himself."

As to Barbaroux, like a true visionary, he dreamed of I know not what rose-water insurrection. "They should not have entered the apartments of the palace," he has said, "but merely blockaded them. Had this plan been followed, the blood of Frenchmen and Swiss, ignorant victims of court perfidy, would not have been shed on the 10th of August, the republic would have been founded without convulsions or massacres, and we, corroded by popular gangrene, should not have become the horror of all nations." The demagogues were not at all certain of success. Robespierre was to spend the 10th of August in the discreet darkness of a cellar. Danton was prudently to await the end of the combat before arming himself with a big sabre and marching at the head of the Marseilles battalion as the hero of the day. Barbaroux says in his *Memoirs* that on the 1st, 3rd, and 7th of August, Marat implored him to take him to Marseilles, and that on the evening of the 9th he renewed this prayer more urgently than ever, adding that he would disguise himself as a jockey in order to get away.

In spite of their many weaknesses, the majority of the Assembly were royalists and constitutionalists still. The proof is that on August 8, in spite of the violent menaces of the galleries, they decided by 406 against 244 votes, that there was no occasion to impeach Lafayette, so abhorred by the Jacobins. This vote excited the wrath of the revolutionists to fury. The conservative deputies were insulted, pursued, and struck. Several of them barely escaped assassination. The sessions became stormier from day to day. Not only were the large galleries of the Assembly overthronged by violent crowds, but the courtyards, the approaches, and the corridors were obstructed. Many sat or stood on the exterior entablatures of the high windows.

The upper part of the hall, where the Jacobins sat, received many strangers, in spite of the often-reiterated opposition of the right. Below this Mountain sat the members of the centre, the *Ventrus*. There were not seats enough for them, and they were crowded up in a ridiculous manner. At the bottom of the hall, almost entirely deserted, were the forty-four members of the right. They were easily marked and counted by their future executioners, who threatened them by voice and gesture. Every day the petitioners who were admitted to the honours of the session avoided the empty benches of the right and seated themselves with the Mountain or the centre, where they crowded still more the already overcrowded deputies. The discussions were like formidable tempests.

"The effect produced by such a spectacle," says Count de Vaublanc in his *Memoirs*, "was still greater on those who entered the hall during one of those terrible moments. I received this impression several times myself, and it will never be effaced from my mind; I seek vainly for expressions by which to describe it. Long afterwards, M. de Caux, then

177

Minister of War, said to me: 'You made the profoundest impression on me which I ever received in my life. I was young at the time. I entered the galleries just as you were standing out against the furious shouts of a part of the deputies and the people in the galleries.'"

Meanwhile the end was approaching. Faithful royalists still proposed schemes of flight to Louis XVI. Bertrand de Molleville, who is so ill disposed toward Madame de Staël, says concerning this: "There was nobody, even to Madame de Staël, who, either in the hope of being pardoned the injury her intrigues had done the King, or else through her continual need of intrigue, had not invented some plan of escape for His Majesty." Louis XVI. declined them all. He would owe nothing to Lafayette. He relied on the money he had given to Danton and other demagogues, and hoped that the insurrectionary bands would be repulsed by the royalists of the National Guard and the Swiss regiment.

August 8th, in the evening, this fine regiment left its Courbevoie barracks and arrived at the Tuileries at daybreak next morning. Under various idle pretexts it had been deprived of its twelve pieces of artillery, and also of three hundred men who had been given the commission, true or false as may be, to watch over the transportation of corn in Normandy. Only seven hundred and fifty, officers and soldiers, remained; but all of them had said: "We will let ourselves be killed to the last man rather than fail in honour or betray the sanctity of our oaths." In company with a handful of noblemen, these were to be the last defenders of the throne.

The fatal hour was approaching. The section of the *Cordeliers* had decided that if the Assembly had not pronounced the King's deposition by the evening of August 9th, the drums should beat the general alarm at the stroke of midnight, and the insurrection march against the Tuileries. The revolutionists were to carry out their plan, and the Swiss to keep their word.

27

The Night of August Ninth to Tenth

The night was serene, the sky clear and sown with stars. The calmness of nature contrasted with the revolutionary passions that had been unchained. On account of the heat, all the windows of the Tuileries had been left open, and from a distance the palace could be seen illuminated as if for a *fête*. It had just struck midnight. The Revolution was executing the programme of the *Cordeliers'* section. The tocsin was sounding all over the city. Everybody named the church whose bell he thought he recognized. The people of the *faubourgs* were out of bed in their houses. The drums mingled with the tocsin. The revolutionists beat the general alarm, and the royalists the call to arms.

No one was asleep at the Tuileries. There was no further question of etiquette. The night reception in the royal bedchamber was omitted for the first time. Certain old servitors, faithful guardians of tradition, in vain recalled that it was not permissible to sit down in the sovereign's apartments. The courtiers of the last hour seated themselves in armchairs, on tables and consoles. Louis XVI. stayed sometimes in his chamber and sometimes in his Great Cabinet, also called the Council Hall, where the assembled ministers received constant tidings of what was happening without. The pious monarch had summoned his confessor, Abbé Hébert, and shutting himself up with this venerable priest, he besought from Heaven the resignation and courage he needed to pass through the final crisis. Madame Elisabeth showed the faithful Madame Campan the carnelian pin which fastened her *fichu*. These words, surrounding the stalk of a lily, were engraved on it: "Forget offences, pardon injuries."

"I fear much," said the virtuous Princess, "that this maxim has little influence over our enemies, but it must be none the less dear to us."

Louis XVI. did not wear his padded vest. "I consented to do so on the 14th of July," said he, "because on that day I was merely going to a ceremony where an assassin's dagger might be apprehended. But on a day when my party may be forced to fight with the revolutionists, I should think it cowardly to preserve my life by such means."

Marie Antoinette was grave and tranquil in her heroism. There was nothing affected about her, nothing theatrical, neither passion, despair, nor the spirit of revenge. According to the expressions of Roederer, who never left her, "she was a woman, a mother, a wife in peril; she feared, she hoped, she grieved, and she took heart again." She was also a queen, and the daughter of Maria Theresa. Her anxiety and grief were restrained or concealed by her respect for her rank, her dignity, and her name. When she reappeared amidst the courtiers in the Council Hall, after having dissolved in tears in Thierry's room, the redness of her cheeks and eyes had disappeared. The courtiers said to each other: "What serenity! what courage!"

The struggle might still seem doubtful. Something like two hundred noblemen who had spontaneously repaired to the King, seven hundred and fifty Swiss, and nine hundred mounted *gendarmes* posted at the approaches of the Tuileries were the last resources of the commander-in-chief of the French army. The Swiss, who through some one's extreme imprudence had not cartridges enough, were posted in the apartments, the chapel, and at the entry of the Royal Court. Baron de Salis, as the oldest captain of the regiment, commanded at the stairways.

A reserve of three hundred men, under Captain Durler, was stationed in the Swiss Court, before the Pavilion of Marsan. The National Guards belonging to the sections *Petits-Pères* and the *Filles-Saint-Thomas* showed themselves well disposed toward the King; but it was different with the other companies. As to the mounted *gendarmes*, Louis XVI. could not count on them, and before the riot ended they were to join the insurgents in spite of all the efforts made by their royalist officers. The artillerists of the National Guard, charged with serving the cannons placed in the courts and before the palace doors to defend the entry, were to act in the same manner.

Like the Swiss, the two hundred noblemen, martyrs to the old French ideas of honour, had resolved to be loyal unto death. With their silk coats and drawing-room swords, they seemed as if they had come to a *fête* instead of a combat. The servants of the *château* joined them. Some of them had pistols and blunderbusses. Some, for lack of other weapons, had taken the tongs from the chimneys. They jested with each other over their accoutrements. No, no; there was nothing laughable in these champions of misfortune. They represented the past, with its ancient fidelity to the altar and the throne. A great poet who had the spirit of divination, Heinrich Heine, wrote on November 12, 1840, as if he foresaw February 24, 1848:

"The middle classes will possibly make less resistance than the aristocracy would do in a similar case. Even in its most pitiable weakness, its enervation by immorality and its degeneration through flattery, the old nobility was still alive to a certain point of honour unknown to our middle classes, who have become prosperous by industry, but who will perish by it also. Another 10th of August is predicted for these middle classes; but I doubt whether the industrial Knights of the throne of July will prove themselves as heroic as the powdered marquises of the old *régime* who, in silk coats and flimsy dress swords, opposed the people who invaded the Tuileries."

The greater part of these noblemen, volunteers for the last conflict, were old men with white hair. There were also children among them. M. Mortimer-Ternaux, author of the *Histoire de la Terreur*, has remarked:

Was not this a time to exclaim with Racine:—

See what avengers arm themselves for the quarrel?

Who could have told Louis XIV., when in the midst of the splendours of his court he was present at the performance of *Athalie*, that the poet was predicting, through the mouth of Joad, the fate reserved for his great-grandson?

The royalist National Guards who were in the apartments considered the volunteer noblemen as companions in arms. They shook hands with each other amid cries of "Long live the King! Long live the National Guard!" But the troops outside did not share these sentiments. Jealous of the royalists assembled in the palace, they wanted to have them sent out. A regimental commander having come to make known this desire to Louis XVI., Marie Antoinette exclaimed:"Nothing can separate us from these gentlemen; they are our most faithful friends. They will share the dangers of the National Guard. They will obey us. Put them at the cannon's mouth, and they will show you how men die for their King."

Meantime what had become of Pétion, whose business it was, as mayor, to defend the palace? Summoned to the Tuileries, he arrived there at eleven in the evening. As Louis XVI. said to him: "It seems there is a great deal of commotion?"

"Yes, sire," he replied, "the excitement is great." And he enlarged upon the measures he claimed that he had taken, and his pretended haste to wait upon the King.

In going out, he came face to face with M. de Mandat, who, as general-in-chief of the National Guard, was in command of all military forces. "Why," exclaimed he, "have the police refused cartridges to the National Guard when they have wasted them on the Marseillais? My men have only four charges apiece; some of them have not one. No matter; I answer for everything; my measures are taken, providing I am authorized, by an order signed by you, to repel force by force."

Not daring to avow his complicity with the riot, Pétion signed the order demanded. Then he made his escape under pretext of inspecting the gardens, and fell amongst some royalist National Guards, who reprimanded him severely. He began to fear being kept at the Tuileries as a hostage, to guarantee the palace against the attempts of the populace, and went to the Assembly. It had adjourned at ten o'clock the evening before, but on account of the crisis had met again at two in the morning.

The Assembly knew the gravity of the danger as well as the King did; but through a ridiculous and culpable point of honour, it affected not to recognize it, and devoted to the reading of a colonial report the moments it should have employed in saving that Constitution it had sworn to maintain. Pétion merely put in an appearance in the Hall of the Manège. But he took good care not to return to the Tuileries. At half-past three in the morning the rolling of a carriage was heard from the palace. It was that of the mayor, going back empty. He had not dared to get into it, and had only sent his coachman an order to return when he found himself in safety at the mayoralty, whither he had made his way on foot.

Meanwhile, some hundred unknown individuals, who gathered at the Hôtel-de-Ville, and surreptitiously made their way into one of the halls, had formed an insurrectionary Commune. On their own authority they appointed commissaries of sections, and dismissed the staff of the National Guard, who were very much in their way; but retained in office Manuel as procurator and Pétion as mayor. This new municipality, whose very existence was unknown at the palace, had just learned that Mandat, general-in-chief of the National Guard, had a document in his pocket by which Pétion authorized him to oppose force to force. It was necessary to get rid of this document at any cost.

The municipality sent Mandat an order to come to the Hôtel-de-Ville. He knew nothing about the revolution that had just taken place there. And yet he hesitated to obey. A secret presentiment took possession of his soul. Finally, at the instance of Roederer, he decided, towards five in the morning, to leave the Tuileries and go to that Hôtel-de-Ville, which was to be so fatal to him. When he came before the municipality he was surprised to see new faces.

He was accused of having intended to disperse "the innocent and patriotic column of the people," and sentenced to be taken to the Abbey prison. It was a sentence of death. Mandat was massacred on the steps of the Hôtel-de-Ville. A pistol-shot brought him down. Pikes and sabres finished him. His body was thrown into the Seine. Such was the first exploit of the new Commune. It preluded thus the massacres of September.

"Mandat's death," says Count de Vaublanc in his *Memoirs*, "was, beyond any doubt, the chief cause of the calamities of the day. If he had attacked the rebels as soon as they came near the palace, he could have dispersed them with ease. They took a long time to form and set off; and, being undecided and uneasy, they often halted. No troop marching from a given point in this immense city knew whether it was seconded by the rebels from other quarters, and lost much time in making sure."

The second exploit of the Commune was to confine Pétion at the mayoralty under the guard of six men. A voluntary captive, this accomplice of the insurrection rejoiced at a measure which sheltered him from every danger. As M. Mortimer-Ternaux has observed: "On this fatal night, when the passion of the royalty was fulfilled, Pétion doubled the parts of Judas and Pontius Pilate. Like Judas, he went at nightfall to give the kiss of peace to Louis XVI. by assuring him of his loyalty; like the Roman governor, he proclaimed at daybreak the impotence with which he had stricken himself, and washed his hands of all that was to happen."

When the first fires of this fatal day were kindling in the sky, Marie Antoinette experienced a profound emotion. Looking with melancholy at the horizon which began to lighten: "Sister," said she to Madame Elisabeth, "come and see the sun rise." It was the sun that was to illumine the death-struggle of royalty. Sinister omen! the sun was red

28

The Morning of August Tenth

The fatal day began. It was five o'clock in the morning. The Queen made her children rise, lest the swords of the insurgents should surprise them in their beds. The *Dauphin*, unaccustomed to being called so early, stared with surprise at the spectacle presented by the court and garden. "Mamma," said he, "why should anyone harm papa? He is so good!" Then, turning to a little girl who was his usual companion in his games, he addressed her these words, which prove how well, in spite of his age, he knew the peril he was in: "Here, Josephine, take this lock of my hair, and promise to wear it as long as I am in danger."

Led by their chief, Marshal de Mailly, an old man of eighty-six, the two hundred noblemen, who had assembled in the Gallery of Diana, passed in review before the royal family with those of the National Guards who were royalists. "Sire," exclaimed the old marshal, bending his knee, "here are your faithful nobles who have hastened to re-establish Your Majesty on the throne of your ancestors."

"For this once," responded Louis XVI., "I consent that my friends should defend me; we will perish or save ourselves together." The last defenders of the throne shed tears of fidelity and tenderness. They kneeled before Marie Antoinette, and entreated the honour of kissing her hand. Never had the Queen appeared more gracious and majestic. The National Guards, enchanted, loaded their arms with transport.

The Queen seized the *Dauphin* in her arms and held him above their heads like a living standard. The young men shouted: "Long live the Kings of our fathers!" And the old men cried: "Long live the King of our children!"

At the gates of the Tuileries the tide was rising. Vanguards of the insurrection, the Marseillais arrived unhindered. The municipality had succeeded in removing the cannons which were to have prevented approach by way of the Pont-Neuf and the Pont-Royal. Mandat was no longer there to issue orders. Nothing impeded the march of the *faubourgs*.

And yet resistance might still have been possible. It is Barbaroux, the fierce revolutionist himself, who says so.

> All the faults committed by the insurrection, the wretched arrangement of the attacking party, the terror of some and the ignorance of others, the forces at the palace, all made the victory of the court certain, if the King had not left his post. If he had shown himself on horseback, a large majority of the people of Paris would have pronounced for him.

Napoleon, who was an eye-witness, had said the night before to Pozzo di Borgo, that with two battalions of Swiss and some cavalry he would undertake to give the rioters a lesson they would remember. In the evening of August 10, he wrote to his brother Joseph:

> According to what I saw of the temper of the crowd in the morning, if Louis XVI. had mounted a horse, he would have gained the victory.

Very few of the insurgents were seriously determined on a revolt. Most of them marched blindly, not knowing, and not even asking, whither they went.

Westermann had been obliged to threaten Santerre, and even to put his sword against his breast, in order to induce him to march. A great number of the people of the *faubourgs*, uneasy as to the result of the enterprise, said that, considering the preparations made by the palace, it would be better to defer the matter to another day. The unarmed crowd followed through mere curiosity, and were ready to take flight at the first discharge of musketry. According to Count de Vaublanc, the Swiss, if they had been commanded by a good officer from four o'clock in the morning, would have sufficed to disperse the multitude as they came up, and possibly might have won the day for the King without bloodshed. "Thus, the best of princes rendered useless the courage of his defenders, and to spare the blood of his enemies accomplished the ruin of his friends. All his virtues turned against him and brought him to his ruin."

M. de Vaublanc says again in his *Memoirs*:

> At six in the morning those who were in revolt had not yet assembled. How much time had been lost, how much was still to be lost! It was too evident that no military judgment had pre-

sided over that strange disposition of troops, so placed within and without the palace as to be unable to give each other mutual support; a military man knows too well the value of the briefest moments, he knows too well how quickly victory can be decided by attacking the flank of a multitude with a small number of brave men. If the King had appointed one of the generals near him absolute master of operations, no doubt this general would have given the rebels no time to unite. . . . Alas! Louis XVI. had three times more courage than was necessary to conquer, but he knew not how to avail himself of it.

Such also was the opinion of M. Thiers, who, in his *Histoire de la Révolution française*, says:

It must be repeated, the unfortunate Prince feared nothing for himself. He had, in fact, refused to wear a wadded vest, as he had done on July 14, saying that on a day of combat he ought to be as much exposed as the least of his servants. Courage did not fail him then, and afterwards he displayed a bravery that was noble and elevated enough; but he lacked boldness to take the offensive. . . . It is certain, as has been frequently said, that if he had mounted a horse and charged at the head of his troops, the insurrection would have been put down.

Toward six o'clock the King went out on the balcony. He was saluted with acclamations. Then he went down the great staircase with the Queen to inspect the troops stationed in the courtyards. As one of his gentlemen-of-the-chamber, Emmanuel Aubier, has remarked: "He had never made war himself during his reign; there had never been a war on the continent; he was so unfortunate as to be wanting in grace, even awkward, and to look thoughtful rather than energetic,—a thing displeasing to French soldiers." Instead of putting on a uniform and mounting a horse, he wore a purple coat, of the shade used as mourning for kings, on this fatal day when he was to wear mourning for the monarchy.

Unspurred, unbooted, shod as if for a drawing-room, with white silk stockings, his hat under his arm, his hair out of curl and badly powdered, there was nothing martial, nothing royal about him. At this hour, when what was needed was the attitude and the fire of a Henry IV., he looked like an honest country gentleman talking with his farmers. The first condition of inspiring confidence is to possess it. Louis XVI.'s aspect was much more that of a victim than a sovereign.

The cries of "Long live the King!" which would have been enthusiastic for a prince ready to battle for his rights and reconquer his realm at the sword's point, were few and sad. After having inspected the troops in the courts, Louis XVI. decided to inspect those in the garden also. The Queen returned to the palace, and he continued his rounds.

The loyal National Guards, comprising the companies of the *Petits-Pères* and the *Filles-Saint-Thomas*, were drawn up on the terrace between the palace and the garden. They received the King sympathetically and advised him to continue his inspection as far as the Place Louis XV. At this moment a battalion of the National Guards from the Saint-Marceau section defiled before him, uttering shouts of hatred and fury. Louis XVI. was undisturbed by this. He remained calm, and when this battalion had got into position, he tranquilly reviewed it. Then he walked on again and crossed the entire garden. The battalion of the *Croix-Rouge*, which was on the terrace beside the water, cried from a distance: "Down with the *veto*! Down with the traitor!"

On the te

rrace of the Feuillants, at the other side, there was an equally violent crowd. The King, calm as ever, went on to the swing-bridge by which the Tuileries was entered from Place Louis XV. He was well enough received by the troops stationed there. But his return to the palace could not but be difficult. The National Guards of the *Croix-Rouge* had broken rank and come down from the terrace beside the river to the garden, and pressed around the King with menacing shouts.

The unfortunate monarch could only re-enter the palace where he had but a few moments more to stay, by calling to his aid a double row of faithful grenadiers. The ministers who were at the windows became alarmed. One of them, M. de Bouchage, cried: "Great God! it is the King they are hooting! What the devil are they doing down there? Quick; we must go after him!" And he hastened to descend into the garden with his colleague, Bigot de Sainte-Croix, to meet his master. The Queen, who beheld the sight, shed tears. The two ministers brought back Louis XVI. He came in out of breath, and fatigued by the heat and the exercise he had taken, but otherwise seeming very little moved.

"All is lost," said the Queen. "This review has done more harm than good."

From this moment bad tidings succeeded each other without interruption. They were apprised of the formation of the new Commune, Mandat's murder, the march of the *faubourgs*, and the arrival of the first detachments of rioters. The Marseillais debouched into the Carrousel, and sent an envoy to demand that the gate of the Royal Court should be opened. As it remained closed, they knocked on it with repeated blows, while the National Guards said: "We will not fire on our brothers."

Would resistance have been possible even at this moment; that is to say, between seven and eight in the morning? M. de Vaublanc thought so. "I do not know," he writes, "to what section the first band that arrived on the Carrousel belonged; it was in disorder and badly armed. If the King had marched towards this troop at the head of a battalion of the National Guard, if he had pronounced these words: 'I am your King; I order you to lay down your arms,' the success would have been decided. The flight of a single battalion of rebels would have sufficed to frighten and disperse the others, even before they were formed into line."

It was at this time that Roederer, instead of counselling resistance, implored Louis XVI. to seek shelter in the Assembly for the royal family. "Sire," he said in an urgent tone, "Your Majesty has not five minutes to lose; there is no safety for you except in the National Assembly. In the opinion of the department, it is necessary to go there without delay. There are not men enough in the courtyards to defend the palace; nor are they perfectly well-disposed. On the mere recommendation to be on the defensive, the cannoneers have already unloaded their cannons."

"But," said the King, "I did not see many persons on the *Carrousel*."

"Sire," returned Roederer, "there are a dozen pieces of artillery, and an immense crowd is arriving from the *faubourgs*."

The idea of a flight before the insurrection revolted the Queen's pride. "What are you saying, Sir?" cried she; "you are proposing that we should seek shelter with our most cruel persecutors! Never! never! I will be nailed to these walls before I consent to leave them. Sir, we have troops."

"*Madame*, all Paris is on the march. Resistance is impossible. Will you cause the massacre of the King, your children, and your servants?"

Louis XVI. still hesitating, Roederer vehemently insisted. "Sire," said he, "time presses; this is no longer an entreaty nor even a counsel we take the liberty of offering you; there is only one thing left for us to do now, and we ask your permission to take you away."

The King looked fixedly at his interlocutor for several seconds; then, turning to the Queen, he said: "Let us go," and rose to his feet.

Madame Elisabeth said: "Monsieur Roederer, do you answer for the King's life?"

"Yes, *Madame*, with my own," responded the communal attorney. Then, turning to the King: "Sire," said he, "I ask Your Majesty not to take any of your court with you, but to have no *cortège* but the department and no escort except the National Guard."

"Yes," replied the King, "there is nothing but that to say."

The Minister of Justice exclaimed: "The ministers will follow the King."

"Yes, they have a place in the Assembly."

"And Madame de Tourzel, my children's governess?" said the Queen.

"Yes, *Madame*; she will accompany you."

Roederer then left the King's chamber, where this conversation had taken place, and said in a loud voice to the persons crowding together in the Council Hall: "The King and his family are going to the Assembly without other attendants than the department, the ministers, and a guard." Then he asked: "Is the officer who commands the guard here?" This officer presenting himself, he said to him: "You must bring forward a double file of National Guards to accompany the King. The King desires it."

The officer replied: "It shall be done."

Louis XVI. came out of his chamber with his family. He waited several minutes in the hall until the guard should arrive, and, going around the circle composed of some forty or fifty persons belonging to his court: "Come, gentlemen," said he, "there is nothing more to do here."

The Queen, turning to Madame Campan, said: "Wait in my apartment; I will rejoin you or else send word to go I don't know where." Marie Antoinette took no one with her except the Princess de Lamballe and Madame de Tourzel. The Princess de Tarente and Madame de la Roche-Aymon, afflicted at the thought of being left at the Tuileries, went down with all the other ladies to the Queen's apartments on the ground-floor.

La Chesnaye, who had succeeded to the command of the National Guard in consequence of Mandat's death, put himself at the head of the escort. This was formed of detachments from the most loyal battalions, the *Petits-Pères*, the *Suite des Moulins*, and the *Filles-Saint-*

Thomas, re-enforced by about two hundred Swiss, commanded by the colonel of the regiment, Marquis de Maillardoz, and the major, Baron de Bachmann. The cortège reached the great staircase by way of the Council Hall, the Royal Bedchamber, the Œil-de-Boeuf, the Hall of the Guards, and the Hall of the Hundred Swiss. As he was passing through the Œil-de-Boeuf, Louis XVI. took the hat of the National Guard on his right, and replaced it by his own, which was adorned with white feathers. The guard, surprised, removed the King's hat from his head and carried it under his arm.

When Louis XVI. arrived at the foot of the stairs in the Pavilion of the Horloge, his thoughts recurred to the faithful adherents who had so uselessly devoted themselves to his defence, and whom he was leaving at the Tuileries without watchword or direction. "What is going to become of all those who have stayed upstairs?" said he.

"Sire," replied Roederer, "it seemed to me that they were all in coloured coats. Those who have swords need only lay them off, follow you, and go out through the garden."

"That is true," returned Louis XVI. In the vestibule, a little further on, as he was about to quit the fatal palace which fate had condemned him never to re-enter, he had a last moment of scruple and hesitation. He said again: "But after all, there are not many people on the *Carrousel*."

"True, Sire," replied Roederer; "but the *faubourgs* will soon arrive, and all the sections are armed, and have assembled at the municipality; besides, there are neither men enough here, nor are they determined enough to resist the actual gathering on the *Carrousel*, which has twelve pieces of artillery."

The die is cast; Louis XVI. abandons the Tuileries. Respect alone restrains the grief and indignation that move the Swiss soldiers and the noblemen whose weapons and whose blood have been refused. They looked down from the windows at the *cortège*, or better, the funeral procession of royalty. It was about seven o'clock in the morning. The escort was drawn up in two lines. The members of the department formed a circle around the royal family. Roederer walked first. Then came the King, with Bigot de Sainte-Croix, Minister of Foreign Affairs, at his side; the Queen followed, giving her left arm to M. du Bouchage, Minister of Marine, and her right hand to the *Dauphin*, who held Madame de Tourzel with the other; then Madame Royale and Madame Elisabeth, with De Joly, Minister of Justice; the Minister of War, D'Abancourt, leading the Princess de Lamballe. The Ministers of the Interior and of Taxes, Champion de Villeneuve and Le Roux de la Ville, closed the procession. The air was pure and the morning radiant. The sun lighted up the garden, the marble sculpture, and the sheets of water. Birds sang under the trees, and nature smiled on this day of mourning as if it were a festival.

Looking at the populace, Madame Elisabeth said: "All those people have gone astray; I should like them to be converted; I should not like them to be punished." Tears stood in the eyes of the little Madame Royale.

The Princess de Lamballe said mournfully: "We shall never return to the Tuileries!"

The Prince de Poix, the Duke de Choiseul, Counts d'Haussonville, de Vioménil, de Hervilly, and de Pont-l'Abbé, the Marquis de Briges, Chevalier de Fleurieu, Viscount de Saint-Priest, the Marquis de Nantouillet, MM. de Fresnes and de Salaignac, the King's equerries, and Saint-Pardoux, the equerry of Madame Elisabeth, followed the sad procession. They passed through the grand alley unobstructed as far as the parterres, then turned to the right, toward the alley of the chestnut trees. There a halt of some minutes occurred, in order to give time for warning the Assembly.

Louis XVI. looked down at a heap of dead leaves which had been swept up by the gardeners after a storm the night before. "There are a good many leaves," said the King; "they are falling early this year." It was only a few days before that Manuel had written in a journal that the King would not last until the falling of the leaves. Perhaps Louis XVI. remembered the prophecy of the revolutionist; the *Dauphin*, with the carelessness belonging to his age, amused himself by kicking about the dead leaves, the leaves that had fallen as his father's crown was falling at this moment.

Before the royal family could enter the Assembly chamber, it was necessary that the step the King had taken should be announced to the deputies. The president of the department undertook this commission. A deputation of twenty-four members was at once sent to meet Louis XVI. They found him in the large alley at the foot of the terrace of the Feuillants, a few steps from the staircase leading up to it, and which goes as far as the lobby through which one enters the hall occupied by the National Assembly. "Sire," said the leader of the deputation, "the Assembly, eager to contribute to your safety, offers to you and your family an asylum in its midst."

During this time, the terrace and the staircase had become thronged

191

by a furious crowd. A man carrying a long pole cried out in rage: "No, no; they shall not enter the Assembly. They are the cause of all our troubles. This must be ended. Down with them!"

Roederer, standing on the fourth step of the staircase, cried: "Citizens, I demand silence in the name of the law. You seem disposed to prevent the King and his family from entering the National Assembly; you are not justified in opposing it. The King has a place there in virtue of the Constitution; and though his family has none legally, they have just been authorized by a decree to go there. Here are the deputies sent to meet the King; they will attest the existence of this decree."

The deputies confirmed his words. Nevertheless, the crowd still hesitated to leave the way clear. The man with the pole kept on brandishing it, and crying: "Down with them! down with them!"

Roederer, going on to the terrace, snatched the pole and flung it into the garden. The crowd was so compact that in the midst of the squabble someone stole the Queen's watch and her purse. A man with a sinister face approached the *Dauphin*, took him from Marie Antoinette, and lifted him in his arms. The Queen uttered a cry. "Do not be frightened," said the man; "I will do him no harm."

Another person said to Louis XVI.: "Sire, we are honest men; but we are not willing to be betrayed any longer. Be a good citizen, and don't forget to drive away your shavelings and your wife." Insults and threats resounded from all sides. Finally, after an actual struggle, the royal family succeeded in opening a passage. They made their way with difficulty through the narrow lobby, choked with people, penetrated the crowd, and entered the session chamber. It was there that royalty, humiliated and overcome, was to lie at the point of death under the eyes of its implacable enemies.

29

The Box of the Logograph

The royal family has just entered the session chamber. It will find there not an asylum, but the vestibule of the prison and the scaffold. The man who had taken the *Dauphin* from the Queen's arms at the door of the Assembly set him down on the secretary's desk with an air of triumph, and the young Prince was greeted with applause. Marie Antoinette advanced with dignity. According to Vaublanc's expression, she would not have had a different bearing or a more august serenity on a day of royal pomp. Louis XVI. took a place near the president. The Queen, her daughter, Madame Elisabeth, and Madame de Tourzel sat down on the ministerial benches. As soon as the *Dauphin* was left to himself, he sprang towards his mother.

A voice cried: "Take him to the King! The Austrian woman is unworthy of the people's confidence." An usher attempted to obey this injunction. However, the child began to cry, people were affected, and he was allowed to remain with the Queen.

At this moment some armed noblemen made their appearance at the extremity of the hall. "You compromise the King's safety!" exclaimed someone, and the nobles retired.

Order was restored. Louis XVI. began to speak. "I came here," said he, "to prevent a great crime, and I think that I could be nowhere more secure than amidst the representatives of the nation." Alas! the crime will not be prevented, but only adjourned. Vergniaud occupied the president's chair.

"Sire," he replied, "you may count on the firmness of the National Assembly. It knows its duties; its members have sworn to die in defending the rights of the people and the constituted authorities."

So they still called Louis XVI. Sire; presently they will call him nothing but Louis Capet. They allow him to take an armchair near the president; but in a few minutes they will find this place too good for him. And it is the voice of this very Vergniaud who, a few hours from now, will pronounce his deposition, and five months later his sentence of death.

Hardly had the unhappy King sat down when Chabot, the unfrocked Capuchin, claimed that a clause of the Constitution forbade the Assembly to deliberate in presence of the sovereign. Under this pretext his place was changed, and Louis XVI. with all his family was shut up in the reporters' gallery, sometimes called the box of the Logograph. This miserable hole, about six feet high by twelve wide, was on a level with the last ranks of the Assembly, behind the president's chair and the seats of the secretaries.

It was ordinarily set apart for the editors, or rather for the stenographers of a great newspaper which reported the proceedings, and which was called the *Journal logographique*, or the *Logotachygraphe*, usually abbreviated into the *Logographe*. Louis XVI. seated himself in the front of the box, Marie Antoinette half-concealed herself in a corner, where she sought a little shelter against so many humiliations. Her children and their governess took places on a bench with Madame Elisabeth and the Princess de Lamballe. Several noblemen, the latest courtiers of misfortune, stood up behind them.

Roederer, who was at the bar, then made a report in the name of the municipal department, in which he explained all that had taken place. He declared that he had said to the soldiers and National Guard detailed for the defence of the Tuileries:

> We do not ask you to shed the blood of your brethren nor to attack your fellow-citizens; your cannons are there for your defence, not for an attack; but I require this defence in the name of the law, in the name of the Constitution. The law authorizes you, when violence is used against you, to repress it vigorously. ... Once more, you are not to be assailants, but to act on the defensive only.

Roederer added that the cannoneers, instead of complying with his urgent exhortations, gave no response save that of unloading their pieces before him. After having explained how greatly the defence was disorganized, he thus ended his report:

> We felt ourselves no longer in a position to protect the charge confided to us; this charge was the King; the King is a man; this man is a father. The children ask us to assure the existence of

the father; the law asks us to assure the existence of the King of France; humanity asks of us the existence of the man. No longer able to defend this charge, no other idea presented itself than that of entreating the King to come with his family to the National Assembly. . . . We have nothing to add to what I have just said, except that, our force being paralyzed, and no longer in existence, we can have none but that which it shall please the National Assembly to communicate. We are ready to die in the execution of the orders it may give us. We ask, while awaiting them, to remain near it, being useless everywhere else.

The Assembly, not then suspecting that it would so soon depose Louis XVI., applauded without contradiction from the galleries. The president said to Roederer: "The Assembly has listened to your account with the greatest interest; it invites you to be present at the session."

The advice given by Roederer to the King has been greatly blamed. The event has seriously influenced the judgment since passed upon it. If Louis XVI. had received the support he had a right to count on from the representatives, things would have appeared in quite another light.

Count de Vaublanc, in his *Memoirs*, has rendered full justice to the loyal intentions of the municipal attorney. "The advice he gave has been accounted a crime," says M. de Vaublanc; "I think it is an unjust reproach. Until then he had done all that lay in his power to contribute to the defence of the palace. He must have seen clearly that as the King would not defend himself, he could no longer be defended. If the rebels had been attacked, neither M. Roederer nor anyone else would have proposed going to the Assembly; but since they were on the defensive, and without any recognized leader, the magistrate might doubtless have been struck with a single thought: The King and his family are about to be massacred. The King put an end to all irresolution in saying these words: 'There is nothing more to do here.'"

At first, Louis XVI. seemed not to repent of the step he had been obliged to take. Even in that wretched hole, the Logograph box, his face at first was calm and even confident. As the shouting had increased outside, Vergniaud ordered the removal of the iron grating separating this box from the hall, so that in case the populace made an irruption into the lobbies, the King could take refuge in the midst of the deputies. In default of workmen and tools, the deputies nearest at hand, the Duke de Choiseul, Prince de Poix, and the ministers, undertook to tear away the grating, and Louis XVI. himself, accustomed to the rough work of a locksmith, joined his efforts to theirs. The fastenings having been broken in this manner, the unfortunate sovereign seemed not to doubt the sentiments of the National Assembly. He pointed out the most remarkable deputies to the *Dauphin*, chatted with several among them, and looked on at the session like a mere spectator in a box at the theatre.

The royal family had been nearly two hours at the Assembly when all of a sudden a frightful discharge of musketry and artillery was heard. The deputies of the left grew pale with fear and anger, thinking themselves betrayed. Casting glances of uneasiness and wrath at the feeble monarch, they accused him of having ordered a massacre, and said that all was lost. An officer of the National Guard rushed in, crying: "We are pursued, we are overpowered!" The galleries, affrighted, imagined that the Swiss would arrive at any moment. Excitement was at its height. Sinister, imposing, dreadful moment! Solemn hour, when the monarchy, amidst a frightful tempest, was like a venerable oak which lightning has just stricken; when terror, wrath, and pity disputed the possession of men's souls, and when the King, already captive, was present like Charles V. at his own funeral.

Marie Antoinette had started. At the sound of the cannon her cheeks kindled and her eyes blazed. A vague hope animated her. Perhaps, she said within herself, the monarchy is at last to be avenged; perhaps the Swiss are about to give the insurrection a lesson it will remember; perhaps Louis XVI. will re-enter in triumph the palace of his forefathers. The daughter of Cæsars prayed God in silence, and supplicated Him to grant victory to the defenders of the throne.

Chimeras! vain hopes! Louis XVI. has no longer but one idea: to cast off all responsibility for events. He mustered up, so to say, the little authority he had yet remaining, to write hastily, in pencil, the last order he was to sign: the order to stop firing. He flattered himself that the prohibition to shoot would justify him completely in the sight of the National Assembly, and induce them to treat him with more consideration. But he asked himself anxiously who would be bold enough to carry his order as far as the palace. Would not so perilous a mission intimidate even the most heroic?

M. d'Hervilly, who was at this moment in the box of the Logograph, offered himself. As the King and Queen at first refused his offer, and pointed out all the dangers of such an errand: "I beg Their Majesties," cried he, "not to think of my danger; my duty is to brave everything in their service; my place is in the midst of the firing, and if I were afraid of it I should be unworthy of my uniform."

These words determined Louis XVI. to give M. d'Hervilly the order signed by his own hand; the valiant nobleman, bearing this order which was to have such disastrous consequences for the defenders of the palace, went hastily out of the Assembly hall and made his way to the Tuileries through a rain of balls and canister.

30

The Combat

What had taken place at the Tuileries after the departure of the royal family for the Assembly? At the very moment when they abandoned this palace which they were never to see again, the Marseillais, the vanguard of the insurrection, were pounding at the gate of the principal courtyard, furious because it was not opened. A few minutes later, the column of the Faubourg Saint-Antoine, after passing through the rue Saint-Honoré, debouched on the Carrousel. It was under command of the Pole, Lazouski, and Westermann, who directed it toward the gate of the Royal Court. As the Marseillais had not yet succeeded in forcing this, Westermann had it broken open. The cannoneers, whose business it was to defend the palace, at once declared on the side of the riot and turned their pieces against the Tuileries. With the exception of the domestics there were now in the palace only the seven hundred and fifty Swiss, about a hundred National Guards, and a few nobles. The sole instructions the Swiss received came from old Marshal de Mailly: "Do not let yourselves be taken."

Louis XVI. had said absolutely nothing on going away, and his departure discouraged his most faithful adherents. Add to this that the Swiss had not enough cartridges. What was to be the fate of this fine regiment, this *corps d'élite*, which everywhere and always had set the example of discipline and military honour; which ever since the Revolution began had haughtily repulsed every attempt to tamper with it; and whose red uniforms alone struck terror into the populace? These brave soldiers guarded respectfully the traditions of their ancestors who, at the famous retreat of Meaux, had saved Charles IX.

"But for my good friends the Swiss," said that prince, "my life and liberty would have been in a bad way." What the Swiss of the sixteenth century had done for one King of France, the Swiss of the eighteenth century would have done for his successor. They would have saved Louis XVI. if he would have let himself be saved.

A major-general who had remained at the Tuileries, judging that it was impossible to defend the courts with so few soldiers, cried: "Gentlemen, retire to the palace!"

"They had to leave six cannon in the power of the enemy and to abandon the courts. It should have been foreseen that it would be necessary to retake these under penalty of being burned in the palace; the common soldiers said so loudly. Meanwhile they obeyed, and were disposed as well as time and the localities permitted. The stairs and windows were lined with soldiers." (Account of Colonel Pfyffer d'Altishoffen, published at Lucerne in 1819.)

One post occupied the chapel, and another the vestibule and grand staircase. There were Swiss also at the windows looking into the courts. "Down with the Swiss!" cried the Marseillais. "Down! down! Surrender!" However, the struggle had not yet begun. Nearly fifteen minutes elapsed between the invasion of the Royal Court and the first shot. The Marseillais brandished their pikes and guns, but they were not confident, for at first they dared not cross the court more than halfway. The Swiss and National Guards who were at the windows made gestures to induce the populace to quiet down and go away.

The throng of insurgents grew greater every minute. They had just got their cannon into battery against the Tuileries. What the Swiss specially intended was to defend the grand staircase, so as to prevent the apartments on the first floor from being invaded. This staircase, afterwards destroyed, was in the middle of the vestibule of the Horloge Pavilion. The chapel, whose site was afterwards changed, was on the level of the first landing; and from this landing, two symmetrical flights, at right angles with the first, led to the Hall of the Hundred Swiss (the future Hall of the Marshals). Westermann, bolder than the other insurgents, had advanced as far as the vestibule with several Marseillais. He began to parley with the soldiers, trying to set them against their officers and induce them to lay down their arms.

Sergeant Blazer answered Westermann: "We are Swiss, and the Swiss only lay down their weapons with their lives."

The officers caused a barricade of pieces of wood to be raised on the first landing at the head of the stairs, to prevent new deputations from coming to demoralize their men. The Marseillais attempted to take it by main force. Some of them were armed with halberds terminating in hooks. These they thrust below the barricade, trying to catch the men defending it. They seized an adjutant in this way and disarmed him. At the foot of the stairs "they seized the first Swiss sentry and afterwards five others. They laid hold of them with hooked pikes which they thrust into their coats and drew them forwards, disarming them at once of their sabres, guns, and cartridge-boxes, amidst shouts of laughter. Encouraged by the success of this forlorn hope, the whole crowd pressed towards the foot of the stairs and there massacred the five Swiss already taken and disarmed." (M. Peltier's *Relation*.) Then a pistol-shot was heard. From which side did it come? Was it the Marseillais who provoked the combat? Was it the Swiss who sought to avenge their comrades, the sentries? Whoever it was, this pistol-shot was the signal for the fight, which began about half-past ten in the morning.

At first the Swiss had the advantage. Every shot they fired from the windows told. Among the people crowding the courtyards were many who had not come to fight, but through mere curiosity. Pale with fright, they fled toward the Carrousel through the gate of the Royal Court, which was strewn in an instant with guns, pikes, and cartridge-boxes. Some of the insurgents fell flat on their faces and counterfeited death, rising occasionally and gliding along the walls to gain the sentry-boxes of the mounted sentinels as best they could. Even the majority of the cannoneers deserted their pieces and ran like the rest. The courts were cleared in an instant.

Two Swiss officers, MM. de Durler and de Pfyffer, instantly made a sortie at the head of one hundred and twenty soldiers, took four cannon, and found themselves once more masters of the door of the Royal Court. A detachment of sixty soldiers formed themselves into a hollow square before this door and kept up a rolling fire on the rioters remaining on the Carrousel until the place was completely swept. At the same time, on the side of the garden, another detachment of Swiss, under Count de Salis, seized three cannon and brought them to the palace gate. Napoleon, who witnessed the combat from a distance, says:

The Swiss handled their artillery with vigour; in ten minutes the Marseillais were chased as far as the rue de l'Echelle, and never came back until the Swiss were withdrawn by the King's order.

It was now, in fact, that M. d'Hervilly arrived, hatless and unarmed, through the fusillade of grape. They wanted to show him the dispositions they had just made on the garden side. "There is no question of that," said he; "you must go to the Assembly; it is the King's order."

The unfortunate soldiers flattered themselves that they might still be of use. "Yes, brave Swiss," cried Baron de Viomesnil, "go and find the King. Your ancestors did so more than once." In spite of their chagrin at abandoning the field of which they had just become masters, they obeyed. Their only thought was to repair to that Assembly where a last humiliation awaited them. The officers had the drums beat the call to arms, and, in spite of the rain of balls from every side, they succeeded in marshalling the soldiers as if for a dress parade in front of the palace, opposite the garden.

The signal for departure was given. An unforeseen peril was reserved for these heroes. The battalions of the National Guard, stationed at the door of the Pont Royal, at that of the Manège court, and the beginning of the terrace of the Feuillants, had stood still, with their weapons grounded, since the affray began. But hardly had the Swiss entered the grand alley than these battalions, neutral until now, detailed a number of individuals who hid behind the trees, and fired, with their muzzles almost touching the troops. On reaching the middle of the alley, the Swiss, who hardly deigned to return this fire, divided into two columns.

The first, turning to the right under the trees, went towards the staircase leading to the Assembly from the terrace of the Feuillants. The second, which followed at a short distance and acted as a rearguard, went on as far as the Place Louis XV., where it found the mounted *gendarmes*. If this body of cavalry had done its duty, it would have united with the Swiss. But, far from that, it declared for the insurrection, and sabred them. It is said that the officers and soldiers killed in this retreat across the garden were interred at the foot of the famous chestnut whose exceptional forwardness has earned the surname of the tree of March 20. Thus the Bonapartist tree of popular tradition owes its astonishing strength of vegetation solely to the human compost furnished by the corpses of the last defenders of royalty.

The first column, that which was on its way to the Assembly, presented itself resolutely in front of the terrace of the Feuillants, which was full of people. These took flight, and the Swiss entered the corridors of the Assembly. Carried away by his zeal, one of their officers, Baron de Salis, entered the hall with his naked sword in his hand. The left uttered a cry of affright. A deputy went out to order the commander, Baron de Durler, to make his troop lay down their arms. M.

de Durler, having refused, he was conducted to the King.

"Sire," said he, with sorrowful indignation, "they want me to lay down arms."

Louis XVI. responded: "Put them in the hands of the National Guard; I am not willing that brave men like you should perish."

To surrender arms! Did Louis XVI. fully comprehend that for soldiers like these such an outrage was a hundred times worse than death? The King's words were like a thunderbolt to them. They wept with rage. "But," said they, "even if we have no more cartridges, we can still defend ourselves with our bayonets!"

Such devotion, such courage, such discipline, such heroism to end like this! And yet the unfortunate Swiss, though grieved to the heart, resigned themselves to the last sacrifice their master required from their fidelity, laid down their arms, and were imprisoned in the ancient church of the Feuillants, to the number of about two hundred and fifty. It was all that remained of this magnificent regiment. The others had been killed in the garden or had their throats cut in the palace, and the greater part of the survivors were to be assassinated in the massacres of September.

Thus ended the French King's regiment of Swiss Guards, like one of those sturdy oaks whose prolonged existence has affronted so many storms, and which nothing but an earthquake can uproot. It fell the very day on which the ancient French monarchy also fell. It counted more than a century and a half of faithful services rendered to France. To destroy this worthy corps a combination of unfortunate events had been required; it had been necessary to deprive the Swiss of their artillery, their ammunition, their staff, and the presence of the King; to enfeeble them five days before the combat by sending away a detachment of three hundred men; to forbid the two hundred men who accompanied the King to the Assembly to fire a shot; to render useless the wise dispositions of MM. de Maillardoz and de Bachmann by an ill-advised order at the moment of the attack; and to have M. d'Hervilly come at the moment of victory to divide and enfeeble the defence. (*Relation* of Colonel Pfyffer d'Altishoffen.)

The Swiss republic has honoured the memory of these sons who died for a king. At the entrance of Lucerne, in the side of a rock, a grotto has been hollowed out, in which may be seen a colossal stone lion, the work of Thorwaldsen, the famous Danish sculptor. This lion, struck by a lance, and lying down to die, holds tight within his claws the royal *escutcheon* upon a shield adorned with *fleurs-de-lis*. Underneath the lion are engraved the names of the Swiss officers and soldiers who died between August 10 and September 2, 1792. Above it may be read this inscription cut in the rock:—

HELVETIORUM FIDEI AC VIRTUTI.
To the fidelity and courage of the Swiss.

Louis XVI. had to repent his weakness bitterly. The wretched monarch had at last reached the bottom of the abyss where the slippery descent of concessions ends, and for having been willing to spare the blood of a few criminals, he was to see that of his most loyal and faithful adherents shed in torrents.

It is said that Napoleon, who witnessed the combat from a distance, cried several times, in speaking of Louis XVI.:

What, then, wretched man! Have you no cannon to sweep out this rabble?

Behind the people of the 10th of August, the man of *Brumaire* already appeared as a conqueror.

Work away, then, insurgents! This unknown young man, this "straight-haired Corsican," hidden in the crowd, will be the master of you all! He will crush the Revolution, he will made himself all-powerful in that palace of the Tuileries where the riot is lording it at this moment! And after him, the brother of the King whom you insult today and will kill tomorrow, the Count de Provence, that *émigré* who is the object of your hatred, will triumphantly enter the palace of his forefathers. And each of them in his turn, the Corsican gentleman and the brother of Louis XVI., will be received with the same transports in that fatal palace which is now red with the blood of the Swiss! How surprised these people would be if they could foresee what the future has in store for them! Among these frenzied demagogues, these ultra-revolutionists, these dishevelled Marseillais with lips blackened by powder, and jackets all blood, how many will be the fanatical admirers and soldiers of a Cæsar!

31

The Results of the Combat

The results of the combat were, at the Assembly, the decree of suspension, or, rather, the decree of deposition; at the Tuileries, devasta-
tion, massacre, and conflagration. From the moment when he ordered
his last defenders to lay down their arms, Louis XVI. was but the
phantom of a king.

While the fight was going on, Robespierre had remained in hiding; Marat had not quitted the bottom of a cellar. Even Danton, the
man of "audacity," did not show himself until after the last shot had
been fired. But now that fate had declared for the Revolution, those
who were trembling and hesitating a moment since, were those who
talked the loudest. Louis XVI., who had been dreaded a few minutes
ago, was insulted and jeered at. The National Assembly, royalist in the
morning, became the accomplice of the republicans during the day. It
perceived, moreover, that the 10th of August was aimed at it not less
than at the throne, and that its own downfall would be contempora-
neous with that of royalty.

Huguenin, the president of the new Commune, came boldly to
the bar, and said to the deputies: "The people is your sovereign as well
as ours!"

Another individual, likewise at the bar, exclaimed in a menacing
tone:

For a long time the people has asked you to pronounce the
deposition, and you have not even yet pronounced the suspension! Know that the Tuileries is on fire, and that we shall not
extinguish it until the vengeance of the people has been satisfied!

Vergniaud, who in the morning had promised the King the support of the Assembly, no longer even attempted to stem the revolutionary tide. He came down from the president's chair, and went to a desk to write the decree which should give a legislative form to the will of the insurrection. In virtue of this decree, which Vergniaud read from the tribune, and which was unanimously adopted, the royal power was suspended and a National Convention convoked. In reality this was a veritable deposition, and yet the Assembly still hesitated to give the last shock which should uproot the royal tree that had sheltered beneath its branches so many faithful generations. It declared that in default of a civil list, a salary should be granted to the King during his suspension; that Louis XVI. and his family should have a palace, the Luxembourg, for a residence, and that he should be appointed governor of the Prince-royal.

Concerning this, Madame de Staël has remarked in her *Considerations sur les principaux événements de la Révolution française*: "Ambition for power mingled with the enthusiasm of principles in the republicans of 1792, and several among them offered to maintain royalty if all the ministerial places were given to their friends. . . . The throne they attacked served to shelter them, and it was not until after they had triumphed that they found themselves exposed before the people." What the Girondins wanted was merely a change in the ministry; it was not a revolution. Vergniaud felt that he had been distanced. When he read the act of deposition, his voice was sad, his attitude dejected, and his action feeble. Did he foresee that the King and himself would die at the same place, on the same scaffold, and only nine months apart?

Louis XVI. listened to the invectives launched against him, and to the decree depriving him of royal power, without a change of colour. At the very moment when the vote was taken, he bent towards Deputy Coustard, who sat beside the box of the *Logographe*, and said with the greatest tranquillity: "What you are doing there is not very constitutional." Impassive, and speaking of himself as of a king who had lived a thousand years before, he leaned his elbows on the front of the box, and looked on, like a disinterested spectator, at the lugubrious spectacle that was unrolled before him.

Marie Antoinette, on the contrary, was shuddering. So long as the combat lasted, a secret hope had thrilled her. But when she saw them bringing to the Assembly and laying on the table the jewel-cases, trinkets, and portfolios which the insurgents had just taken from her bedroom at the Tuileries; when she heard the victorious cries of the rioters; when Vergniaud's voice sounded in her ears like a funeral knell—she could hardly contain her grief and indignation. For one instant she closed her eyes. But presently she haughtily raised her head.

The tide was rising, rising incessantly. Petitioners demanded sometimes the deposition, and sometimes the death, of the King. This dialogue was overheard between the painter David and Merlin de Thionville, who were talking together about Louis XVI.: "Would you believe it? Just now he asked me, as I was passing his box, if I would soon have his portrait finished."

"Bah! and what did you say?"

"That I would never paint the portrait of a tyrant again until I should have his head in my hat."

"Admirable! I don't know a more sublime answer, even in antiquity."

The demands of the Revolution grew greater from minute to minute. In the decree of deposition which had been voted on Vergniaud's proposition, it was stipulated that the ministers should continue to exercise their functions. A few instants later, Brissot caused it to be decreed that they had lost the nation's confidence. A new ministry was nominated during the session. The three ministers dismissed before June 20—Roland, Clavière, and Servan—were reinstalled by acclamation in the ministries of the Interior, of Finances, and of War. The other ministers were chosen by ballot: Danton was nominated to that of Justice by 282 votes, Monge to the Marine by 150, and Lebrun-Tondu to Foreign Affairs by 100. This ballot established the fact that out of the 749 members composing the Assembly, but 284 were present.

Two days before, 680 had voted on the question concerning Lafayette, and now, at the moment of the final crisis, not more than 284 could be found! All the others had disappeared, through fear or through disgust. The Revolution was accomplished by an Assembly thus reduced, and a Commune whose members had appointed themselves. Marie Antoinette, in her pride as Queen, was unable to conceive that there could be anything serious in such a government. When Lebrun-Tondu's appointment was announced, she leaned towards Bigot de Sainte-Croix, and said in his ear: "I hope you will none the less believe yourself Minister of Foreign Affairs."

The unfortunate royal family were still prisoners in the narrow box of the *Logographe*. The heat there was horrible: the sun scorched the white walls of this furnace where the captives listened, as in a place of torture, to the most ignoble insults and the most sanguinary threats.

At seven o'clock in the evening, Count François de la Rochefoucauld succeeded in approaching the box of the *Logographe*. He thus describes its aspect at this hour: "I approached the King's box; it was unguarded except by some wretches who were drunk and paid no attention to me, so that I half-opened the door. I saw the King with a fatigued and downcast face; he was sitting on the front of the box, coldly observing through his *lorgnette* the scoundrels who were talking, sometimes one after another, and sometimes all together.

Near him was the Queen, whose tears and perspiration had completely drenched her *fichu* and her handkerchief. The *Dauphin* was asleep on her lap, and resting partly also on that of Madame de Tourzel. Mesdames Elisabeth, de Lamballe, and Madame the King's daughter were at the back of the box. I offered my services to the King, who replied that it would be too dangerous to try to see him again, and added that he was going to the Luxembourg that evening. The Queen asked me for a handkerchief; I had none; mine had served to bind up the wounds of the Viscount de Maillé, whom I had rescued from some pikemen. I went out to look for a handkerchief, and borrowed one from the keeper of the refreshment-room; but as I was taking it to the Queen, the sentinels were relieved, and I found it impossible to approach the box."

We have just seen what occurred at the Assembly after the close of the combat. Cast now a glance at the Tuileries. What horrible scenes, what cries of grief, how many wounded, dead, and dying, what streams of blood! What had become of those Swiss who, either in consequence of their wounds, or through some other motive, had been obliged to remain at the palace? Eighty of them had defended the grand staircase like heroes, against an immense crowd, and died after prodigies of valour. Seventeen Swiss who were posted in the chapel, and who had not fired a shot since the fight began, hoped to save their lives by laying down their arms. It was a mistake. They had their throats cut like the others. Two ushers of the King's chamber, MM. Pallas and de Marchais, sword in hand, and hats pulled down over their eyes, said: "We don't want to live any longer; this is our post; we ought to die here!" and they were killed at the door of their master's chamber.

M. Dieu died in the same way on the threshold of the Queen's bedroom. A certain number of nobles who had not followed the King to the Assembly succeeded in escaping the blows of the assassins. Passing through the suite of large apartments towards the Louvre Gallery, they rejoined there some soldiers detailed to guard an opening contrived in the flooring, so as to prevent the assailants from entering by that way. They crossed this opening on boards, and reached the extremity of the gallery unhindered; then, going down the staircase of Catharine de Medici, they managed to gain the streets near the Louvre. These may have been saved. But woe to all men, no matter what their conditions, who remained in the Tuileries! Domestic servants, ushers, labourers, every soul was put to death. They killed even the dying, even the surgeons who were caring for the wounded.

It is Barbaroux himself who describes the murderers as "cowardly fugitives during the action, assassins after the victory, butchers of dead bodies which they stabbed with their swords so as to give themselves the honours of the combat. In the apartments, on roofs, and in cellars, they massacred the Swiss, armed or disarmed, the chevaliers, soldiers, and all who peopled the *château* . . . Our devotion was of no avail," says Barbaroux again; "we were speaking to men who no longer recognized us."

And the women, what was their fate? When the firing began, the Queen's ladies and the Princesses descended to Marie Antoinette's apartments on the ground-floor. They closed the shutters, hoping to incur less danger, and lighted a candle so as not to be in total darkness. Then Mademoiselle Pauline de Tourzel exclaimed: "Let us light all the candles in the chandelier, the sconces, and the torches; if the brigands force open the door, the astonishment so many lights will cause them may delay the first blow and give us time to speak."

The ladies set to work. When the invaders broke in, sabre in hand, the numberless lights, which were repeated also in the mirrors, made such a contrast with the daylight they had just left, that for a moment they remained stupefied. And yet, the Princess de Tarente, Madame de La Roche-Aymon, Mademoiselle de Tourzel, Madame de Ginestons, and all the other ladies were about to perish when a man with a long beard made his appearance, crying to the assassins in Pétion's name: "Spare the women; do not dishonour the nation."

Madame Campan had attempted to go up a stairway in pursuit of her sister. The murderers followed her. She already felt a terrible hand against her back, trying to seize her by her clothes, when someone cried from the foot of the stairs: "What are you doing up there?"

"Hey!" said the murderer, in a tone that did not soon leave the trembling woman's ears.

The other voice replied: "We don't kill women."

The Revolution goes fast; it will kill them next year. Madame Campan was on her knees. Her executioner let go his hold. "Get up, hussy," he said to her, "the nation spares you!"

In going back she walked over corpses; she recognized that of the old Viscount de Broves. The Queen had sent word to him and to another old man as the last night began, that she desired them to go home. He had replied: "We have been only too obedient to the King's orders in all circumstances when it was necessary to expose our lives to save him; this time we will not obey, and will simply preserve the memory of the Queen's kindness."

What a sight the Tuileries presented! People walked on nothing but dead bodies. A comic actor drank a glass of blood, the blood of a Swiss; one might have thought himself at a feast of Atreus. The furniture was broken, the secretaries forced open, the mirrors smashed to pieces. Prudhomme, the journalist of the *Révolutions de Paris*, thinks that "Medicis-Antoinette has too long studied in them the hypocritical look she wears in public."

What a sinister carnival! Drunken women and prostitutes put on the Queen's dresses and sprawl on her bed. Through the cellar gratings one can see a thousand hands groping in the sand, and drawing forth bottles of wine. Everywhere people are laughing, drinking, killing. The royal wine runs in streams. Torrents of wine, torrents of blood. The apartments, the staircase, the vestibule, are crimson pools. Disfigured corpses, pictures thrust through with pikes, musicians' stands thrown on the altar, the organ dismounted, broken,—that is how the chapel looks. But to rob and murder is not enough: they will kindle a conflagration. It devours the stables of the mounted guards, all the buildings in the courts, the house of the governor of the palace: eighteen hundred yards of barracks, huts, and houses.

Already the fire is gaining on the Pavilion of Marsan and the Pavilion of Flora. The flames are perceived at the Assembly. A deputy asks to have the firemen sent to fight this fire which threatens the whole quarter Saint-Honoré. Somebody remarks that this is the Commune's business. But the Commune, to use a phrase then in vogue, thinks it has something else to do besides preventing the destruction of the tyrant's palace. It turns a deaf ear. The messenger returns to the Assembly. It is remarked that the flames are doing terrible damage. The president decides to send orders to the firemen. But the firemen return, saying: "We can do nothing. They are firing on us. They want to throw us into the fire."

What is to be done? The president bethinks himself of a "patriot" architect, Citizen Palloy, who generally makes his appearance whenever there are "patriotic" demolitions to be accomplished. It is he whom they send to the palace, and who succeeds in getting the flames extinguished. The Tuileries are not burned up this time. The work of the incendiaries of 1792 was only to be finished by the *petroleurs* of 1871.

Night was come. A great number of the Parisian population were groaning, but the revolutionists triumphed with joy. Curiosity to see the morning battle-field, urged the indolent, who had stayed at home all day, towards the quays, the Champs-Elysées, and the Tuileries. They looked at the trees under which the Swiss had fallen, at the windows of the apartments where the massacres had taken place, at the ravages made by the hardly extinguished fire. The buildings in the three courts: Court of the Princes, Court Royal, Court of the Swiss, had been completely consumed. Thenceforward these three courts formed only one, separated from the *Carrousel* by a board partition which remained until 1800, and was replaced by a grating finished on the very day when the First Consul came to install himself at the Tuileries. The inscription which was placed above the wooden partition: "*On August 10 Royalty was abolished; it will never rise again*," disappeared even before the proclamation of the Empire.

Squads of labourers gathered up the dead bodies and threw them into tumbrels. At midnight an immense pile was erected on the Carrousel with timbers and furniture from the palace. There the corpses of the victims that had strewed the courts, the vestibule, and the apartments were heaped up, and set on fire.

The National Guard had disappeared; it figured with the King and the Assembly itself, among the vanquished of the day. Instead of its bayonets and uniforms one saw nothing in the stations and patrols that divided Paris but pikes and tatters. "Someone came to tell me," relates Madame de Staël, "that all of my friends who had been on guard outside the palace, had been seized and massacred. I went out at once to learn the news; the coachman who drove me was stopped at the bridge by men who silently made signs that they were murdering on the other side. After two hours of useless efforts to pass I learned that all those in whom I was interested were still living, but that most of them had been obliged to hide in order to escape the proscription with which they were threatened. When I went to see them in the evening, on foot, and in the mean houses where they had been able to find shelter, I found armed men lying before the doors, stupid with drink, and only half waking to utter execrable curses. Several women of the people were in the same state, and their vociferations were more odious still. Whenever a patrol intended to maintain order made its appearance, honest people fled out of its way; for what they called maintaining order was to contribute to the triumph of assassins and rid them of all hindrances."

At last the city was going to rest a while after so much emotion! It was three o'clock in the morning. The Assembly, which had been in session for twenty-four hours, adjourned. Only a few members remained in the hall to maintain the permanence proclaimed at the beginning of the crisis. The inspectors of the hall came for Louis XVI. and his family, to conduct them, not to the Luxembourg, but to the upper story of the convent of the Feuillants, above the corridor where the offices and committees of the Assembly had been established. It was there, in the cells of the monks, that the royal family were to pass the night. Then all was silent once more. Royalty was dying!

32

The Royal-Family in the Convent of the Feuillants

What a strange prison was this dilapidated old monastery, these little cells, not lived in for two years, with their flooring half-destroyed, and their narrow windows looking down into courts full of men drunken with wine and blood! By the light of candles stuck into gun-barrels the royal family entered this gloomy lodging. Trembling for her son, who was frightened, the Queen took him from M. Aubier's arms and whispered to him. The child grew calmer. "Mamma," said he, "has promised to let me sleep in her room because I was very good before all those wicked men."

Four cells, all opening by similar small doors upon the same corridor, comprised the quarters of the royal family. What a night! The souvenirs of the previous day came back like dismal dreams. Their ears were still deafened with furious cries. They seemed to see the blood of the Swiss flowing like a torrent, the pyramids of corpses in red uniforms, the flames of the terrible conflagration sweeping the approaches to the Tuileries. Marie Antoinette seems under an hallucination; her emotions break her down. Is this woman, confided to the care of an unknown servant, in this deserted old convent, really she? Is this the Queen of France and Navarre? This the daughter of the great Empress Maria Theresa? What uncertainty rests over the fate of her most faithful servitors! What news will she yet learn? Who has fallen? Who has survived the carnage? The hours of the night wear on; Marie Antoinette has not been able to sleep a moment.

The Marquis de Tourzel and M. d'Aubier remained near the King's bedside. Before sleeping, he talked to them with the utmost calmness of all that had taken place. "People regret," said he, "that I did not have

212

the rebels attacked before they could have forced the Assembly; but besides the fact that in accordance with the terms of the Constitution, the National Guards might have refused to be the aggressors, what would have been the result of this attack? The measures of the insurrection were too well taken for my party to have been victorious, even if I had not left the Tuileries. Do they forget that when the seditious Commune massacred M. Mandat, it rendered his projected defence of no avail?"While Louis XVI. was saying this, the men placed under the windows were shouting loudly for the Queen's head. "What has she done to them?" cried the unfortunate sovereign.

The next morning, August 11, several persons were authorized to enter the cells of the convent. Among them was one of the officers of the King's bedchamber, François Hue, who had incurred the greatest dangers on the previous day. Cards of admission were distributed by the inspector of the Assembly hall. A large guard was stationed at all the issues of the corridor. No one could pass without being stopped and questioned. After surmounting all obstacles, M. Hue reached the cell of Louis XVI.

The King was still in bed, with his head covered by a coarse cloth. He looked tenderly at his faithful servant. M. Hue, who could scarcely speak for sobbing, apprised his unhappy master of the tragic death of several persons whom His Majesty was especially fond of, among others, the Chevalier d'Allonville, who had been under-governor to the first *Dauphin*, and several officers of the bedchamber: MM. Le Tellier, Pallas, and de Marchais. "I have, at least," said Louis XVI., "the consolation of seeing you saved from this massacre!"

All night long, Madame Elisabeth, the Princess de Lamballe, and Madame de Tourzel had prayed and wept in silence at the door of the chamber where Marie Antoinette watched beside her sleeping children. It was not until morning, after cruel insomnia, that the wretched Queen was at last able to close her eyes. And when, after a few minutes, she opened them again, what an awakening!

At eight o'clock in the morning Mademoiselle Pauline de Tourzel arrived at the Feuillants. "I cannot say enough," she writes in her *Souvenirs de Quarante Ans*, "about the goodness of the King and Queen; they asked me many questions about the persons concerning whom I could give them any tidings. *Madame* and the *Dauphin* received me with touching signs of affection; they embraced me, and *Madame* said: 'My dear Pauline, do not leave us anymore!'"

The courtiers of misfortune came one after another. Madame

Campan and her sister, Madame Auguié, saw the Prince de Poix, M. d'Aubier, M. de Saint-Pardou, Madame Elisabeth's equerry, MM. de Goguelat, Hue, and de Chamilly in the first cell; in the second they found the King. They wanted to kiss his hand, but he prevented it, and embraced them without speaking. In the third cell they saw the Queen, waited on by an unknown woman. Marie Antoinette held out her arms. "Come!" she cried; "come, unhappy women! come and see one who is still more unhappy than you, since it is she who has been the cause of all your sorrow!"

She added:

We are ruined. We have reached the place at last to which they have been leading us for three years by every possible outrage; we shall succumb in this horrible revolution, and many others will perish after us. Everybody has contributed to our ruin: the innovators like fools, others like the ambitious, in order to aid their own fortunes; for the most furious of the Jacobins wanted gold and places, and the crowd expected pillage. There is not a patriot in the whole infamous horde; the emigrants had their schemes and manoeuvres; the foreigners wanted to profit by the dissensions of France; everybody has had a part in our misfortunes.

Here the *Dauphin* entered with his sister and Madame de Tourzel. "Poor children!" cried the Queen. "How cruel it is not to transmit to them so noble a heritage, and to say: All is over for us!" And as the little *Dauphin*, seeing his mother and those around her weeping, began to shed tears also: "My child," the Queen said, embracing him, "you see I have consolations too; the friends whom misfortune deprived me of were not worth as much as those it gave me." Then Marie Antoinette asked for news of the Princess de Tarente, Madame de la Roche-Aymon, and others whom she had left at the Tuileries. She compassionated the fate of the victims of the previous day.

Madame Campan expressed a desire to know what the foreign ambassadors had done in this catastrophe. The Queen replied that they had done nothing, but that the English ambassadress, Lady Sutherland, had just displayed some interest by sending linen for the *Dauphin*, who was in need of it.

What memories must not that little cell in the Feuillants convent have left in the souls of those who were privileged to present there the homage of their devotion to the Queen! "I think I still see," Madame

Campan has said in her *Memoirs*, "I shall always see, that little cell, hung with green paper, that wretched couch from which the dethroned sovereign stretched out her arms to us, saying that our woes, of which she was the cause, aggravated her own. There, for the last time, I saw the tears flowing and heard the sobs of her whose birth and natural gifts, and above all the goodness of whose heart had destined her to be the ornament of all thrones and the happiness of all peoples."

During the 11th and 12th of August the tortures of the 10th were renewed for the royal family. They were obliged to occupy the odious box of the *Logographe* during the sessions of the Assembly, and from there witness, as at a show, the slow and painful death-struggle of royalty. As she was on her way to this wretched hole, Marie Antoinette perceived in the garden some curious spectators on whose faces a certain compassion was depicted. She saluted them. Then a voice cried: "Don't put on so many airs with that graceful head; it is not worthwhile. You'll not have it much longer."

From the box of the *Logographe* the royal family listened to the most offensive motions; to decrees according the Marseillais a payment of thirty *sous* a day, ordering all statues of kings to be overthrown, and petitions demanding the heads of all the Swiss who had escaped the massacre. At last the Assembly grew tired of the long humiliation of the august captives.

On Monday, August 13, they were not present at the session, and during the day they were notified that in the evening they were to be incarcerated, not in the Luxembourg,—that palace being too good for them,—but in the tower of the Temple. When Marie Antoinette was informed of this decision, she turned toward Madame de Tourzel, and putting her hands over her eyes, said: "I always asked the Count d'Artois to have that villanous tower of the Temple torn down; it always filled me with horror!"

Pétion told Louis XVI. that the Communal Council had decreed that none of the persons proposed for the service of the royal family should follow them to their new abode. By force of remonstrance the King finally obtained permission that the Princess de Lamballe, Madame de Tourzel and her daughter should be excepted from this interdiction, and also MM. Hue and de Chamilly, and Mesdames Thibaud, Basire, Navarre, and Saint-Brice. The departure for the Temple took place at five in the evening. The royal family went in a large carriage with Manuel and Pétion, who kept their hats on.

The coachman and footmen, dressed in gray, served their masters for the last time. National Guards escorted the carriage on foot and with reversed arms. The passage through a hostile multitude occupied not less than two hours. The vehicle, which moved very slowly, stopped for several moments in the Place Vendôme. There Manuel pointed out the statue of Louis XIV., which had been thrown down from its pedestal.

At first the descendant of the great King reddened with indignation, then, tranquillizing himself instantly, he calmly replied: "It is fortunate, Sir, that the rage of the people spends itself on inanimate objects." Manuel might have gone on to say that on this very Place Vendôme "Queen Violet," one of the most furious vixens of the October Days, had just been crushed by the fall of this equestrian statue of Louis XIV. to which she was hanging in order to help bring it down. The statue of Henry IV. in the Place Royale, that of Louis XIII. in the Place des Victoires, and that of Louis XV. in the place that bears his name, had fallen at the same time.

The royal family arrived at the Temple at seven in the evening. The lanterns placed on the projecting portions of the walls and the battlements of the great tower made it resemble a catafalque surrounded by funeral lights. The Queen wore a shoe with a hole in it, through which her foot could be seen. "You would not believe," said she, smiling, "that a Queen of France was in need of shoes." The doors closed upon the captives, and a sanguinary crowd complained of the thickness of the walls separating them from their prey.

33

The Temple

There are places which, by the very souvenirs they evoke, seem fatal and accursed. Such was the dungeon that was to serve as a prison for Louis XVI. and his family. The great tower for which Marie Antoinette had felt a nameless instinctive repugnance in the happiest days of her reign, arose at the extremity of Paris like a gigantic phantom, and recalled in a sinister fashion the tragedies of the Middle Ages and the sombre legends of the Templars. It was formerly the manor, the fortress, of that religious and military Order of the Temple, founded in the Holy Land at the beginning of the twelfth century, to protect the pilgrims, and which, after the fall of the Kingdom of Jerusalem, had spread all over Europe. The great tower was built by Frère Hubert, in the early years of the thirteenth century, in the midst of an enclosure surrounded by turreted walls. There ruled, by cross and sword, those men of iron, in white habits, who took the triple vows of poverty, chastity, and obedience, and who excited royal jealousy by the increase of their power.

It was there that Philippe le Bel went on October 13, 1307, with his lawyers and his archers, to lay his hand on the grand-master, seize the treasures of the order, and on the same day, at the same hour, cause all Templars to be arrested throughout the realm. Then began that mysterious trial which has remained an insoluble problem to posterity, and after which these monastic knights, whose bravery and whose exploits have made so prolonged an echo, perished in prisons or on scaffolds. Pursued by horrible accusations, they had confessed under torture, but they denied at execution.

When the grand-master, Jacques de Molay, and the commander of Normandy were burned alive before the garden of Philippe le Bel, March 11, 1314, even in the midst of flames, they did not cease to attest the innocence of the Order of the Temple. The people, astonished by their heroism, believed that they had summoned the Pope and the King to appear in the presence of God before the end of the year. Clement V., on April 20, and Philippe IV., on November 29, obeyed the summons.

The possessions of the order were given to the Hospitallers of Saint John of Jerusalem, who transformed themselves into Knights of Malta toward the middle of the sixteenth century. The Temple became the provincial house of the grand-prior of the Order of Malta for the *nation* or *language* of France, and the great tower contained successively the treasure, the arsenal, and the archives. In 1607, the grand-prior, Jacques de Souvré, had a house built in front of the old manor, between the court and the garden, which was called the palace of the grand-prior. His successor, Philippe de Vendôme, made his palace a rendezvous of elegance and pleasure.

There shone that *Anacreon* in a cassock, the gay and sprightly Abbé de Chaulieu, who died a fervent Christian in the voluptuous abode where he had dwelt a careless Epicurean. There young Voltaire went to complete the lessons he had begun in the sceptical circle of Ninon de l'Enclos. The office of grand-prior, which was worth sixty thousand *livres* a year, passed afterwards to Prince de Conti, who in 1765 sheltered Jean-Jacques Rousseau there, as *lettres de cachet* could not penetrate within its privileged precinct. Under Louis XVI. the palace of the grand-prior had served as a passing hostelry to the young and brilliant Count d'Artois when he came from Versailles to Paris. The flowers of the entertainments given there by the Prince were hardly faded when Louis XVI. suddenly entered it as a prisoner.

It was seven o'clock in the evening when the wretched King and his family, coming from the convent of the Feuillants, arrived at the Temple. Situated near the Faubourg Saint-Antoine, not far from the former site of the Bastille, the Temple enclosure at this period was not more than two hundred yards long by nearly as many wide. The rest of the ancient precinct had disappeared under the pavements or the houses of the great city. Nevertheless, the enclosure still formed a sort of little private city, sometimes called the Ville-Neuve-du-Temple, the gates of which were closed every night. In one of its angles stood the house called the grand-prior's palace.

This was the first stopping-place of the royal family, which had been entrusted by Pétion to the surveillance of the municipality and the guard of Santerre. The municipal officers stayed close to the King, kept their hats on, and gave him no title except *"Monsieur."* Louis XVI., not doubting that the palace of the grand-prior was the residence assigned him by the nation until the close of his career, began to visit its apartments. While the municipal officers took a cruel pleasure in this error, thinking of the still keener one they would enjoy when they disabused him of it, he pleased himself by allotting the different rooms in advance. The word palace had an unpleasant sound to the persecutors of royalty.

The Temple tower looked more like a prison. Toward eleven o'clock, one of the commissioners ordered the august captives to collect such linen and other clothing as they had been able to procure, and follow him. They silently obeyed, and left the palace. The night was very dark. They passed through a double row of soldiers holding naked sabres. The municipal officers carried lanterns. One of them broke the dismal silence he had observed throughout the march. "Thy master," said he to M. Hue, "has been accustomed to gilded canopies. Very well! he is going to find out how we lodge the assassins of the people."

The lamps in the windows of the old quadrangular dungeon lighted up its high pinnacles and turrets, its gigantic profile and gloomy bulk. The immense tower, one hundred and fifty feet high, and with walls nine feet thick, rose, menacing and fatal, amidst the darkness. Beside it was another tower, narrower and not so high, but which was also flanked by turrets. Thus the whole dungeon was composed of two distinct yet united towers. The second of these, called the little tower, to distinguish it from the great one, was selected as the prison of the former hosts of Versailles, Fontainebleau, and the Tuileries.

The little tower of the Temple, which had no interior communication with the great one against which it stood, was a long quadrangle flanked by two turrets. Four steps led to the door, which was low and narrow, and opened on a landing at the end of which began a winding staircase shaped like a snail-shell. Wide from its base as far as the first story, it grew narrower as it climbed up into the second. The door, which was considered too weak, was to be strengthened on the following day by heavy bars, and supplied with an enormous lock brought from the prisons of the Châtelet.

The Queen was put on the second floor, and the King on the third. On entering his chamber, Louis XVI. found a miserable bed in an alcove without tapestry or curtains. He showed neither ill humour nor surprise. Engravings, indecent for the most part, covered the walls.

He took them down himself. "I will not leave such objects before my children's eyes," said he. Then he lay down and slept tranquilly.

The first days of captivity were relatively calm. The prisoners consoled themselves by their family life, reading, and, above all, prayer. Forgetting that he had been a king, and remembering that he was a father, Louis XVI. gave lessons to the *Dauphin*. "It would have been worthwhile for the whole nation to be present at these lessons; they would have been both surprised and touched at all the sensible, cordial, and kindly things the good King found to say when the map of France lay spread out before him, or concerning the chronology of his predecessors. Everything in his remarks showed the love he bore his subjects and how greatly his paternal heart desired their happiness. What great and useful lessons one could learn in listening to this captive king instructing a child born to the throne and condemned to share the captivity of his parents." (*Souvenirs de Quarante Ans*, by Madame de Béarn, *née* de Tourzel.)

All those who had been authorized to follow the royal family to the Temple—the Princess de Lamballe, Madame de Tourzel and her daughter, Mesdames Thibaud, Basire, Navarre, MM. de Chamilly and François Hue—surrounded the captives with the most respectful and devoted attentions. But these noble courtiers of misfortune, these voluntary prisoners who were so glad to be associated in their master's trials, were not long to enjoy an honour they had so keenly desired. In the night of August 18-19, two municipal officers presented themselves, who were commissioned to fetch away "all persons not belonging to the Capet family." The Queen pointed out in vain that the Princess de Lamballe was her relative. The Princess must go with the others.

"In our position," has said Madame de Tourzel, the governess of the children of France, "there was nothing to do but obey. We dressed ourselves and then went to the Queen, to whom I resigned that dear little Prince, whose bed had been carried into her room without awaking him." It was an indescribable torture for Madame de Tourzel to abandon the *Dauphin*, whom she cherished so tenderly, and whom she had educated since 1789.

"I abstained from looking at him," she adds, "not only to avoid weakening the courage we had so much need of, but in order to give no room for censure, and so come back, if possible, to a place we left with so much regret. The Queen went instantly into the chamber of the Princess de Lamballe, from whom she parted with the utmost grief. To Pauline and me she showed a touching sensibility, and said to me in an undertone: 'If we are not so happy as to see you again, take good care of Madame de Lamballe. Do the talking on all important occasions, and spare her as much as possible from having to answer captious and embarrassing questions.'"

The two municipal officers said to Hue and Chamilly: "Are you the *valets-de-chambre?*" On their affirmative response, the two faithful servants were ordered to get up and prepare for departure. They shook hands with each other, both of them convinced that they had reached the end of their existence.

One of the municipal officers had said that very day in their presence: "The guillotine is permanent, and strikes with death the pretended servants of Louis." When they descended to the Queen's antechamber, a very small room in which the Princess de Lamballe slept, they found that Princess and Madame de Tourzel all ready to start, and clasped in one embrace with the Queen, the children, and Madame Elisabeth. Tender and heart-breaking farewells, presages of separations more cruel still!

All these exiles from the prison left at the same time. Only one of them, M. François Hue, was to return. He was examined at the Hôtel-de-Ville, and at the close of this interrogation an order was signed permitting him to be taken back to the tower. "How happy I was," he writes, "to return to the Temple! I ran to the King's chamber. He was already up and dressed, and was reading as usual in the little tower. The moment he saw me, his anxiety to know what had occurred made him advance toward me; but the presence of the municipal officers and the guards who were near him made all conversation impossible. I indicated by a glance that, for the moment, prudence forbade me to explain myself. Feeling the necessity of silence as well as myself, the King resumed his reading and waited for a more opportune moment. Some hours later, I hastily informed him what questions had been asked me and what I had replied." (*Dernières Années de Louis XVI., par François Hue.*)

The unfortunate sovereign doubtless believed that the others were also about to return. Vain hope! During the day Manuel announced to the King that none of them would come back to the Temple.

"What has become of them?" asked Louis XVI. anxiously.

"They are prisoners at the Force," returned Manuel.

"What are they going to do with the only servant I have left?" asked the King, glancing at M. Hue.

"The Commune leaves him with you," said Manuel; "but as he cannot do everything, men will be sent to assist him."

"I do not want them," replied Louis XVI.; "what he cannot do, we will do ourselves. Please God, we will not voluntarily give those who have been taken from us the chagrin of seeing their places taken by others!"

In Manuel's presence, the Queen and Madame Elisabeth aided M. Hue to prepare the things most necessary for the new prisoners of the Force. The two Princesses arranged the packets of linen and other matters with the skill and activity of chambermaids.

Behold the heir of Louis XIV., the King of France and Navarre, with but a single servant left him! He has but one coat, and at night his sister mends it. Behold the daughter of the German Cæsars, with not even one woman to wait upon her, and who waits on herself, incessantly watched, meanwhile, by the inquisitors of the Commune; who cannot speak a word or make a gesture unwitnessed by a squad of informers who pursue her even into the chamber where she goes to change her dress, and who spy on her even when she is sleeping! And yet neither the calmness nor the dignity of the prisoners suffers any loss.

There was but one thing that keenly annoyed Louis XVI. It was when, on August 24, they deprived him, the chief of gentlemen, of his sword, as if taking away his sceptre were not enough. He consoled himself by prayer, meditation, and reading. He spent hours in the room containing the library of the keeper of archives of the Order of Malta, who had previously occupied the little tower. One day when he was looking for books, he pointed out to M. Hue the works of Voltaire and Jean-Jacques Rousseau. "Those two men have ruined France," said he in an undertone.

On another day he was pained by overhearing the insults heaped on this faithful servant by one of the Municipal Guards. "You have had a great deal to suffer today," he said to him. "Well! for the love of me, continue to endure everything; make no answer."

At another time he slipped into his hand a folded paper. "This is some of my hair," said he; "it is the only present I can give you at this moment."

M. Hue exclaims in his pathetic book:

O shade forever cherished! I will preserve this precious gift to my latest day! The inheritance of my son, it will pass on to my descendants, and all of them will see in this testimonial of Louis

XVI.'s goodness, that they had a father who merited the affection of his King by his fidelity.

In the evenings the Queen made the *Dauphin* recite this prayer:

Almighty God, who created and redeemed me, I adore Thee. Spare the lives of the King, my father, and those of my family! Defend us against our enemies! Grant Madame de Tourzel the strength she needs to support the evils she endures on our account.

And the angel of the Temple, Madame Elisabeth, recited every day this sublime prayer of her own composition:

What will happen to me today, O my God! I do not know. All I know is, that nothing will happen that has not been foreseen by Thee from all eternity. It is enough, my God, to keep me tranquil. I adore Thy eternal designs, I submit to them with my whole heart; I will all, I accept all; I sacrifice all to Thee; I unite this sacrifice to that of Thy dear Son, my Saviour, asking Thee by His sacred heart and His infinite merits, the patience in our afflictions and the perfect submission which is due to Thee for all that Thou wiliest and permittest

One day when she had finished her prayer, the saintly Princess said to M. Hue:

It is less for the unhappy King than for his misguided people that I pray. May the Lord deign to be moved, and to look mercifully upon France!"

Then she added, with her admirable resignation: "Come, let us take courage. God will never send us more troubles than we are able to bear."

The prisoners were permitted to walk a few steps in the garden every day to get a breath of fresh air. But even there they were insulted. As they passed by, the guards stationed at the base of the tower took pains to put on their hats and sit down. The sentries scrawled insults on the walls. Colporteurs maliciously cried out bad tidings, which were sometimes false. One day, one of them announced a pretended decree separating the King from his family. The Queen, who was near enough to hear distinctly the voice which told this news, not exact as yet, was struck with a terror from which she did not recover.

And yet there were still souls that gave way to compassion. From the upper stories of houses near the Temple enclosure there were eyes looking down into the garden when the prisoners took their walk. The common people and the workmen living in these poor abodes were affected. Sometimes, to show her gratitude for the sympathy of those unknown friends, Marie Antoinette would remove her veil, and smile. When the little *Dauphin* was playing, there would be hands at the windows, joined as if to applaud. Flowers would sometimes fall, as if by chance, from a garret roof to the Queen's feet, and occasionally it happened that when the captives had gone back to their prison, they would hear in the darkness the echo of some royalist refrain, hummed by a passer-by in the silence of the night.

The Temple tower is no longer in existence. Bonaparte visited it when he was Consul. "There are too many souvenirs in that prison," he exclaimed. "I will tear it down." In 1811 he kept his promise. The palace of the grand-prior was destroyed in 1853. No trace remains of that famous enclosure of the Templars whose legend has so sombre a poetry. But it has left an impress on the imagination of peoples which will never be effaced. It seems to rise again gigantic, that tower where the son of Saint Louis realized not alone the type of the antique sage of whom Horace said: *Impavidum ferient ruinae*, but also the purest ideal of the true Christian.

Does not the name Temple seem predestinated for a spot which was to be sanctified by so many virtues, and where the martyr King put in practice these verses of the *Imitation of Jesus Christ*, his favourite book: "It needs no great virtue to live peaceably with those who are upright and amiable; one is naturally pleased in such society; we always love those whose sentiments agree with ours. But it is very praiseworthy, and the effect of a special grace and great courage to live in peace with severe and wicked men, who are disorderly, or who contradict us. . . . He who knows best how to suffer, will enjoy the greatest peace; such a one is the conqueror of himself, master of the world, the friend of Jesus Christ, and the inheritor of heaven."

34

The Princess de Lamballe's Murder

The Princess de Lamballe, after being taken from the Temple in the night of August 18-19, had been examined by Billaud-Varennes at the Hôtel-de-Ville, and then sent, at noon, August 19, to the Force. This prison, divided into two distinct parts, the great and the little Force, was situated between the rues Roi-de-Sicile, Culture, and Pavée. In 1792 it supplemented the Abbey and Châtelet prisons, which were overcrowded. The little Force had a separate entry on the rue Pavée to the Marais, while the door of the large one opened on the rue des Ballets, a few steps from the rue Saint-Antoine. The register of the little Force, which is preserved in the archives of the prefecture of police, records that, at the time of the September massacres, this prison in which the Princess de Lamballe was immured, contained one hundred and ten women, most of them not concerned with political affairs, and in great part women of the town. Here, from August 19 to September 3, the Princess suffered inexpressible anguish. She never heard a turnkey open the door of her cell without thinking that her last hour had come.

The massacres began on September 2. On that day the Princess de Lamballe was spared. In the evening she threw herself on her bed, a prey to the most cruel anxiety. Toward six o'clock the next morning, the turnkey entered with a frightened air: "They are coming here," he said to the prisoners. Six men, armed with sabres, guns, and pistols, followed him, approached the beds, asked the names of the women, and went out again. Madame de Tourzel, who shared the Princess de Lamballe's captivity, said to her:

This threatens to be a terrible day, dear Princess; we know not what Heaven intends for us; we must ask God to forgive our faults. Let us say the *Miserere* and the *Confiteor* as acts of contrition, and recommend ourselves to His goodness.

The two women said their prayers aloud, and incited each other to resignation and courage.

There was a window which opened on the street, and from which, although it was very high, one could see what was passing by mounting on Madame de Lamballe's bed, and thence to the window ledge. The Princess climbed up, and as soon as her head was noticed on the street, a pretence of firing on her was made. She saw a considerable crowd at the prison door.

Very little doubt remained concerning her fate. Neither she nor Madame de Tourzel had eaten since the previous day. But they were too greatly moved to take any breakfast. They dared not speak to each other. They took their work, and sat down to await the result of the fatal day in silence.

Toward eleven o'clock the door opened. Armed men filled the room and demanded Madame de Lamballe. The Princess put on a gown, bade *adieu* to Madame de Tourzel, and was led to the great Force, where some municipal officers, wearing their insignia, subjected the prisoners to a pretended trial. In front of this tribunal stood executioners with ferocious faces, who brandished bloody weapons. The atmosphere was sickening: full of the steam of carnage, and the odours of wine and blood. Madame de Lamballe fainted. When she recovered consciousness she was interrogated: "Who are you?"

"Marie Louise, Princess of Savoy."

"What is your rank?"

"Superintendent of the Queen's household."

"Were you acquainted with the conspiracies of the court on August 10?"

"I do not know that there were any conspiracies on August 10, but I know I had no knowledge of them."

"Swear liberty, equality, hatred to the King, the Queen, and royalty."

"I will swear the first two without difficulty; I cannot swear the last; it is not in my heart."

Here an assistant said in a whisper to Madame de Lamballe: "Swear it! if you do not swear, you are a dead woman." The Princess made no answer; she put her hands up to her eyes, covered her face with them and made a step toward the wicket.

The judge exclaimed: "Let someone release *Madame*!" This phrase was the death signal. Two men took the victim roughly by the arms, and made her walk over corpses. Hardly had she crossed the threshold when she received a blow from a sabre on the back of her head, which made her blood flow in streams. In the narrow passage leading from the rue Saint-Antoine to the Force, and called the Priests' *cul-de-sac*, she was despatched with pikes on a heap of dead bodies. Then they stripped off her clothes and exposed her body to the insults of a horde of cannibals. When the blood that flowed from her wounds, or that of the neighbouring corpses, had soiled the body too much, they washed it with a sponge, so that the crowd might notice its whiteness better. They cut off her head and her breasts. They tore out her heart, and of this head and this heart they made horrible trophies. The pikes which bore them were lifted high in air, and they went to carry around these excellent spoils of the Revolution.

At the very moment when the hideous procession began its march, Madame de Lebel, the wife of a painter, who owed many benefits to Madame de Lamballe, was trying to get near the prison, hoping to hear news of her. Seeing the great commotion in the crowd, she inquired the cause. When someone replied: "It is Lamballe's head that they are going to carry through Paris," she was seized with horror, and, turning back, took refuge in a hairdresser's shop on the Place Bastille. Hardly had she done so when the crowd entered the Place. The murderers came into the shop and required the hairdresser to arrange the head of the Princess. They washed it, and powdered the fair hair, all soiled with blood.

Then one of the assassins cried joyfully: "Now, at any rate, Antoinette can recognize her!" The procession resumed its march. From time to time they called a halt before a wine-shop. Wishing to empty his glass, the scoundrel who had the Princess's head in his hand, set it flat down on the lead counter. Then it was put back on the end of a pike. The heart was on another pike, and other individuals dragged along the headless corpse. In this manner they arrived in front of the Temple. It was three o'clock in the afternoon.

On that day the royal family had been refused permission to go into the garden. They were in the little tower when the cries of the multitude became audible. The workmen who were then employed in tearing down the walls and buildings contiguous to the Temple dungeon, mingled with the crowd, increased also by innumerable curious spectators, and uttered furious shouts. One of the Municipal Guards at the Temple closed doors and windows, and pulled down curtains so that the captives could see nothing.

On the street in front of the enclosure a tricolored ribbon had been fastened across, with this inscription: "*Citizens, you who know how to ally the love of order with a just vengeance, respect this barrier; it is necessary to our surveillance and our responsibility.*" This was the sole dike they meant to oppose to the torrent. At the side of this ribbon stood a municipal officer named Danjou, formerly a priest, who was called Abbé Six-feet, on account of his height. He mounted on a chair and harangued the crowd. He felt his face touched by Madame de Lamballe's head, still on the end of a pike which the bearer shook about and gesticulated with, and also by a rag of her chemise, soaked with blood and mire, which another individual also carried on a pike. The naked body was there likewise, with its back to the ground and the front cut open to the very breast. Danjou tried to make the crowd of assassins who wanted to invade the Temple understand that at a moment when the enemy was master of the frontiers, it would be impolitic to deprive themselves of hostages so precious as Louis XVI. and his family.

"Moreover," he added, "would it not demonstrate their innocence if you dare not try them? How much worthier it is of a great people to execute a king guilty of treason on the scaffold!"

Thus, while preventing an immediate massacre, he held the scaffold in reserve. Danjou said that the Communal Council, in order to show its confidence in the citizens composing the mob, had decided that six of them should be admitted to make the rounds of the Temple garden, with the commissioners at their head. The ribbon was then raised and several persons entered the enclosure. They were those who carried the remains of Madame de Lamballe. With these were the labourers who had been at work on the demolitions. Voices were heard demanding furiously that Marie Antoinette should show herself at a window, so that someone might climb up and make her kiss her friend's head. As Danjou opposed this infernal scheme, he was accused of being on the side of the tyrant. Was the dungeon of the Temple to be forced? Were the assassins about to seize the Queen, tear her in pieces, and drag her, like her friend, through streets and squares to the rolling of drums and the chanting of the *Marseillaise* and the *Ça ira?*

A municipal officer entered the tower and began a mysterious parley with his colleagues. As Louis XVI. asked what was going on, someone replied: "Well, sir, since you desire to know, they want to show you Madame de Lamballe's head."

Meanwhile the cries outside were growing louder. Another municipal came in, followed by four delegates from the mob. One of them, who carried a heavy sabre in his hand, insisted that the prisoners should present themselves at the window, but this was opposed by the municipal officers, who were less cruel. This man said to the Queen in an insulting tone:

> They want us to hide the Princess de Lamballe's head from you when we brought it to let you see how the people avenge themselves on their tyrants. I advise you to show yourself if you don't want the people to come up.

Marie Antoinette fainted on learning her friend's death in this manner. Her children burst into tears and tried by their caresses to bring her back to consciousness. The man did not go away.

"Sir," the King said to him, "we are prepared for the worst, but you might have dispensed yourself from informing the Queen of this frightful calamity."

Cléry, the King's valet, was looking through a corner of the window blinds, and saw Madame de Lamballe's head. The person carrying it had climbed up on a heap of rubbish from the buildings in process of demolition. Another, who stood beside him, held her bleeding heart. Cléry heard Danjou expostulating the crowd in words like these: "Antoinette's head does not belong to you; the departments have their rights in it also. France has confided these great criminals to the care of Paris; and it is your business to assist us in guarding them until national justice shall avenge the people."

Then, addressing himself to these cannibals as if they were heroes whose courage and exploits he praised, he added, in speaking of the profaned corpse of the Princess de Lamballe:

> The remains you have there are the property of all. Do they not belong to all Paris? Have you the right to deprive others of the pleasure of sharing your triumph? Night will soon be here. Make haste, then, to quit this precinct, which is too narrow for your glory. You ought to place this trophy in the Palais Royal or the Tuileries garden, where the sovereignty of the people has been so often trampled underfoot, as an eternal monument of the victory you have just won.

Remarks like these were all that could prevent these tigers from entering the Temple and destroying the prisoners. Shouts of "To the Palais Royal!" proved to Danjou that his harangue had been appreciated. The assassins at last departed, after having covered his face with kisses that smelt of wine and blood. They wanted to show their victim's head at the Hôtel Toulouse, the mansion of the venerable Duke de Penthièvre, her father-in-law, but were deterred by the assurance that she did not ordinarily live there, but at the Tuileries. Then they turned toward the Palais Royal. The Duke of Orleans was at a window with his mistress, Madame de Buffon. He left it, but he may have seen the head of his sister-in-law.

Some of the cannibals had remained in the neighbourhood of the Temple. Sitting down at table in a wine-shop, they had the heart of the Princess de Lamballe cooked, and ate it with avidity. "Thus," says M. de Beauchesne in his excellent work on Louis XVII., "this civilization which had departed from God, surpassed at a single bound the fury of savages, and the eighteenth century, so proud of its learning and humanity, ended by anthropophagy." In the evening, when someone was giving Collot d'Herbois an account of the day's performances, he expressed but one regret,—that they had not succeeded in showing Marie Antoinette the remains of the Princess de Lamballe. "What!" he spitefully exclaimed, "did they spare the Queen that impression? They ought to have served up her best friend's head in a covered dish at her table."

35

The September Massacres

Lovers of paradoxes have tried to represent the September massacres as something spontaneous, a passing delirium of opinion, a sort of great national convulsion. This myth was a lie against history and humanity. It exists no longer, Heaven be thanked. The mists with which it was sought to shroud these execrable crimes are now dissipated. Light has been shed upon that series of infernal spectacles which would have made cannibals blush. No; these odious massacres were not the result of a popular movement, an unforeseen fanaticism, a paroxysm of rage or vengeance. They present an ensemble of murders committed in cool blood, a planned and premeditated thing. M. Mortimer-Ternaux, in his *Histoire de la Terreur*, M. Granier de Cassagnac, in his *Histoire des Girondins et des Massacres de Septembre*, have proved this abundantly. They have exhumed from the archives and the record offices such a mass of uncontested and incontestable documents, that not the slightest doubt is now permissible. Edgar Quinet has not hesitated to recognize this in his book, *La Révolution*. He says:

> The massacres were executed administratively; the same discipline was everywhere displayed throughout the carnage. . . .
> This was not a piece of blind, spontaneous barbarism; it was a barbarity slowly meditated, minutely elaborated by a sanguinary mind. Hence it bears no resemblance to anything previously known in history. Marat harvested in September what he had been sowing for three years.

The Parisian populace, eight hundred thousand souls, was inert; it was cowardly, it trembled; but it did not approve, it was not an accomplice. It was a monstrous thing that a handful of cut-throats should be enough to transform Paris into a slaughter-house. One shudders in thinking what a few criminals can accomplish in the midst of an immense population.

The people, the real people—that composed of laborious and honest workmen, ardent and patriotic at heart, and of young *bourgeois* with generous aspirations and indomitable courage— never united for an instant with the scoundrels recruited by Maillard from every kennel in the capital. While the hired assassins of the Committee of Surveillance established in the prisons what Vergniaud called a butcher's shop for human flesh, the true populace was assembled on the Champ-de-Mars, and before the enlistment booths; it was offering its purest blood for the country; it would have blushed to shed that of helpless unfortunates.[1]

In 1871, the murder of hostages and the burning of monuments was no more approved by the population than the massacres in the prisons were in 1792. The crimes were committed at both epochs by a mere handful of individuals. The great majority of the people were guilty merely of apathy and fear.

The hideous *tableau* surpasses the most lugubrious conceptions of Dante's sombre imagination. Paris is a hell. From August 29, it is like a torpid Oriental town. The whole city is in custody, like a criminal whose limbs are held while he is being searched and put in irons. Every house is inspected by the agents of the Commune. A knock at the door makes the inmates tremble. The denunciation of an enemy, a servant, a neighbour, is a death sentence. People scarcely dare to breathe. Neither running water nor solid earth is free. The parapets of quays, the arches of bridges, the bathing and washing boats are bristling with sentries. Everything is surrounded. There is no refuge. Three thousand suspected persons are taken out of houses, and crowded into prisons. The hunt begins anew the following day. The programme of massacres is arranged. The Communal Council of Surveillance has minutely regulated everything. The price of the actual work is settled. The personnel of cut-throats is at its post. Danton has furnished the executioners; Manuel, the victims. All is ready. The bloody drama can begin.

On September 2, Danton said to the Assembly:

The tocsin about to sound is not an alarm signal; it is a charge upon the enemies of the country. To vanquish them, gentlemen,

---

1. M. Mortimer-Ternaux, *Histoire de la Terreur*.

all that is needed is boldness, and again boldness, and always boldness.

Two days before, he had been still more explicit. "The 10th of August," said he, "divided us into republicans and royalists; the first few in number, the second many; we must make the royalists afraid." A frightful gesture, a horizontal gesture, sufficed to express his meaning.

Robbery preceded murder. It was a veritable raid. The Commune caused the palaces, national property, the Garde-Meuble, the houses and mansions of the *émigrés* to be pillaged. One saw nothing but carts and wagons transporting stolen goods to the Hôtel-de-Ville. All the plate was stolen from the churches likewise. "Millions," says Madame Roland in her *Memoirs*, "passed into the hands of people who used it to perpetuate the anarchy which was the source of their domination." When will the men of the Commune render their accounts? Never. Who are the accomplices of Danton and Marat in organizing the massacres? A band of defaulting accountants, faithless violators of public trusts, breakers of locks, swindlers, spies, and men overwhelmed with debts. What interest have they in planning the murders? That of perpetuating the dictatorship they had assumed on the eve of August 10, and, above all, of having no accounts to render. A few weeks later on, Collot d'Herbois will say at the Jacobin Club:

The 2nd of September is the chief article in the creed of our liberty.

The jailors were forewarned. They served the prisoners' dinner earlier, and took away their knives. There was a disturbed and uneasy look in their faces which made the victims suspect their end was near. Toward noon the general alarm was beaten in every street. The citizens were ordered to return at once to their dwellings. An order was issued to illuminate every house when night fell. The shops were closed. Terror overspread the entire city.

It was agreed that at the third discharge of cannon the cut-throats should set to work. The first blood shed was that of prisoners taken from the mayoralty to the Abbey prison. The carriages containing them passed along the Quai des Orfèvres, the Pont-Neuf and rue *Dauphine*, until it reached the Bussy square. Here there was a crowd assembled around a platform where enlistments were going on. The throng impeded the progress of the carriages. Thereupon one of the escort opened the door of one of them, and standing on the step, plunged his sabre into the breast of an aged priest. The multitude shuddered and fled in affright. "That makes you afraid," said the assassin; "you will see plenty more like it."

The rest of the escort followed the example set them. The carriages go on again, and so do the massacres. They kill along the route, and they kill on arriving at the Abbey. Towards five o'clock, Billaud-Varennes presents himself there, wearing his municipal scarf. "People," says he—what he calls people is a band of salaried assassins—"people, thou immolatest thine enemies, thou art doing thy duty." Then he walks into the midst of the dead bodies, dipping his feet in blood, and fraternizes with the murderers. "There is nothing more to do here," exclaims Maillard; "let us go to the Carmelites."

At the Carmelites, one hundred and eighty priests, crowded into the church and convent, were awaiting their fate with pious resignation. Two days before, Manuel had said to them ironically: "In forty-eight hours you will all be free. Get ready to go into a foreign country and enjoy the repose you cannot find here." And on the previous day a *gendarme* had said to the Archbishop of Arles, blowing the smoke from his pipe into his face as he did so: "It is tomorrow, then, that they are going to kill Your Grandeur." A short time before the massacre began, the victims were sent into the garden. At the bottom of it was an orangery which has since become a chapel. Mgr. Dulau, Archbishop of Arles, and the Bishops of Beauvais and de Saintes, both of whom were named de la Rochefoucauld, kneeled down with the other priests and recited the last prayers. The murderers approached. The Archbishop of Arles, who was upwards of eighty, advanced to meet them. "I am he whom you seek," he said; "my sacrifice is made; but spare these worthy priests; they will pray for you on earth, and I in heaven." They insulted him before they struck him. "I have never done harm to anyone," said he.

An assassin responded: "Very well; I'll do some to you," and killed him. The other priests were chased around the garden from one tree to another, and shot down. During this infernal hunt the murderers were shouting with laughter and singing their favourite song: *Dansez la Carmagnole!*

The massacre of the Carmelites is over. "Let us go back to the Abbey!" cries Maillard; "we shall find more game there." This time there is a pretence of justice made. The tribunal is the vestibule of the Abbey; Maillard, the chief cut-throat, is president; the assassins are the judges, and the public, the Marseillais, the *sans-culottes*, the female furies, and men to whom murder was a delightful spectacle. The prisoners are summoned one after another. They enter the vestibule, which has a wicket as a door of exit. They are questioned simply as a matter of form. Their answers are not even listened to. "Conduct this gentleman to the Force!" says the president. The prisoner thinks he is safe; he does not know that this phrase has been agreed upon as the signal of death. On reaching the wicket, hatchet and sabre strokes cut him down in the midst of his dream. The Swiss officers and soldiers who had survived August 10 were murdered thus. Their torture lasted a longer or shorter time, and was accomplished with more or less cruel refinements, according to the caprice of the assassins, who were nearly all drunk.

Night came, and torches were lighted. No shadows; a grand illumination. They must see clearly in the slaughter house. Lanterns were placed near the lakes of blood and heaps of dead bodies, so as plainly to distinguish the work from the workmen. There were some who were bent on losing no details of the carnage. The spectators wanted to take things easy. They were tired of standing too long. Benches for men and others for dames were got ready for them. The death-rattle of the agonizing, the vociferations of the assassins, the emulation between the executioners who kill slowly and the victims who are in haste to die, give joy to the spectators. There is no interruption to the human butchery. There has been so much blood spilled that the feet of the murderers slip on the pavement. A litter is made of straw and the clothes of the victims, and thereafter none are killed except upon this mattress. In this way the work is more commodiously accomplished. The assassins have plenty of assurance. Morning dawns on the continuation of the murders, and the wives of the murderers bring them something to eat.

On September 2, the only persons handed over to the cut-throats, were at the Abbey, the Carmelites, and Saint-Firmin. On September 3, the massacre became more general. The assassins had said: "If there is no more work, we shall have to find some." Their desire realizes itself. Work will not be lacking. There is still some at the Force, where the Princess de Lamballe, the preferred victim, is murdered. The assassins, who at the Abbey had been paid at the rate of eight *francs* a day, get only fifty *sous* at the Force. They work with undiminished zeal, even at this reduction. If necessary, they would work for nothing. To drink wine and shed blood is the essential thing. The negro Delorme, servant to Fournier "the American," distinguishes himself among them all. His black skin, reddened with blood, his white teeth and ferocious eyes, his bestial laugh, his ravenous fury, make him a choice assassin.

There is work too at the Conciergerie, at the great and little Châtelet, the Salpêtrière, and the Bicêtre. A great number of those detained are people condemned or accused of private crimes which had absolutely nothing in common with politics. No matter; blood is wanted; they kill there as elsewhere. At the Grand Châtelet, work is so plenty, and the assassins so few, that they release several individuals imprisoned for theft, and impress them into their service.

One of these unfortunate accidental executioners begins in a hesitating way, strikes a few undecided blows, and then throws down the hatchet placed in his hands. "No, no," he cries, "I cannot. No, no! Rather a victim than a murderer! I would rather receive death from scoundrels like you, then give it to innocent, disarmed people. Strike me!" And at once the veteran murderers kill the inexperienced cutthroat.

There was a woman, known on account of her charms as the Beautiful Flower Girl, who was accused of having wounded her lover, a French guard, in a fit of jealousy. Théroigne de Mericourt, an Amazon of the gutters, was her rival. She pointed her out to the assassins. They fastened her naked to a post, her legs apart and her feet nailed to the ground. They burned her alive. They cut off her breasts with sabre strokes. They impaled her on a hot iron. Her shrieks carried dismay as far as the outer banks of the Seine. Théroigne was at the height of felicity.

At the Salpêtrière there was still another spectacle. This prison for fallen women is a place of correction for the old, of amendment for the young, and an asylum for those who are still children. More than forty children of the lower classes were slain during these horrible days. The delirium of murder reached its height. Gorged with wine mingled with gunpowder, intoxicated with the fumes and reek of carnage, the assassins experienced a devouring, inextinguishable thirst for blood which nothing could quench. More blood, and yet more blood! And where can it now be found? The prisons are empty. There are no more nobles, no more priests, to put to death. Very well! for lack of anything better, they will go to an asylum for the poor, the sick, and the insane; to the Bicêtre. Vagabonds, paupers, fools, thieves, steward, chaplains, janitor, all is fish that comes to their net. The butchery lasts five days and nights without stopping. Massacre takes every form; some are drowned in the cellars, others shot in the courts. Water, fire, and sword, every sort of torture.

The cut-throats can at last take some repose. They have worked all the week. There are still some, however, who have not yet had enough, and who are going to continue the massacres of Paris in the provinces. The Communal Council of Surveillance has taken care to send to every commune in France a circular bearing the seal of the Minister of Justice, inviting them to follow the example of the capital.

September 9, the prisoners who had been detained at Orleans to be tried there by the Superior Court, entered Versailles on carts. At the moment when they approached the grating of the Orangery, assassins sent from Paris under the lead of Fournier "the American" sprang upon them and immolated every one. Thus perished the former Minister of Foreign Affairs, de Lessart, and the Duke de Brissac, former commander of the Constitutional Guard. Fournier "the American"[2] returned on horseback to Paris and began to caracole on the Place Vendôme; Danton loudly felicitated him on the success of the expedition, from the balcony of the Ministry of Justice.

During all this time, what efforts had the Assembly made to put a stop to the murders? None, absolutely none. Never has any deliberative body shown a like cowardice. Neither Vergniaud's voice nor that of any other Girondin was heard in protest. Indignation, pity, found not a single word to say. Speeches, discussions, votes on different questions, went on as usual. Concerning the massacres, not a syllable. During that infamous week, neither the ministers, the virtuous Roland not more than the others, neither Pétion, the mayor of Paris, nor the commander of the National Guard sent a picket guard of fifty men to any quarter to prevent the murders.

A population of eight hundred thousand souls and a National Guard of fifty thousand men bent their necks under the yoke of a handful of bandits, of two hundred and thirty-five assassins (the exact number is known). People trembled. At the Assembly the old moderate party had disappeared. There were not more than two hundred odd deputies present at the shameful and powerless sessions. Terrorized Paris was in a state of stupor and prostration.

The murderers ended by execrating themselves. Tormented by remorse, they could see nothing before them but vivid faces, reeking entrails, bleeding limbs. "Among the cut-throats," M. Louis Blanc has said, "some gave signs of insanity that led to the supposition that some

---

2. Claude Fournier-Lhéritier, was born in Auvergne, 1745, and served as a volunteer in Santo Domingo, 1772-85, with Toussaint l'Ouverture, whence his *sobriquet* "the American."

mysterious and terrible drug had been mingled with the wine they drank." Some of them became furious madmen. Others sought refuge in suicide, killing themselves the moment they had no one else to kill. Others enlisted. They were chased out of the army. Among these was the man who had carried the head of the Princess de Lamballe on a pike. One day when he was boasting of his murders, the soldiers became indignant and put him to death.

Others still were tried as Septembrists and sent to the scaffold. The guilty received their punishment, even on this earth. Well! there are people nowadays who would like to rehabilitate them! In vain has Lamartine, the founder of the Second Republic, exclaimed in a burst of noble wrath: "Has human speech an execration, an anathema, which is equal to the horror these crimes of cannibals inspire in me, as in all civilized men?"

In vain have the most celebrated historians of democracy, Edgar Quinet and Michelet, expressed in eloquent terms their indignation against these crimes. In vain has M. Louis Blanc said:

Every murder is a suicide. In the victim the body alone is killed; but what is killed in the murderer is the soul.

There are men who would not alone excuse, but glorify the assassinations and the assassins!

36

Madame Roland
During the Massacres

Madame Roland's hatred was appeased. The ambitious *bourgeoise* throned it for the second time at the Ministry of the Interior, and the Queen groaned in captivity in the Temple tower. The Egeria of the Girondins had not felt her heart swell with a single movement of pity for Marie Antoinette. The fatal 10th of August had seemed to her a personal triumph in which her pride delighted. The *parvenue* enjoyed the humiliations of the daughter of the German Cæsars. Her jealous instincts feasted on the afflictions of the Queen of France and Navarre.

Lamartine, indignant at this cruelty on Madame Roland's part, has repented of the eulogies he gave her in his *Histoire des Girondins*. In his *Cours de Littérature* (Volume 13. Conversation 23.), he says:

I glided over that medley of intrigue and pomposity which composed the genius, both feminine and Roman, of this woman. In so doing, I conceded more to popularity than to truth. I wanted to give a Cornelia to the Republic. As a matter of fact, I do not know what Cornelia was, that mother of the Gracchi who brought up conspirators against the Roman Senate, and trained them to sedition, that virtue of ambitious commoners. As to Madame Roland, who inflated a vulgar husband by the breath of her feminine anger against a court she found odious because it did not open to her upstart vanity, there was nothing really fine in her except her death. Her *rôle* had been a mere parade of true greatness of soul.

What Lamartine finds fault with most of all is her hostility to the martyr Queen. He adds:

> She inspired the Girondins, her intimate friends, with an implacable hatred against the Queen, already so humiliated and so menaced; she had neither respect nor pity for this victim; she points her out to the rebellious multitude. She is no longer a wife, a mother, or a Frenchwoman. She poses as Nemesis at the door of the Temple, when the Queen is groaning there over her husband, her children, and herself, between the throne and the scaffold. This ostentatious stoicism of implacability is what, in my view, kills the woman in this female demagogue.

Alas! if Madame Roland was guilty, she was to be punished cruelly. The colleague of the *virtuous* Roland was the organizer of the September massacres. The republican sheepfold dreamed of by the admirer of Jean-Jacques Rousseau was invaded by ferocious beasts. Human nature had never appeared under a more execrable aspect than since its so-called regeneration. Madame Roland was filled with a naïve astonishment. After having sown the wind she was utterly surprised to reap the whirlwind. What! she said to herself, my husband is minister, or, to speak with great exactness, I am the minister myself, and yet there are people in France who are dissatisfied! Ungrateful nation, why dost thou not appreciate thy happiness?

Madame Roland resembled certain politicians, who, having attained to power, would willingly disembarrass themselves of those by whose aid they reached it. For the second time she had just arrived at the goal of her ambition. Who dared, then, to pollute her joy? Why did that marplot, Danton, come with his untimely massacres to destroy such brilliant projects and banish such delightful dreams? The man who, as if in derision and antithesis, allowed himself to be called the Minister of Justice, produced the effect of a monster on Madame Roland. The republic as conceived by him had not the head of a goddess, but of a Gorgon. Its eyes glittered with a sinister lustre. The sword it held was that of an assassin or a headsman.

Madame Roland was greatly astonished when, on Sunday, September 2, 1792, toward five in the evening, when the massacres had already begun, she saw two hundred men of forbidding appearance arrive at the Ministry of the Interior and ask for her husband, who was absent. Lucky for him he was; for albeit a minister, they had come to arrest him in virtue of a mandate of the Communal Council of Surveillance. Not finding Roland, the two hundred men retired. One of them, with his shirt-sleeves rolled up to his elbows, and a sabre in his hand, declaimed furiously against the treachery of ministers. A few minutes later, Danton said to Pétion: "Do you know what they have taken into their heads? If they haven't issued a decree to arrest Roland!"

"Who did that?" demanded the mayor. "Eh! those devils of committeemen. I have taken the mandate; hold! here it is!"

What was Madame Roland doing the next day, when the worst of the massacres were going on? She gave a dinner, and allowed the Prussian, Anacharsis Clootz, who came, moreover, uninvited, to make a regular defence of these horrible murders. "The events of the day," she says in her *Memoirs*, "formed the subject of conversation. Clootz pretended to prove that it was an indispensable and salutary measure; he uttered a good many commonplaces about the people's rights, the justice of their vengeance, and of its utility to the welfare of the species; he talked a long while and very loudly, ate still more, and fatigued more than one listener."

And yet, revolutionary passions had not extinguished every notion of humanity and justice in Madame Roland's soul. On that very day she induced her husband to write a letter to the National Assembly concerning the massacres. But how weak and undecided is this letter, and how public opinion must have been lowered and debased when it could regard Roland as a courageous minister! In place of scathing the murderers with the energy of an honest man, he pleads extenuating circumstances in their favour.

"It is in the nature of things and according to the human heart," he said in his pale missive, "that victory should lead to some excesses. The sea, agitated by a violent storm, continues to roar long after the tempest; but everything has its limits and must finally see them determined. Yesterday was a day over whose events we ought, perhaps, to draw a veil. I know that the terrible vengeance of the people carries with it a sort of justice; but how easy it is for scoundrels and traitors to abuse this effervescence, and how necessary it is to arrest it!"

This language produced not the least effect. The massacres went on, and Roland remained minister; although in his letter of September 3 he had written: "I ask the privilege of resigning if the silence of the laws does not permit me to act."

The *virtuous* Roland sat in the Council beside his colleague, the organizer of this human butchery. September 13, he addressed a letter to the Parisians in which he burnt incense to himself, bragged about his character, his actions, and his firmness, and carried his infatuation so far as to write: "I have twice accepted a burden which I felt myself able to bear." Ah! how difficult it is to renounce even a shadow of power, and of what compromises with their consciences are not ministers capable in order to retain for a few days longer the portfolios that are slipping from their hands! In the depths of his soul Roland, like his wife, had the profoundest horror of the murders and the murderers. And yet notice how he extenuates them in his letter to the Parisians:

> I admired August 10; I trembled over the results of September 2; I carefully considered what the betrayed patience of the people and their justice had produced, and I did not blame a first impulse too inconsiderately; I believe that its further progress should have been prevented, and that those who were seeking to perpetuate it were deceived by their imagination or by cruel and evil-minded men. If the erring brethren recognize that they have been deceived, let them come; my arms are open to them.

That was a very prompt amnesty. Already the assassins are but erring brethren, and the minister welcomes them to his arms!

The Gironde kept silence, or, if it spoke, it was to attribute, like Vergniaud, the massacres "to the *émigrés* and the satellites of Coblentz." Later on, they were horrified by the crimes, but it was when others were to profit by them. Each taken by himself, the Girondins did not hesitate to condemn the murders; but taken as a whole, they considered merely the interests of their party. Were not three of them still in the Ministerial Council? What had they to complain of, then? The September massacres are the most striking expression of what abominations the ambitious may commit or allow to be committed in order to maintain themselves a few weeks longer in power.

But there is a voice in the depths of conscience which neither interest nor ambition can succeed in stifling. Madame Roland could not blind herself. The odious reality appeared to her. At last she saw the yawning gulf beneath her feet, and she uttered a cry of terror. A secret voice warned her that her fate would be like that of the September victims. After the 9th of that fatal month her imagination was vividly impressed. Bloody phantoms rose before her. She wrote on that day to Bancal des Issarts:

> If you knew the frightful details of these expeditions. . . . You

know my enthusiasm for the Revolution; well, I am ashamed of it; it has become hideous. In a week ... how do I know what may happen? It is degrading to remain in office, and we are not permitted to leave Paris. We are detained so that we may be destroyed at the propitious moment.

From that time a rising anger and indignation took possession of the mind and heart of the Egeria of the Girondins, and constantly increased until the hour when she ascended the steps of the scaffold. She writes in her *Memoirs*, *apropos* of the September massacres:

All Paris witnessed these horrible scenes executed by a small number of wretches (there were but fifteen at the Abbey, at the door of which only two National Guards were stationed, in spite of the applications made to the Commune and the commandant). All Paris permitted it to go on. All Paris was accursed in my eyes, and I no longer hoped that liberty might be established among cowards, insensible to the worst outrages that could be perpetrated against nature and humanity, cold spectators of attempts which the courage of fifty armed men could have prevented with ease.... It is not the first night that astonishes me; but four days!—and inquisitive people going to see this spectacle! No, I know nothing in the annals of the most barbarous peoples which can compare with these atrocities.

What a striking lesson for those who play with anarchical passions and end by falling themselves into the snares they have laid for others! Nothing is more deserving of study than this retaliatory punishment which is found, one may say, on every page of revolutionary histories. The hour was coming when the Girondins and their heroine would repent of the means they had employed to overset the throne. This was when the same means were employed against them, when they recognized their own weapons in the wounds they received. Then, when they had no more interest in keeping silence, they sought to escape a complicity that gained them nothing. Instead of the luminous heights which in their golden dreams they had aspired to gain, they fell, crushed and overwhelmed, into a dismal gulf, full of tears and blood.

How bitter then were their recriminations against men and things! It was only to virtue that the dying Brutus said: "Thou art but a name." The Girondins said it also to glory, to country, and to liberty. Those among them who did not succeed in fleeing, disavowed, denounced, and insulted each other before the revolutionary tribunal. At the Conciergerie they intoned the *Marseillaise*, but parodying the demagogic chant in this wise:—

> *Contre nous de la tyrannie[1]*
> *Le couteau sanglant est levé.*

Read the *Memoirs* of Louvet, Buzot, Barbaroux, Pétion, and Madame Roland, and you will see to what extremes of bitterness the language of deceived ambition can go. They are paroxysms of rage, howls of anger, shrieks of despair. Consider the difference between philosophy and religion! The philosophers curse, and the Christian pardons. Yes, as Edgar Quinet has said, "Louis XVI. alone speaks of forgiveness on that scaffold to which the others were to bring thoughts of vengeance and despair. And by that he seems still to reign over those who were to follow him in death with the passions and the furies of earth." Louis XVI. will be magnanimous and calm. A celestial sweetness will overspread his royal countenance. An infernal rage will distort the heart and the features of the Girondins. What pains, what tortures, in their death-struggle! Earth fails them, and they do not look to heaven. What accents of disgust and hatred when they speak of their former accomplices, now become their executioners!

"Great God!" Buzot will say, "if it is only by such men and such infamous means that republics can arise and be consolidated, there is no government more frightful on this earth nor more fatal to human happiness." He will address these insults, worthy of the imprecations of Camillus, to the city of Paris: "I say truly, that France can expect neither liberty nor happiness except from the irreparable destruction of that capital."

Barbaroux will be still more severe. His anathemas are launched not only at Paris, but at all France. "The people," he says, "do not deserve that one should become attached to them, for they are essentially ungrateful. It is the absurdest folly to try to conduct to liberty people without morals, who blaspheme God and adore Marat. These people are no more fit for a philosophic government than the *lazzaroni* of Naples or the cannibals of America. . . . Liberty, virtue, sacred rights of men, today you are nothing but empty names." Pétion, before dying, will write to his son this letter, which is like the testament of the Gironde: "My greatest torment will be to think that so many crimes went unpunished; vengeance is here the most sacred of duties.

---

1. The bloody *knife* of tyranny is lifted against us.

. . . My son, either the murderers of thy father and thy country will be delivered to the severities of the law and expiate their crimes upon the scaffold, or thou art under obligation to free thy country from them. They have broken all the ties of society; their crimes are of such a nature that they do not fall under ordinary rules. From such monsters everyone is authorized to purge the earth."

Madame Roland will be not less vehement than Buzot, Barbaroux, and Pétion. She will address these severe but just reproaches to her friends who had not been valiant enough in their own defence:

They temporized with crime, the cowards! They were to fall in their turn, but they succumb shamefully, pitied by nobody, and with nothing to expect from posterity but utter contempt. . . . Rather than obey their tyrants, than descend from the bar and go out of the Assembly like a timid flock about to be branded by the butcher, why did they not do justice to themselves by falling on the monsters to annihilate them rather than be sentenced by them?

It is not her friends alone whom her anger will lash, but the sovereign people, the people once so flattered, whom she will pursue with her anathemas. "The people," she will say, "can feel nothing but the cannibal joy of seeing blood flow, in order that they may run no risk of shedding their own. That predicted time has come when, if they ask for bread, dead bodies will be given them; but their degraded nature takes pleasure in the spectacle, and the satisfied instinct of cruelty makes the dearth supportable until it becomes absolute."

The Egeria of the Girondins will comprehend that all is lost, that even her blood will be sterile, and that France is condemned either to anarchy or a dictatorship. "Liberty," she will exclaim, "was not made for this corrupt nation, which leaves the bed of debauchery or the dunghill of poverty only to brutalize itself in license, and howl as it wallows in the blood streaming from scaffolds." Like the damned souls in Dante, Madame Roland will leave all hope behind, and when, a few days after Marie Antoinette, she ascends the steps of the guillotine, instead of thinking of heaven, like the Queen, she will address this sarcastic speech to the plaster statue which has replaced that of Louis XV.: "O Liberty! how they have betrayed thee!"

But let us not anticipate. The Girondins are still to have a glimmer of joy. The Republic is about to be proclaimed.

37

The Proclamation of the Republic

"One of the astonishing things in the French Revolution," says one of the most eminent writers of the democratic school, Edgar Quinet, "is the unexpectedness with which the great changes occur. The most important events, the destruction of the monarchy and the advent of the Republic, came about without any previous warning." The most ardent republicans were royalists, not merely under the old *régime*, but after 1789, and even up to August 10, 1792. Marat wrote, in No. 374 of the *Ami du Peuple*, February 17, 1791:

"I have often been represented as a mortal enemy of royalty, but I claim that the King has no better friend than myself."

And he added:

As to Louis XVI. personally, I know very well that his defects are chargeable solely to his education, and that by nature he is an excellent sort of man, whom one would have cited as a worthy citizen if he had not had the misfortune to be born on the throne; but, such as he is, he is at all events the King we want. We ought to thank Heaven for having given him to us. We ought to pray that he may be spared to us.

Marat praying, Marat thanking Heaven! and for whom? For the King. Does not that prove what deep root royalty had taken in France? April 20, 1792, the same Marat bitterly reproached Condorcet with "shamelessly calumniating the Jacobin Club, and perfidiously accusing it of wishing to destroy the monarchy" (*L'Ami du Peuple*, No. 434). June 13, he attacked those who violated the oath taken at the time of the Federation, and said: "To defend the Constitution is the same thing as to be faithful to the nation, the law, and the King" (*L'Ami du Peuple*, No. 448).

During the entire continuance of the Legislative Assembly, when Robespierre, having left the tribune, was pretending to educate the people by means of his journal, what he defended to the utmost was the royal Constitution. Madame Roland relates that after the flight to Varennes, when the prospect of a republic loomed up, possibly for the first time, at a secret meeting, Robespierre, grinning as usual, and biting his nails, asked ironically what a republic might be. In June, 1792, the entire Jacobin Club was royalist still. It proposed to drop Billaud-Varennes, because Billaud-Varennes had dared to put the monarchical principle in question. On the 7th of July following, two months and a half, that is, before the opening of the Convention, at the time of the famous Lamourette Kiss, all the members of the Assembly swore to execrate the Republic forever. Three weeks after September 2, Danton alleged the paucity and the weakness of the republicans, compared with the royalists, as motives for the massacres. Pétion has said:

When the insurrection of August 10 was undertaken, there were but five men in France who desired a republic.

Buzot, Madame Roland's idol, has written:

A wretched mob, unintelligent and unenlightened, vomited forth insults against royalty; the rest neither desired nor willed anything but the Constitution of 1791, and spoke of the republicans just as one speaks of extremely honest fools. This people is republican only through force of the guillotine.

And yet, September 21, 1792, the Convention, holding its first sitting in the Hall of the Manège, began by proclaiming the Republic.

Buzot, in his *Memoirs*, has thus described the deputations that were sent to the bar, and the public that occupied the galleries:

It seemed as if the outlet of every sewer in Paris and other great cities had been searched for whatever was most filthy, hideous, and infected. Villainously dirty faces, surmounted by shocks of greasy hair, and with eyes half sunk into their heads, they spat out, with their nauseating breath, the grossest insults mingled with the sharp snarls of carnivorous beasts. The galleries were worthy of such legislators: men whose frightful aspect betokened crime and poverty, and women whose shameless faces expressed the filthiest debauchery. When all these with hands and feet and voice made their horrible racket, one seemed to be in an assembly of devils.

When the session opened, Collot d'Herbois was the first speaker.

He said:

> There is a matter which you cannot put off until tomorrow, which you cannot put off until this evening, which you cannot defer for a single instant without being unfaithful to the wishes of the nation; it is the abolition of royalty.

Quinet having objected that it would be better to present this question when the Constitution was to be discussed, Grégoire, constitutional Bishop of Blois, exclaimed:

> Certainly, no one will ever propose to us to preserve the deadly race of kings in France. All the dynasties have been breeds of ravenous beasts, living on nothing but human flesh; still it is necessary to reassure plainly the friends of liberty; this magic talisman, which still has power to stupefy so many men, must be destroyed.

Bazire remarked that it would be a frightful example to the people to see an Assembly which they had entrusted with their dearest interests, resolve upon anything in a moment of enthusiasm and without thorough discussion. Grégoire replied with vehemence:

> Eh! what need is there of discussion when everybody is of the same mind? Kings, in the moral order, are what monsters are in the physical order. Courts are the workshop of crime and the lair of tyrants. The history of kings is the martyrology of nations; we are all equally penetrated by this truth. What is the use of discussing it?

Then the question, put to vote in these terms: "The National Convention declares that royalty is abolished in France," was adopted amidst applause.

At four in the afternoon of the same day, a municipal officer named Lubin, surrounded by mounted *gendarmes* and a large crowd of people, came to read a proclamation before the Temple tower. The trumpets were sounded. A great silence ensued, and Lubin, who had a stentorian voice, read loud enough to be heard by the royal family confined in the dungeon, this proclamation, the death knell of monarchy: "Royalty is abolished in France. All public acts will be dated from the first year of the Republic. The seal of State will be inscribed with this motto: *Republique française.* The National Seal will represent a woman seated on a sheaf of arms, holding in one hand a pike surmounted by a liberty-cap." Hébert (the famous Père Duchesne) was at this moment on guard near the royal family. Sitting on the threshold of their chamber, he sought to discover a movement of vexation or anger, or any other emotion on their faces. He was unsuccessful.

While listening to the revolutionary decree which snatched away his throne, the descendant of Saint Louis, Henry IV., and Louis XIV. experienced not the slightest trouble. He had a book in his hand, and he quietly went on reading it. As impassive as her spouse, the Queen neither made a movement nor uttered a word. When the proclamation was finished, the trumpets sounded again. Cléry then went to the window, and the eyes of the crowd turned instantly towards him. As they mistook him for Louis XVI., they overwhelmed him with insults. The *gendarmes* made threatening gestures, and he was obliged to withdraw so as to quiet the tumult. While the populace was unchained around the Temple prison, one man alone was calm, one man alone seemed a stranger to all anxiety: it was the prisoner.

A new era begins. The death-struggle of royalty is over. Royalty is dead, and the King is soon to die. Grégoire, who had stolen the vote (there were but 371 conventionists present; 374 were absent; that is to say, more than half), is both surprised and enthusiastic about what he has done. He confesses that for several days his excessive joy deprived him of appetite and sleep. Such joy will not last very long. M. Taine compares revolutionary France to a badly nourished workman, poor, and overdriven with toil, and yet who drinks strong liquors. At first, in his intoxication, he thinks he is a millionaire, loved and admired; he thinks himself a king.

> But soon the radiant visions give place to black and monstrous phantoms . . . At present, France has passed through the period of joyous delirium, and is about to enter on another that is sombre; behold it, capable of daring, suffering, and doing all things, whenever its guides, as widely astray as itself, shall point out an enemy or an obstacle to its fury.

How quickly the disenchantments come! Already Lafayette, the man of generous illusions, has had to imitate the conduct of those *émigrés* on whom he has been so severe. He has fled to a foreign land, and found there not a refuge, but a prison. He will remain more than five years in the gloomy fortress of Olmutz. The victor of Valmy, Dumouriez, will hardly be more fortunate. He will go over to the enemy, and live in exile on a pension from foreign powers. How close together deceptions and recantations come! Marat, who had already said to the inhabitants of the capital:

Eternal cockneys, with what epithets would I not assail you in the transports of my despair, if I knew any more humiliating than that of Parisians?[1]

Marat, who had said to all Frenchmen: "No, no; liberty is not made for an ignorant, light, and frivolous nation, for cits brought up in fear, dissimulation, knavery, and lying, nourished in cunning, intrigue, sycophancy, avarice, and swindling, subsisting only by theft and rapine, aspiring after nothing but pleasures, titles, and decorations, and always ready to sell themselves for gold!"[2] Marat will write, May 7th, 1793, that is to say, at the apogee of his favourite political system: "All measures taken up to the present day by the assemblies, constituent, legislative, and conventional, to establish and consolidate liberty, have been thoughtless, vain, and illusory, even supposing them to have been taken in good faith. The greater part seem to have had for their object to perpetuate oppression, bring on anarchy, death, poverty, and famine; to make the people weary of their independence, to make liberty a burden, to cause them to detest the Revolution, through its excessive disorders, to exhaust them by watching, fatigue, want, and inanition, to reduce them to despair by hunger, and to bring them back to despotism by civil war."[3]

There were six ministers appointed on August 10. Two of them, Claviére and Roland, will kill themselves; two others, Lebrun-Tondu and Danton, will be guillotined; the remaining two, Servan and Monge, are destined to become, one a general of division under Napoleon, and the other a senator of the Empire and Count of Péluse; and when, at the beginning of his reign, the Emperor complains to the latter because there are still partisans of the Republic to be found: "Sire," the former minister of August 10 will answer, "we had so much trouble to make them republicans! may it please Your Majesty kindly to allow them at least a few days to become imperialists!" Of the two men who had so enthusiastically brought about the proclamation of the Republic, one, Collot d'Herbois, will be transported to Guiana by the republicans, and die there in a paroxysm of burning fever; the other, Grégoire, will be a senator of the Empire, which will not, however, prevent him from promoting the deposition of Napoleon as he had promoted that of Louis XVI.

There are men who will exchange the jacket of the *sans-culotte*

1. *Ami du Peuple*, No. 429.
2. *Ami du Peuple*, No. 539.
3. *La Publiciste de la République*, No. 211.

for the gilded livery of an imperial functionary. The conventionists and regicides are transformed into dukes and counts and barons. David, the official painter of the Empire, Napoleon's favourite, will paint with joy the picture of a pope, and be very proud of his great picture of the new Charlemagne's coronation. But listen to Edgar Quinet:

> When I see the orators of deputations taking things with such a high hand at the bar, and lording it so proudly over mute and complaisant assemblies, I should like to know what became of them a few years later.

And thereupon he sets out to discover their traces. But after considerable investigation he stops. "If I searched any further," he exclaims, "I should be afraid of encountering them among the petty *employés* of the Empire. It was quite enough to see Huguenin, the indomitable president of the insurrectionary Commune, so quickly tamed, soliciting and obtaining a post as clerk of town gates as soon as absolute power made its reappearance after the 18th *Brumaire*. The terrible Santerre becomes the gentlest of men as soon as he is pensioned by the First Consul. Hardly had Bourdon de l'Oise and Albitte, those men of iron, felt the rod than you see them the supplest functionaries of the Empire. The great king-taker, Drouet, thrones it in the *sub-prefecture* of Sainte-Menehould. Napoleon has related that, on August 10, he was in a shop in the Carrousel, whence he witnessed the taking of the palace. If he had a presentiment then, he must have smiled at the chaos which he was to reduce so easily to its former limits. How many furies, and all to terminate so soon in the accustomed obedience!"

Is not history, with its perpetual alternatives of license and despotism, like a vicious circle? And do not the nations pass their time in producing webs of Penelope, whose bloody threads they weave and unweave again with tears? All governments, royalties, empires, republics, ought to be more modest. But all, profoundly forgetful of the lessons of the past, believe themselves immortal. All declare haughtily that they have closed forever the era of revolutions.

With the advent of the Republic a new calendar had been put in force. The equality of days and nights at the autumnal equinox opened the era of civil equality on September 22.

> Who would have believed that this human geometry, so profoundly calculated, was written in the sand, and that in a few years no traces of it would remain? . . . The heavens have continued to gravitate, and have brought back the equality of days and

nights; but they have allowed the promised liberty and equality to perish, like meteors that vanish in empty space. . . . The *sans-culottes* have not been able to make themselves popular among the starry peoples. . . . An ancient belief which the men of the Revolution had neglected through fear or through contempt was again met with; a spectre had appeared; a chilly breath, like that of Samuel, had made itself felt; and lo, the edifice so sagely constructed, and leaning on the worlds, has vanished away.[4]

There lies at the foundation of history a supreme sadness and melancholy. This never-ending series of illusions and deceptions, errors and afflictions, faults and crimes; this rage, and passion, and folly; so many efforts and fatigues, so many dangers, tortures, and tears, so much blood, such revolutions, catastrophes, cataclysms of every sort,—and all for what? Wretched humanity, rolling its stone of Sisyphus from age to age, inspires far more compassion than contempt. The painful reflections caused by the annals of all peoples are perhaps more sombre for the French Revolution than for any other period. Edgar Quinet justly laments over the inequality between the sacrifices of the victims and the results obtained by posterity. He affirms that in other histories one thing reconciles us to the fury of men, and that is the speedy fecundity of the blood they shed; for example, when one sees that of the martyrs flow, one also sees Christianity spread over the earth from the depth of the catacombs; while amongst us, the blood which streamed most abundantly and from such lofty sources, did not find soil equally well prepared.

And the illustrious historian exclaims sadly:

The supreme consolation has been refused to our greatest dead; their blood has not been a seed of virtue and independence for their posterity. If they should reappear once more, they would feel themselves tortured again, and on a worse scaffold, by the denial of their descendants; they would hurl at us again the same *adieu*: 'O Liberty! how they have betrayed thee!'

---

4. Edgar Quinet, *La Révolution*, t. 11.

LEONAUR

ALSO FROM LEONAUR
AVAILABLE IN SOFTCOVER OR HARDCOVER WITH DUST JACKET

THE FALL OF THE MOGHUL EMPIRE OF HINDUSTAN *by H. G. Keene*—By the beginning of the nineteenth century, as British and Indian armies under Lake and Wellesley dominated the scene, a little over half a century of conflict brought the Moghul Empire to its knees.

LADY SALE'S AFGHANISTAN *by Florentia Sale*—An Indomitable Victorian Lady's Account of the Retreat from Kabul During the First Afghan War.

THE CAMPAIGN OF MAGENTA AND SOLFERINO 1859 *by Harold Carmichael Wylly*—The Decisive Conflict for the Unification of Italy.

FRENCH'S CAVALRY CAMPAIGN *by J. G. Maydon*—A Special Correspondent's View of British Army Mounted Troops During the Boer War.

CAVALRY AT WATERLOO *by Sir Evelyn Wood*—British Mounted Troops During the Campaign of 1815.

THE SUBALTERN *by George Robert Gleig*—The Experiences of an Officer of the 85th Light Infantry During the Peninsular War.

NAPOLEON AT BAY, 1814 *by F. Loraine Petre*—The Campaigns to the Fall of the First Empire.

NAPOLEON AND THE CAMPAIGN OF 1806 *by Colonel Vachée*—The Napoleonic Method of Organisation and Command to the Battles of Jena & Auerstädt.

THE COMPLETE ADVENTURES IN THE CONNAUGHT RANGERS *by William Grattan*—The 88th Regiment during the Napoleonic Wars by a Serving Officer.

BUGLER AND OFFICER OF THE RIFLES *by William Green & Harry Smith*—With the 95th (Rifles) during the Peninsular & Waterloo Campaigns of the Napoleonic Wars.

NAPOLEONIC WAR STORIES *by Sir Arthur Quiller-Couch*—Tales of soldiers, spies, battles & sieges from the Peninsular & Waterloo campaigns.

CAPTAIN OF THE 95TH (RIFLES) *by Jonathan Leach*—An officer of Wellington's sharpshooters during the Peninsular, South of France and Waterloo campaigns of the Napoleonic wars.

RIFLEMAN COSTELLO *by Edward Costello*—The adventures of a soldier of the 95th (Rifles) in the Peninsular & Waterloo Campaigns of the Napoleonic wars.